Scripting Death

Scripting Death

STORIES OF ASSISTED DYING
IN AMERICA

Mara Buchbinder

UNIVERSITY OF CALIFORNIA PRESS

University of California Press
Oakland, California

© 2021 by Mara Buchbinder

Library of Congress Cataloging-in-Publication Data

Names: Buchbinder, Mara, author.
Title: Scripting death : stories of assisted dying in America / Mara
    Buchbinder.
Other titles: California series in public anthropology ; 50.
Description: Oakland, California : University of California Press, [2021] |
    Series: California series in public anthropology ; 50 | Includes
    bibliographical references and index.
Identifiers: LCCN 2020035428 (print) | LCCN 2020035429 (ebook) |
    ISBN 9780520380202 (hardcover) | ISBN 9780520380219
    (paperback) | ISBN 9780520380226 (epub)
Subjects: LCSH: Assisted suicide—Vermont—Case studies—21st century.
Classification: LCC R726 .B788 2021 (print) | LCC R726 (ebook) |
    DDC 179.7—dc23
LC record available at https://lccn.loc.gov/2020035428
LC ebook record available at https://lccn.loc.gov/2020035429

Manufactured in the United States of America

30 29 28 27 26 25 24 23 22 21
10 9 8 7 6 5 4 3 2 1

For my parents,
Harriet Bogin Yogel and Stephen Buchbinder

Contents

Introduction

"I am going to start by stating the obvious: you are going to die."

The speaker, Barbara Mancini, a sixty-year-old blonde dressed in a conservative suit, paused to let her opening statement sink in. She stood at the front of a large auditorium filled mostly with men and women in their sixties and seventies. They had come to attend a public "Death with Dignity" educational event in Chapel Hill, North Carolina, and Mancini was the plenary speaker.

Mancini, a former nurse, had become an advocate for medical aid in dying after helping her terminally ill ninety-three-year-old father overdose on a bottle of morphine, at his request. In a television interview with Anderson Cooper on *60 Minutes* in October 2014, Mancini said, "He asked me to hand him the bottle and I did. I had the dosing syringe in my hand, and he took the cap off, and he drank what was remaining in the bottle."[1]

What followed was a horrifying sequence of events that rattled Mancini even in retelling them two years later. She told the hospice nurse what she had done, the nurse called 911, and her father was treated for an overdose. Mancini was arrested and charged with abetting an attempted suicide. At the hospital, her father was declared incompetent, and it fell to her mother to decide whether to treat the overdose (which he clearly did not want), or to let him die, which would have been worse for Mancini's legal case. Her mother chose the former. Her father was irate, telling the hospital staff not to hurt his daughter. He died four days later of pneumonia. A yearlong prosecution ensued, during which Mancini amassed thousands of dollars in legal fees and was forced to take unpaid leave from her job until a judge finally dismissed the case. In the aftermath, Mancini became a staunch advocate for Compassion & Choices, a national nonprofit organization committed to expanding end-of-life choices.

At the end of her account, Mancini offered the audience three takeaway points: (1) end-of-life care should align with the patient's values, preferences, and wishes; (2) this could happen again; and (3) medical aid in dying should be an option. Her closing line, "Who gets to tell you how you will die?" was met with a standing ovation.

How did American society get to a place where choosing how you will die would seem like an obvious right and a reasonable expectation? How did death become something one *does* rather than something that happens? And what had prompted this large crowd of seniors to attend this event, even though aid in dying was not a legal option in North Carolina?

Medical aid in dying has expanded rapidly in recent years and has quickly captured the public's imagination. At the time of this writing, ten jurisdictions permit physicians to prescribe terminally ill adult patients a lethal dose of medication, provided certain preconditions are met, making this end-of-life option legally available to one in five Americans.[2] Similar legislation is under consideration in many additional states, and is expanding to new groups of patients in countries like the Netherlands and Belgium, which have longer histories with assisted death. This growing sociopolitical movement heralds the possibility of a new era of choice in dying, motivated by a desire to control the timing and circumstances of death and avoid dependence on others.[3] Yet social studies of medicine have repeatedly demonstrated that the realities of policies in action often fall short of advocacy visions, raising questions about how much choice and control aid in dying actually affords.[4]

Advocates like Barbara Mancini presume a straightforward path, in which a terminally ill patient desiring to hasten death requests assistance from a trusted physician, who will accede to the patient's wishes. If only medical aid in dying had been a legal option in Pennsylvania, Mancini wants us to believe, much of her father's end-of-life suffering could have been avoided. Yet this narrative overlooks the many roadblocks to accessing aid in dying in states where it is legal, including identifying a physician willing to prescribe, paying for the medication, and following a complex bureaucratic protocol to ensure all of the legislative safeguards are met. Mancini's father might have been able to navigate these challenges with the help of his daughter, who, as a nurse, was experienced with the health care system. However, this book treats his ability to do so as a starting point for investigation, rather than a foregone conclusion, as the advocacy narrative suggests.

Until now, very little has been publicly known about how medical aid-in-dying laws affect ordinary citizens once they are put into practice. This book offers an in-depth account of how patients, caregivers, and health care providers navigate aid in dying as a new medical frontier in the aftermath of legalization. It chronicles two years of research I undertook to document the implementation of Vermont's 2013 Patient Choice and Control at End of Life Act. My primary research materials are interviews with 144 Vermont patients, caregivers, health care providers, activists, legislators, and other policy stakeholders, as well as participant observation in advocacy and educational events and professional medical conferences.[5]

Between May 31, 2013, and June 30, 2017, paperwork for fifty-two individuals using this law was filed with the Vermont Department of Health. Forty-eight of them had a death certificate on file, of which twenty-nine had ingested the lethal prescription as of January 2018. Of the remaining individuals, seventeen died from their underlying disease, one died from other causes, and one had an unknown cause of death.[6] The most common diagnoses were cancer (43) and amyotrophic lateral sclerosis (ALS) (7). While these absolute numbers are relatively low, they correspond with utilization rates from a twenty-year report of Oregon's Death with Dignity Act, which found that 64 percent of those who had received a prescription ultimately ingested the medication and assisted deaths accounted for nineteen per ten thousand total deaths.[7]

These utilization statistics underscore that, although medical aid in dying has captivated the public's imagination over the past twenty years, only a small segment of American society is likely to experience it themselves. This is a matter not only of personal preference but also of eligibility, including having one of the diagnoses better suited to medical aid in dying. Roughly 25 percent of people in Vermont, and 23 percent in the United States overall, died from cancer between 2009 and 2018; for ALS, the figures were 0.4 percent and 0.2 percent, respectively.[8]

At the same time, the cultural impact of medical aid in dying stretches much further than these numbers suggest. Studies from the Netherlands and Oregon demonstrate that it is discussed far more than it is performed, and that it can serve as a gateway for conversations about other end-of-life concerns.[9] As I will describe in this book, my own research supports such findings, as many health care providers shared how questions about aid in dying had opened up larger discussions of patients' hopes, desires, and fears surrounding the dying process, or other ways of hastening death, such as through voluntarily stopping eating and drinking.[10] Therefore, the significance of legalization for the culture of death in America is much greater than the number of reported deaths implies: it changes the conversation about control over dying and invites new ways of thinking about scripting death.

In the pages that follow, I illustrate how medical aid in dying enables some terminally ill people to exercise agency over death against a backdrop of existential uncertainty, bureaucratic regulation, and the biomedicalization of end-of-life care. However, this opportunity to "script" one's death is not evenly distributed but instead favors individuals from more privileged socioeconomic backgrounds. Two interlocking premises of the book, therefore, are that scripting death distributes agency over the dying process and certain people have more control over dying than others.

Medical aid in dying is known alternatively as physician-assisted suicide, physician aid in dying, and death with dignity. A politics of language underlies these choices: proponents find the language of suicide offensive and inaccurate (because terminally ill proponents very much want to live), while opponents view "aid in dying" as euphemistic and misleading and assert that there are many other ways to die "with dignity." ("We have death with dignity," one hospice nurse told me. "It's called hospice.") While I was working on this project, proponents in the United States deliberately shifted their terminology from physician-assisted death to aid in dying or medical aid in dying to decenter the role of physicians. To further complicate matters, outside of the United States, *aid in dying* is an umbrella term that may include physician-administered medication (widely known as euthanasia) and patient-administered medication (widely known as assisted suicide), whereas, in the United States, only the latter is legally permitted and thus denoted by this term.[11] In Vermont, many patients, clinicians, and policy stakeholders avoid the language of death entirely and refer to the Patient Choice and Control at End of Life Act as simply Act 39. One hospice employee told me that advocates chose this language intentionally, to avoid alienating opponents.

This fraught language has presented me with a conundrum in writing this book. The labels used to describe this practice unavoidably signal meaningful social, political, and moral values for advocates on both sides of the debate. I have tried to maintain a neutral stance on the ethics and politics of assisted dying, and I remain quite ambivalent about the practice, as I explain further below. I have chosen to use the term *medical aid in dying* out of deference to proponents, for whom the stakes of avoiding suicide stigma are more consequential, in my view, than the moral stakes of their opponents. I recognize the consequence of this choice: that some readers will see this language as expressing a bias. However, it is a choice increasingly made by professional medical societies, and one that I believe reflects a shifting public conversation about terminal illness and gaining control over death.

SCRIPTING DEATH

The desire for control over dying is a powerful cultural force in contemporary American society, but it is not universally shared. Brenda Jones,[12] a Vermont hospice and palliative care physician, explained to me that control over death is a bit like control over birth. Just as many expectant mothers today create elaborate birth plans, she said, "There are people who want to script the whole thing as best that they can. And others are kind of like, 'Well, I'm just going to see what happens.'" Although it would be several years before I realized it, Brenda had handed me the title for my book.

Anthropologists and cultural observers have long recognized that pregnant women in the United States often seek control over the uncertainty of childbirth through meticulous planning,[13] yet the notion that death may likewise be scripted has been less fully explored. Like birth, whether or not one desires to script death is shaped by a range of social factors, such as religion, race, and class. It may also depend on individual characteristics, such as personality and family background, and circumstances, such as diagnosis, prognosis, and the anticipated mechanism of death. Some who seek to script their deaths follow a nonmedical path. One activist I spoke with was adamant that, if things got to a certain point, she would simply have her daughters push her into a moonlit lake in a leaky canoe. (Drowning, I learned while working on this project, can be a relatively painless way to die. Whether or not her daughters would acquiesce to this plan is another matter.) Similarly, the nonprofit organization Final Exit Network supports "safe, certain, painless and peaceful methods for self-deliverance," such as self-asphyxiation with helium.[14]

Yet many who seek to script their deaths crave the cultural legitimacy of a legally and medically authorized form of hastened death. In exploring such desires, I use the term *aspirational death* to signal the aesthetic, affective, and ethical preferences that inform orientations to dying as a matter of personal choice and careful choreography. Aspirational deaths form in relation to culturally specific, idealized notions of what constitutes a "good death."[15] For example, in many societies, a death that is foreseeable is generally considered to be good.[16] In contrast, a death may be labeled bad if it is traumatic, unexpected, or comes to someone who is too young. The activist who imagined being launched to her death in a leaky canoe was reacting to her father's death, which was nothing like what he had wanted. "It was tragic, and it was awful, and it disrespected who he was as a human being," she told me. He had planned everything out, from his funeral arrangements to his intended self-asphyxiation using a garden hose and an exhaust pipe. But in the end, he was diagnosed with a debilitating form of cancer four days before he died and spent his last days bedridden. "Having seen a bad death," she explained, "you kind of start envisioning what you would like to have happen when you are ready to go."

Understandings of the good death make use of cultural scripts for dying, mental models, or templates for dying well that vary culturally and historically.[17] In many cases, cultural scripts for dying are shaped by religious frameworks that imbue suffering with meaning and orient the dying

person and mourners toward preparation for the afterlife. In contemporary Western societies, however, the growth of secularization has led medicine to replace religion in assuming institutional control over death.[18]
The term *aspirational* also suggests that the desired form of death may be
out of reach or unattainable. In the case of medical aid in dying, this might
be a result of living in a state where it is not legally authorized, being
unable to find a physician to write the lethal prescription, or failing to
meet the statutory requirements (e.g., mental competence, a six-month
prognosis, or the ability to self-administer the medication).

By posing scripting as a central analytic concept for understanding
human control over death, I play on several distinct meanings of scripts,
including norms or expectations for behavior; protocols and procedures
that order work processes and institutional practices; and written documents, such as written prescriptions for medication. Scripts, as textual
documents, make explicit those practices or routines that might otherwise
go unnoticed, and help to outline the possible consequences when processes are laid out in official documents, such as laws or hospital policies.
Scripting also encompasses staging or choreographing death to fulfill
preferences about how, when, where, and with whom one dies. One rami-
fication of scripting death, therefore, is making tacit the aspects of death
and dying that might otherwise go unstated—such as the tendency for
bodies to expel fluids as they cross the threshold from life to death. At the
same time, because scripts go only so far in determining action and events,
the concept also invites questions about how people improvise when
things do not proceed as expected.[19]

CONTROL AND AGENCY IN DYING

Social scientists have traditionally investigated expanding human control
over death and dying through the lens of technology and its presumed
threat to nature. Technological progress in medicine over the past fifty
years has led to increasing societal debates about how people understand
the boundaries between life and death and the prolongation of life through
biomedical technologies.[20] The cultural legacy of controversial decisions
regarding families' rights to discontinue mechanical ventilation (such as in

the case of Karen Ann Quinlan) and artificial feeding (such as in the case of Terri Schiavo) is that death has become something that can be controlled through human intervention, and not merely something that happens.

Nowhere has the struggle for human control over death been more culturally and ethically fraught than with the concept of brain death. The concept was adopted in 1968 by a Harvard University committee tasked with considering potential criteria to define the permanent and irreversible cessation of brain function. Two technological developments in medicine precipitated their charge: the development of intensive care medicine and the expanded use of mechanical ventilation, and the advent of organ transplantation.[21] Introducing neurological criteria for death meant patients could be declared dead while a ventilator maintained their lung function, keeping vital organs and tissue "alive" and available for procurement and transfer to people in need. Subsequently, because the patient was effectively dead, mechanical ventilation could be stopped.

The introduction of neurological criteria for death responded to a pressing practical need and the laudable policy goal of increasing the supply of vital organs for transplantation. Yet it also introduced conceptual problems. As the anthropologist Sharon Kaufman has written, "With a ventilator, one could be declared dead while still appearing to be alive. It was a radical stance that gave rise to an unintended, unprecedented question that continues to haunt us: was the body, pronounced brain dead and connected to a breathing machine, actually alive or dead? No longer would dead mean dead. Death was in this sense doubled."[22] In addition to this crisis of meaning, the scientific logic of brain death has been challenged over time. Patients who meet the criteria for neurological death may retain a range of vital functions (such as sexual maturation and wound healing). This flies in the face of the judgment that they are in any sense dead and makes easy demarcations between person and corpse difficult.[23]

While scientists have grappled with uncertainty regarding the boundaries of biological life, social scientists have recognized that the cessation of biological life may not always coincide with the social death of the person[24]—that is, a loss of one's identity, social roles and activities, and social connectedness that results in their being treated as less than fully human.[25] In her ethnography of euthanasia in the Netherlands, the anthropologist Frances Norwood suggests that seeking an assisted death enables people to avoid a situation in which social death precedes the bio-logical death of the person.[26] Because the extended use of life-prolonging technologies may lead to social death,[27] it may be tempting to view medical aid in dying as offering salvation from the modern scourge of technology.[28] Indeed, when asked to described bad deaths, many health care providers invoke technology, such as the nurse who recounted the following:

> We had a gentleman who had had a massive stroke and was on a ventilator and really, no hope of him recovering. And his son, for whatever reason, didn't want to let him go. And who knows why. No idea what the history was there. But we basically chemically coded this gentleman for five days, and because it's a teaching facility they did a lot of stuff on him. You know, they put chest tubes in, and they drained his abdomen, and I just felt so bad for that man, who had no voice to say if he wanted it or if he didn't want it.

Owing to stories like these, some sociologists have suggested that the assisted-death movement reflects a crisis of faith in biomedicine as the lynchpin to end-of-life care. From this perspective, medical aid in dying poses an antitechnological solution to redress the problems wrought by technologically mediated hospital deaths.[29]

However, it would be a mistake to view the assisted-death movement as simply a reaction to the growth of medical technologies and their expanded role in controlling death. The historian Shai Lavi has shown that efforts to legalize euthanasia in the United States can be dated to the early twentieth century and preceded the advent of contemporary biomedical technologies. Lavi argues that the growth of life-prolonging technologies and the euthanasia movement were both products of a broader Enlightenment desire to master the dying process.[30] Therefore, as the anthropologists Naomi Richards and Marian Krawcyzk recently argued, life-extending and death-hastening techniques are "two sides of the same coin," and both "can be understood as manifestations of a Western *denial of dying.*"[31]

A fundamental proposition of this book is that scripting death through medical aid in dying fundamentally alters dying by permitting people to control its trajectory—for example, by shortening the dying process or sanitizing it to avoid the "dirty," the bodily decay and deterioration that accompany natural death.[32] Yet it also permits people to control the cultural and personal meanings of death. Staging an aspirational death that includes being surrounded by loved ones and saying heartfelt goodbyes enables people to imbue death with a sense of continuity and coherence with one's life as lived, avoiding the sense of painful rupture that often comes with dying. This distinguishes medical aid in dying from other attempts at controlling death, such as writing advance directives for end-of-life care.[33]

Pairing agency with control as constitutive components of scripting death underscores how pursuing assisted death can be seen as the ultimate enactment of independence and personal choice. If control represents the desired effect, agency is the pathway through which it is realized. Agency is closely related to the bioethical concept of autonomy: the ability to make decisions about one's body and the freedom to do so. To simplify a lively set of bioethical debates, proponents generally maintain that assisted-dying laws promote autonomy by expanding the range of possible choices that a terminally ill person can make and providing them with control over the timing and circumstances of death. In addition to retaining autonomy, avoiding dependence on others at the end of life is a key motivating factor. This set of reasons for pursuing assisted death contrasts with popular presumptions about the role of pain, sidestepping challenges to legalization that fixate on the inadequacies of palliative care. The growth and expansion of hospice and the hospice Medicare benefit, which pays for hospice services for Americans over the age of sixty-five, has improved pain control at the end of life over the past several decades.

While it is hard to deny the importance of autonomy to the assisted-death movement, while I was working on this book, I became curious about how it dominated the public conversation about medical aid in dying. Consider Compassion & Choice's slogan: "My life. My death. My choice." Where, in this formulation, is the physician, who is expected to write a prescription to satisfy the speaker's autonomous wishes? What about the speaker's family? Moreover, in an unequal and stratified society, who has the capacity to make such a choice? However powerful the desire for personal control over death may be, it must also be balanced against other values and sociopolitical forces in an interdependent world.[34]

For anthropologists, agency—which I define broadly as the capacity to act with intention—is always located within larger social relations and systems of power.[35] Sherry Ortner suggests that people use agency to pursue cultural projects "that infuse life with meaning and purpose."[36] This view of agency is particularly relevant to my understanding of medical aid in dying as an aspirational death, one that is inflected with culturally informed ideas about what makes certain deaths good. From this perspective, the pursuit of assisted death can be seen as a type of cultural project.

Insofar as agency is always socially embedded, it is never completely free. "Agency," writes Laura Ahearn, "is not synonymous with free will." Instead, "actions are always already socially, culturally, and linguistically constrained."[37] While most bioethicists would not claim that autonomy is the same as free will either, this remark conveys a subtle distinction between agency and autonomy: agency is conceptualized in relation to the social structure. To affirm the role of agency in scripting death is to acknowledge the power to end one's life is never simply given. Rather, agency over death develops within social relationships and structural constraints—such as geographic location, socioeconomic status, and law—all of which differentially shape one's capacity to enact an aspirational death.

With medical aid in dying, both agency and control over death are distributed among a range of actors and institutions. It is not simply the case that the medical system exerts control, while patients exercise agency. Instead, agency and control are necessarily shared between patients, families, health care providers, medical institutions, and the state. Moreover, there are many situations in which the supposed agency of terminally ill people rubs up against a host of situational and structural constraints. In other words, agency and the implied promise of control are frequently illusory. The dynamic nature of agency highlights the social embeddedness of decisional power and authority with respect to care for the dying, which are not easily accounted for in bioethical models of autonomy.

THE VERMONT WAY

Vermont became the fourth state to legalize medical aid in dying when it passed Act 39, the Patient Choice and Control at End of Life Act, in 2013. It was the first state to do so through the state legislature, rather than through a judicial ruling or ballot initiative. Many Vermonters I spoke with were proud of this fact and saw it as a testament to the strength of their grassroots advocacy networks and citizen legislature.[38] However, this early adoption did not mean that aid in dying was swiftly institution-alized in Vermont medical practice. Officially, aid in dying was legal imme-diately when then Governor Peter Shumlin signed the bill into law on May 31, 2013, yet it would be well over a year before a public health apparatus was in place to regulate the practice and physicians felt comfortable pre-scribing, a process I describe further in the next chapter. At the time of my research, aid in dying was still highly stigmatized, and most physicians were relatively private about their participation.

I focused my research in Vermont for conceptual reasons: in 2015, when I began work on this project, Vermont was the state that had most recently legalized aid in dying. I was interested in understanding what happened when aid in dying was new, and its meanings and repercussions were still being worked out on the ground. (I had followed a similar approach in my previous studies of abortion law and newborn-screening policies.) Yet Vermont was an ideal site for practical reasons as well. I grew up in New England and spent six magical summers at a sleepaway camp in central Vermont. Later, I began my research career there, while an undergraduate at Dartmouth College, located just over the Vermont state line. I cut my teeth as an ethnographer visiting adolescents with type 1 diabetes in rural towns in southern Vermont. It was there I discovered driving as a meditative fieldwork practice, finding that traveling long distances over mostly deserted roads affords rare opportunities for uninterrupted thinking. Returning to the familiar landscape with my husband and son in 2015 felt like a home-coming of sorts.

Vermont is similar in many ways to the first three states—Oregon, Washington, and Montana—to legalize medical aid in dying. Its population is majority white, rural, and secular, with a significant libertarian streak. All of these characteristics are critical to the legalization of aid in dying in the United States; race and religion, in particular, are big predictors of utiliza-tion. With 94.2 percent of its residents identifying as white, Vermont is one of the least racially diverse states in the country.[39] According to a 2016 Gallup poll, Vermont is also the least religious state, with only 21 percent of residents considering themselves to be "very religious"[40] and 37 percent having no religious affiliation.[41] Finally, with a population of just over 626,000, Vermont is the least populous state, except for Wyoming.[42]

Vermont is also known for its progressive politics. It was the first state to outlaw slavery in its state constitution, was the first to authorize civil unions (in 2000), and was an early adopter of medical marijuana (2004) and its decriminalization (2013). However, while Vermont is widely known "as a bastion for particular kinds of liberal whiteness,"[43] this image masks a more complicated history of racial politics. The lack of large-scale farms or factories in Vermont meant African Americans had few economic or social incentives to move there during the Great Migration of the twentieth century. More recently, the emphasis on niche dairy and maple farms has worked against the diversification of its workforce that some rural midwestern states have witnessed.[44] Therefore, Vermont's progressive politics has not fostered racial diversity.

Like many rural states, Vermont has an aging population, rendering end-of-life care a pressing issue. Although Vermont embraced hospice early on, enrollment rates have been much lower than in comparable rural states, and it has consistently ranked among the lowest in the nation for hospice utilization.[45] Vermont has also struggled with how to address the labor shortfall facing an aging population. In 2019, in an effort to entice young people, the state began to offer financial incentives to encourage workers to move to Vermont and work remotely.[46]

Apart from their state's demographic characteristics, Vermonters pride themselves on their "Yankee" values of rugged individualism, ingenuity, and determination. Of Vermont's state character, the geographer Robert Vanderbeck writes, "The figure of the Yankee has at different times served both as region-specific icon and a broader symbol of American national identity."[47] The legalization of aid in dying aligns with the Yankee's "do it yourself" mentality, as well as with an underlying respect for personal liberty. As one physician told me, "I think it goes along with sort of why I love Vermont. I'm not from here, I moved here many, many years ago, but I think that Vermonters have strong wills, and I think that they should be able to exercise [those wills], whether we choose to or not [use aid in dying]." As this comment suggests, most Vermonters possess a robust state identity that informs their understanding of the local significance of medical aid in dying, and they refer to this identity in overwhelmingly proud, complimentary terms. This is true even of aid-in-dying opponents, who recognize the role of Vermonters' strong wills in informing the policy discussion, even if they do not agree with the outcome.

Amanda Townshend, a palliative care physician in Vermont and an early champion of the Patient Choice and Control at End of Life Act, explained to me that in the early days of legalization, doctors struggled to understand the legal requirements and procedures, as well as the pharmaceutical protocols. They had to figure out how to implement medical aid in dying on their own, using their personal and professional networks. She saw this as "the Vermont way" and viewed this on-the-job interpretation and innovation as central to how the law works.

The Vermont way was brought into critical relief for me when California passed the End of Life Options Act in 2016. On the surface, Vermont's and California's laws are nearly identical: both permit a physician to write a lethal prescription for a mentally competent adult patient who is expected to die within six months, both require a second physician to confirm the diagnosis and prognosis, and both adopt safeguards to ensure that the patient's request is voluntary. Yet there are also subtle differences that are apparent only from a close reading of the two laws and a thorough understanding of how they have been implemented. In California, all medical institutions and health systems are required to opt in or opt out of participating in aid in dying, and many institutions undertook strategic-planning initiatives immediately after the law passed to determine how to proceed.[48] In Vermont, in contrast, the only "opt out" permitted by law is for medical institutions to prohibit patients from ingesting the lethal medication on their premises. Legally, Vermont physicians are free to decide about their participation on an individual basis, and, at the time of my research, many hospitals had not adopted formal policies to regulate aid in dying. This, then, is the Vermont way: individualistic, independent, and relatively free from government regulation. However, in spite of this liberty, without formal policies in place, health care providers and patients alike have had to rely on their determination and resourcefulness to navigate this unchartered medicolegal terrain.

The distinctive nature of Vermont provides an important backdrop to this book. In the next chapter, I discuss why and how Vermont became the first state to use the state legislature for legalization, as well as the ways in which the desire for assisted death resonate with idealized notions of

Yankee independence. Yet much of this book could have taken place any-where in the United States where aid in dying is legal. The cultural desire to control death and tame uncertainty, which I describe in chapter 2, may be at home in Colorado or New Jersey, as much as in Vermont, and the access barriers identified in chapter 5 have also been reported elsewhere.[49] Similarly, the social phenomenology of assisted death I elucidate in chap-ter 6 could have unfolded in any permissive jurisdiction and is not specific to Vermont. Throughout the book, I also show how debates about medical aid in dying reflect larger national (and, in some cases, international) con-versations about end-of-life planning (chapter 3) and the physician's role in shepherding death (chapter 4).

Therefore, although this is a Vermont story, it has a broader national message. One of the strengths of ethnography is its refusal to compromise between specificity and generality.[50] Just as the Yankee serves as both regional icon and national symbol,[51] the story of medical aid in dying in Vermont is a microcosm of a larger national story, offering insights into cultural ideals, fears, and debates that will resonate across the United States. By linking specific stories and events to broader social, political, and economic contexts, I reveal how the Vermont case offers instructive lessons for assisted death in America more generally.

THE POWER OF STORY

During the course of my research, I heard hundreds of stories about death: sudden, unexpected deaths and long, protracted ones; heartbreaking, traumatic deaths and more anticipated, ordinary ones; deaths at home and deaths in hospital; deaths of close kin and deaths of beloved pets. Many people told me stories of surreptitious assisted deaths undertaken before medical aid in dying was legal. One state legislator recounted how a young aunt had died of cancer in the 1970s. The aunt had been hospital-ized for months, when one day she begged her sister, the legislator's mother, to "help me get this finished" because she could no longer stand seeing her husband's distraught face when he came to visit her. The legisla-tor's mother spoke with the nurse, and they "took care of it." An aid-in-dying activist told me how her father, a famous physician, had been able to hasten death while he was dying from cancer because he had pharmacists and physicians in his circle. While fear and shame permeated the illegal act, it was also beautiful, with family surrounding her father, playing his favorite music, and reading his favorite poetry as he died. Several people told me how the death of a well-known state politician, who shot himself in the head after a terminal cancer diagnosis, catalyzed the movement for aid in dying in Vermont. And an eloquent right-to-life activist told me many stories of beautiful natural deaths she had witnessed, challenging my preconceived assumptions about the nature of dying and suffering.

Stories can heal. Their power to do so is what drew me to study medical anthropology twenty years ago.[52] Yet stories can do even more. They can move us in different ways: stir our emotions, direct our attention, mobilize resources, and even provoke social and political change. No story was a more powerful catalyst for the assisted-death movement than that of Brittany Maynard. Maynard was diagnosed with glioblastoma, an aggressive and fatal brain cancer, at the age of twenty-nine, while she and her new husband were trying to start a family. Maynard left California and spent the last ten months of her life in Oregon, where she could take advantage of the state's Death with Dignity law and end her life on her own terms. She also devoted herself to advocating for aid in dying. On November 1, 2014, Maynard ingested a lethal dose of medication while at home, surrounded by her husband, Dan Diaz, who would later quit his job to work full-time for Compassion & Choices as an aid-in-dying advocate, and her mother, Deborah Ziegler, who would share her daughter's story when she testified before the California state legislature in support of its End of Life Options Act.

Brittany Maynard's story quickly captured national media attention, including a *People* magazine cover.[53] Because of her youth and vitality, she was an unlikely spokesperson for dying with dignity, but she changed the face of the movement. Within two years of her death, California legalized aid in dying, and five years later, the number of permissive jurisdictions in the United States had more than doubled.

Brittany Maynard unmistakably demonstrates the power of a single story. Yet the singularity of her experience also leaves certain questions unanswered. How did her family absorb the social and economic costs of relocating to Oregon and establishing residency, which enabled her to access death with dignity? How was she able to establish care in a new medical system and identify a physician willing to prescribe the lethal medication, when she was already so sick? How did her undeniable privilege as an upper-middle-class, beautiful white woman contribute to her experience of achieving this type of death, and how realistic would this option be for others? What is eclipsed by framing aid-in-dying advocacy through the power of a single narrative?

Brittany Maynard's case suggests that stories operate like theater spotlights: they direct our attention to the protagonist while obscuring parts of the broader backdrop. In this book, I highlight many stories, but I also situate them within their broader cultural, political, and socioeconomic contexts to show the larger patterns that individual stories cannot. In doing so, I aim to illuminate the gaps between dominant advocacy narratives and what assisted death looks like once it is put into practice.

Acknowledging the power of story also requires me to address the thorny question of who has the power to speak for the dead. Some people I approached for my research were reluctant to give an account of a particular person's death because they did not feel authorized to be a spokesperson for the deceased. As an ethnographer and author, I recognize that I, too, have wrested an uncomfortable power in representing the deaths of people I have never met. Several people I interviewed told me they had been unhappy with journalists' accounts of their loved ones' deaths (which were occasionally covered by the media in the early days of Vermont's aid-in-dying law), putting additional pressure on me to both defend my ethnographic approach and do justice to their stories.

Kelly Ray Knight has compared anthropologists to vultures because they collect the wreckage of people's lives and traumas for intellectual consumption.[54] Robert Desjarlais has similarly asked, "How does a person relate the stories of other people's deaths without making a stylistic show of it, without words dancing on the remnants of their lives?"[55] On one level, these descriptions resonate with me. There is something discomfiting about using stories of one person's tragedy for professional gain. At the same time, telling stories that would not otherwise be told can change the way public debates are framed. The tension between these positions— exploitation and memorialization—is one that many ethnographers face. Ultimately, I accept responsibility for telling these stories because I think they ought to be told. A key premise of this book is that the dominant media and advocacy narratives surrounding medical aid in dying in the United States provide only a partial picture of what this practice might mean for agency and control at the end of life.

Advocacy narratives about medical aid in dying may be misleading for another reason: they provide a false sense of completeness. Stories of death are necessarily partial, because we can never access an inside account of the experience of death. The stories I write about in this book were coauthored with many interlocutors, who vacillated between first-person accounts of their own experiences of caring for dying people and third-person accounts that attempted to tell the story from the deceased person's perspective. In this sense, my interview respondents played a crucial role in the knowledge-production process as I tried to piece together lives and events from fragments of narratives that sometimes left holes and unanswered questions. Even when I obtained the account of a particular person's death from three or four different individuals, a crucial perspective was missing. Therefore, collecting stories of death and dying has required me to traffic in multiple, partial narratives that may appear whole and complete.[56]

During my fieldwork, I had one memorable conversation with a woman, about my age, whose mother's story had been documented in a book written by another relative. The book recounted a long course of terminal illness, followed eventually by a medically assisted death. I asked the woman what it was like to have another family member narrate her mother's story, wondering how she might feel about having such intimate moments of suffering and death available for the world to read. Her answer surprised me. She told me she loves talking about her mother and loves having the book to revisit this time. The book was a gift. She compared it to a child reading a story: it's comforting to know how the story will end, and to be able to keep reading it. She also recognized the difference between the story of her mother's death (as a piece of advocacy, a work of policy and politics) and her mother's death as she experienced it. She was comfortable with this difference.

This conversation bolstered me. It gave me hope that the relatives and friends of those whose deaths fill this book might find small gifts in the stories it tells, that they might forgive me for the moments in which my account fails to match their experiences. In accordance with anthropological research ethics, I have used pseudonyms for all names of research participants, and I have occasionally changed or obscured other details to preserve participants' confidentiality. Still, I know that the central figures will recognize themselves in the stories. I hope they will read the inevitable gulf between narrative and experience in the spirit that my interlocutor did, with generosity and compassion.[57] Yet I also encourage them to ask the critical questions that I did of Brittany Maynard's story: What is left out by particular retellings? And how might the ground shift if we told the story a different way?

EMBRACING AMBIVALENCE

When I began this research, I committed myself to a neutral stance on medical aid in dying. I did not want my own preconceived views—which at the time were uninformed, though largely positive—to influence the research. I wanted to understand all sides of the issue, to be open to possible positive or negative effects of legalization. I could not do this if I began with an activist stance or a particular moral agenda.[58] Moreover, I sensed early on that the public conversations about aid in dying were framing the issues far too simplistically—that much of what captured my attention could not be easily contained by the label "pro" or "con."

Over time, however, and with significant effort, I came to see problems with neutrality. In the two decades since Oregon's Death with Dignity law was enacted, several professional medical societies, including the American Academy of Hospice and Palliative Medicine and many state medical societies, have adopted a stance of "studied neutrality" with respect to medical aid in dying.[59] On the one hand, this represents a marked shift from the American Medical Association's long-standing opposition to physician-assisted suicide. On the other hand, neutrality can also offer a convenient alibi for people wanting to avoid genuine engagement. For example, a Vermont hospice employee told me, "We're neutral. We don't get involved." When avoiding involvement means avoiding referring inquisitive patients to information and other resources, as this respondent later suggested to me, neutrality seems much closer to opposition than to support. This may be why several organizations, such as the American Academy of Family Physicians, have more recently adopted a stance of *engaged* neutrality.[60] The more I told stakeholders that I had a neutral stance on aid in dying, as I always did at the start of my interviews, the more it began to feel like an excuse to avoid articulating my views.

At the same time, those views began to shift. While I began my research feeling fairly supportive of medical aid in dying, my perspective swung in the opposite direction during my first summer of fieldwork. A field note excerpt from that summer, written after an interview with an articulate activist, reads, "This interview challenged a lot of my preexisting assumptions about why people would oppose aid in dying. Her main reason—to support a natural death—was nothing like what I would have expected her to say."[61] I began to see that many of the activists who opposed aid in dying felt comfortable with death as a result of frequent exposure in childhood; consequently, death did not scare them, and this had shaped their view that aid in dying was unnecessary. I also began to appreciate the challenges associated with adopting aid in dying as public policy. It was not simply a matter of affirming patients' rights: physicians had to be willing to participate, and there had to be a regulatory apparatus in place to ensure that the law was free from abuse. Aid in dying started to look far more complicated than simply a commitment to patient choice.

Then, after my first summer of research, my views shifted again. As I interviewed more and more people whose loved ones had used aid in dying, I found its positive effects on their lives and deaths to be unquestionable. Seen from this vantage point, it was hard to deny the value of aid in dying. I also noticed something else: physicians' views were changing, too. I spoke with more and more Vermont physicians who had initially opposed aid in dying but had come around over time because of a particular patient's request.

If you asked me today about my views on aid in dying, I would respond that I am ambivalent. I think assisted death is, for some people, a wonderful end-of-life option, one that restores a sense of control in tumultuous times and permits people to find meaning and joy in how they live their remaining days. Importantly, I do not have moral or religious objections to aid in dying; it presents no conflicts to my secular Jewish worldview. Yet I also think it strains health care providers and the institution of medicine more than the average American realizes. And as a matter of public policy and as an object of multimillion-dollar advocacy campaigns, it unquestionably diverts public attention and resources from other policy changes, such as improvements in palliative care, that would help many more Americans have better deaths.

For me, ambivalence means that making sense of the world is a messy undertaking that may require holding multiple competing perspectives at the same time. Ambivalence recognizes that our social, moral, and political commitments may pull us in different directions simultaneously, and the stories that often guide our thinking on morally complex issues are necessarily fragmented and partial. Where neutrality might mean withholding judgment, ambivalence, in my view, is a more engaged stance, one that entails tracking the moral and affective pulls that orient us to a field of study, even if they lead in confusing or conflicting directions. In the case of aid in dying, it means committing to individual choice and to equality—both values that I hold dearly—may lead me down opposing paths. Ultimately, I think ambivalence serves as a better ethnographic ideal than neutrality.

In *Death Is That Man Taking Names,* the legal scholar Robert Burt argued we should embrace ambivalence around death. Burt saw such ambivalence manifested in a cultural commitment on behalf of organized medicine to preserve life at any cost, combined with a private willingness to embrace death in particular cases. He also criticized aid-in-dying activists for failing to acknowledge ambivalence about both the desirability of death and the virtue of self-determination.[62]

I share with Burt a concern for how advocacy rhetoric may overlook the ambivalence embodied in terms such as *choice* and *compassion*, and the multiple pathways through which these values are realized. It may also overlook larger social and political questions about who even gets to exercise choice when it comes to end-of-life care. Maintaining a methodological and analytical commitment to ambivalence throughout this book means I do not view medical aid in dying as either "good" or "bad," or as an option that we ought to either extend to more Americans or work to curtail.[63] Instead, I approach it as a powerful cultural phenomenon and sociopolitical movement that raises both opportunities and challenges for how we think about choice and control at the end of life, as well as how we imagine the experience of dying. I hope readers will absorb the pages that follow in this spirit. If this book renders them even a little ambivalent about aid in dying, where once they felt certain (or worse, neutral), I will have accomplished my goal.

1 Scripting Choice into Law

One of the first surprises for health care providers, patients, and families navigating medical aid in dying in Vermont firsthand was that the Patient Choice and Control at End of Life Act (Act 39) offers little guidance on such matters as which medication to prescribe and at what dose, what pharmacy to send it to, and what constitutes state residency and self-administration. This chapter delves into the legislative and bureaucratic scripting processes involved in the social production of law, to show how a range of uncertainties that emerged in the clinical implementation of Act 39 were built into the legislative process itself. In the remainder of this book, I will focus on the broad and varied consequences of legalizing medical aid in dying, but in this chapter I review the legislative history that made the law possible.

After briefly situating the legalization of aid in dying in Vermont within a broader national landscape, I describe how and why Vermont became the first jurisdiction in the United States to successfully follow a legislative pathway to legalization. I show how many of the challenges that clinicians and patients encountered in implementing medical aid in dying resulted from political compromises required to attain necessary votes. I then illustrate how various ambiguities within the legislative text set the stage for later uncertainty, when health care providers and administrators followed the bureaucratic script of aid in dying. In drawing attention to the inevitable gaps between laws as written and laws as practiced,[1] I demonstrate that the meaning of law is not inscribed a priori in legislative texts. Instead, law is made through interpretive processes as social actors put law into practice at various institutional sites and stages of implementation.

A BRIEF HISTORY OF ASSISTED DEATH IN AMERICA

The passage of Oregon's Death with Dignity Act in 1994 was the result of a decades-long advocacy movement.[2] Instrumental to these efforts was the work of the Hemlock Society, a right-to-die organization that became Compassion in Dying in 1992 and merged with End of Life Choices in 2003 to become Compassion & Choices.[3] The Catholic Church, the American Medical Association, and disability rights groups were their strongest opponents. The religious-based opposition upheld the sanctity of life and viewed medical aid in dying as a form of killing. Other core arguments against aid in dying focused on the Hippocratic oath and the physician's commitment to "do no harm," as well as on concerns that legalization would create a slippery slope by which aid in dying would eventually be extended to an expanding group of patients. Relatedly, some worried that certain groups, such as the elderly, the poor, and people with disabilities, would be vulnerable to coercion by caregivers, whose lives would be easier if they died.

Measure 16, which authorized the Oregon Death with Dignity Act, passed by ballot initiative in 1994 by a thin margin of fifty-one to fortynine. Advocates used previous failed attempts in Washington and California to refine their messaging and build their coalition. They raised a million dollars and developed a carefully crafted advertising campaign that used personal stories to cast proponents as empathic, relatable people, who had been unfairly demonized by religious opponents.[4] To address concerns about the potential for abuse, the architects designed the law to include multiple safeguards. To qualify, a patient must be terminally ill, a resident of Oregon, and at least eighteen years old; make two oral requests spaced at least fifteen days apart; and submit a written request signed in the presence of two witnesses. Two physicians must certify that the patient is expected to die within six months and has decision-making capacity. If either believes that a psychological disorder impairs the patient's judgment, they must refer the patient for a psychological examination. The law also requires that the medication be self-administered, to ensure that lethal medication is not administered against the patient's will.[5] Participation by physicians and health systems is likewise voluntary.[6]

After the successful 1994 vote, the opposition sought to block implementation of the Death with Dignity Act by challenging its constitutionality in federal court, and a lengthy appeal process ensued. A repeal measure was placed on the ballot in 1997, but again aid-in-dying proponents won. Even after the law was implemented in 1997, there were numerous federal challenges. Congressional opposition led to the Assisted Suicide Funding Restriction Act of 1997, a federal law that prohibits the use of federally appropriated funds for the purpose of aid in dying. This law has had important consequences for patients' access to aid in dying because it prevents physicians employed by the Department of Veterans Affairs and those working in federally qualified health centers from prescribing medication under state aid-in-dying laws.[7] It also prevents patients from using Medicare insurance to pay for the lethal medication. On the other hand, an important success for proponents was the Supreme Court's 2005 decision in *Gonzales v Oregon*, which determined that the federal government could not punish Oregon physicians who prescribed under the Death with Dignity Act.

At the same time that activists in Oregon mounted their legalization campaign, advocates in Washington and New York challenged a set of state laws that made assisting or promoting a suicide subject to criminal sanctions. (In 1990, most states had prohibitions on assisted death, and thirty-five had statutes that explicitly criminalized it.[8]) In both cases, the plaintiffs—who included terminally ill patients and physicians—filed petitions claiming that the state's prohibitions on assisted death violated personal liberties ensured by the Fourteenth Amendment's due process and equal protection clauses. In both cases, the relevant circuit courts upheld the petitioners' challenges. In 1997, *Washington v Glucksberg* and *Vacco v Quill* reached the Supreme Court, which voted unanimously to reverse the lower-court decisions overturning these prohibitions. In doing so, the Supreme Court affirmed a distinction between assisting a suicide and withdrawing life-sustaining treatment, the latter of which it had authorized in its 1990 decision in *Cruzan v Director, Missouri Department of Health.*[9]

The Supreme Court's rejection of a constitutional right to die with the assistance of a physician meant that legalization strategies would focus on state-level efforts. In Washington state, where advocacy groups had spearheaded the test case leading to *Washington v Glucksberg,* the momentum for legalization was strong. In 2008, medical aid in dying was authorized in Washington through a ballot initiative approved by 58 percent of voters. Montana followed the next year, when the state Supreme Court determined that the state constitution did not prohibit aid in dying. The test case was brought by Robert Baxter, a man suffering from end-stage cancer, who sued the state because he wanted to access medication to end his life on his own terms. Although Baxter died while his case was working its way through the courts, he ceded an important legacy to the assisted-death movement.[10] Unlike Oregon and Washington and the other states that have since legalized aid in dying, Montana does not have a regulatory statute—there are no safeguards or reporting requirements. Instead, physicians are subject to clinical standards of care, as they are for other medical procedures.[11]

When Vermont passed the Patient Choice and Control at End of Life Act in 2013, it became the fourth state in the United States to legalize medical aid in dying, and the first state to follow a legislative process. While advocates followed the legislative pathway because Vermont does not have a ballot initiative process, they also had confidence in this strategy owing to Vermont's small size and the accessibility of its state legislators. "Any individual can change policy in Vermont," one activist told me. In the next section, I consider why and how this came to pass.

AID IN DYING COMES TO VERMONT

When asked why Vermont was an early adopter of medical aid in dying, my research respondents often mentioned their state's progressive, liberal politics, aging population, and low levels of religiosity. As Anita Clarke, a Catholic activist who opposed aid in dying put it, "We have the highest number of unchurched. So, Vermont has long been a thumb your nose at

God kind of a state where if they believe in Him they go take a walk in the woods and tell Him how they think. You know? So it's fertile ground for that idea of choice. I mean, the choice thing goes way—it's deeply entrenched in Vermont. And now we have the largest number of elderly, greying, and we have almost no new, vital young blood."

In addition to these factors, many also cited particular features of Vermont's legislative system. Julia King, an activist on the proponent side, explained to me that in a small state policy makers are much more accessible. Scott Connelly, a physician ethicist who opposed aid in dying, expressed a similar view: "We are a very small state, so you get, on a proportional basis—you get an impassioned group of a couple hundred people, they're not going to make a whole lot of headway in Texas . . . but here you can get a lot of work done." Vermont also has a citizen legislature, composed of citizens who have full-time occupations outside of their legislative duties. The legislature, which includes 150 members in the House of Representatives and 30 senators, meets on a part-time basis, between January and May. A retired political scientist I spoke with theorized that this made a critical difference to how the legislature functioned, and how its members thought about aid in dying: "These aren't full-time politicians for the most part. So, I think they approach issues differently from people in a bigger state." He went on to suggest that partisan politics plays a less decisive role in Vermont than it does in larger states. In Vermont, he said, legislators are more likely to vote in line with their conscience than with their political party.

Anita Clarke held a more skeptical view, however. For her, the small size meant that political influence was easier to purchase. She explained, "It takes about $200,000 to buy Vermont if you want to get an issue passed, that every Vermonter turning on their television is going to see your ad. You can buy lobbyist teams for probably around $100,000. So, it happens to us a lot. . . . When you want to get something kicked up and started you come to Vermont."

Anita's comments, while cynical, capture an important truth about the role of lobbyists in the passage of Act 39. A bill for medical aid in dying had been introduced in the Vermont legislature as early as 1976, but it was not until early 2002 that legalization became a realistic possibility, in large part because a Vermont-based advocacy group, which had splintered from the Vermont Hemlock Society, hired a local lobbyist firm to help pro-mote their cause. These efforts were bolstered by the Death with Dignity National Center, a national organization aimed at promoting death-with-dignity laws using the Oregon model, which supported this work by offering funding and expert consultation on political strategy.[12]

The campaign grew slowly at first. The advocates cold-called legislators who had voted in favor of civil unions in 2000 to generate interest in their cause. They also visited the annual town meetings held in every Vermont town each March, talking to constituents and passing out brochures. Despite widespread support, however, the opposition was stronger. One of the lobbyists who worked on the campaign explained, "We used the phrase that the support for our issue was a mile wide and an inch deep. Whereas the opposition was fairly narrow in minority interest, but it was really deep. They were able to turn out people for this issue and we were not." Bills were introduced in 2005, 2007, and 2009, but proponents were unable to secure the necessary votes.

In 2010, the lobbyist firm hired Ellen Pennybaker, a Vermont-based political strategist, to bolster the campaign. Ellen recalled a sense of enti-tlement among the group of local advocates that launched the movement in Vermont:

> The thing about Death with Dignity that is a little bit different than a lot of issues is that, at least from my experience, the people who are the most pas-sionate about it were upper-class white people who felt like they were being oppressed because they've been able to do whatever they wanted to their whole lives, and now it's time to die and they can't do what they want to do, right? And so, there was a group of, I don't know, fifteen or twenty, mostly old white men who were just like, "Well, we'll just tell the governor what we want, and then we'll get it." Because that's how they had gotten everything else they ever wanted.

Ellen's comments highlight the subtle role of race and class privilege in advocacy movements surrounding assisted death. It was precisely because the well-to-do advocates were accustomed to having things go their way, she suggests, that they expected autonomy in dying.

With Ellen overseeing a statewide media campaign, advocacy momen-tum grew. The proponents enlisted well-known public figures to write op-eds in newspapers across the state. They hired a media firm to make television commercials and worked on a positive messaging campaign. The strategy was careful and measured: they did not want to shut down their would-be supporters by overwhelming them with grim talk about death. Ellen recounted, "Because it's such an emotionally fraught issue, the legislators, we knew they wouldn't react well if they were getting pounded by people saying, 'I want to die.'" Many advocates' views on legalizing medical aid in dying were similar to those on marriage equality in the civil rights arena. However, as one legislator told me, "In a number of respects, it was very different because the issue around marriage equality was really a celebratory kind of issue. And I think that the aid in dying, it was harder to get people to have sort of joyful feelings about it, right?" When I asked this same legislator how controversial this issue was, he said, "I would say on a scale of one to ten, it was between seven and eight. It's an intensely personal issue." Unlike marriage equality, he explained, it was clear there was not going to be a Democratic caucus position.

By 2013, conditions were favorable for the passage of an aid-in-dying statute. It was the year after an election year, and, because the Vermont legislature operates on a biennium, there is a tacit agreement that controversial issues do not get introduced in an election year. Leading up to the 2012 election, the proponents had done considerable work to identify candidates who would be supportive of aid in dying and get them elected. Governor Peter Shumlin[13] favored aid in dying and had even made legalization part of his campaign platform.[14]

At the start of the 2013 legislative session, proponents had the necessary votes in the House. In the Senate, however, they had only thirteen solid votes and needed sixteen. Acquiring those three votes led to political compromise that had significant consequences for the implementation of aid in dying in Vermont.

THE COMPROMISE

At the heart of this compromise was a fundamental conflict between two models of medical aid in dying: the legislative safeguard model adopted by

Oregon in the Death with Dignity Act and the standard-of-practice model followed in Montana. Oregon's law includes a series of legislative safeguards designed to protect vulnerable groups from coercion and ensure that anyone who ingested lethal medication would be doing so freely. This strategy was aimed at reassuring those opponents who worried that people might be forced into hastening death by family members or doctors with nefarious motives—for example, a desire to expedite one's inheritance or relieve oneself of caregiving obligations. Montana, in contrast, followed a judicial path to legalization and does not have a regulatory statute, leaving physicians to self-regulate their participation using clinical standards. Underlying this alternative model is a belief that the government has no business interfering in the practice of medicine. These two models offer fundamentally different views on the role of the state in scripting death: in the former, government is enlisted to prevent abuse and hold physicians accountable, while in the latter, aid in dying remains within the private sphere of the doctor-patient relationship.

These two models represent neither a straightforward conflict between medicine and the state over control of aid in dying nor a straightforward conflict in values. Many advocates on the proponent side in Vermont believed that Montana's model was ideologically superior but doubted that physicians would participate in aid in dying without legislative safeguards. In contrast, the Oregon model offered oversight and protection. Furthermore, adopting the Oregon model seemed more pragmatic because that model addressed legislators' concerns about abuse and inspired confidence owing to Oregon's reassuring history.

Claire Ruskin, one of the lobbyists who worked on the campaign, explained, "I agree with the concept that this should be a decision between a patient and a doctor and that the government doesn't need to get involved." Claire had worked previously in the reproductive rights arena and was sympathetic to the idea that the government should not legislate morality. On the other hand, she continued, "Politically it's a different story because we, in all of our campaign material and all of our advocacy, relied heavily on the Oregon experience and the Washington experience." The data from Oregon and Washington suggested that there was no abuse of vulnerable groups, such as the elderly or people with disabilities, and there had been no prosecutions or serious investigations. The picture from Oregon and Washington was overwhelmingly reassuring for proponents, whereas no one seemed to know what was happening in Montana.[15]

The conflict between these views played out on a national scale. Ellen Pennybaker told me, "That was the tension between the two national groups. The Death with Dignity National strategy is: the safeguards are a pain in the ass, but they get bills passed. The more states you have with them, the more likely you can get more states. Compassion & Choices was: we don't want the hoops." Representatives from both of these organizations visited Vermont during the lead-up to the passage of Act 39 and met with key stakeholders working on the campaign, vying for their preferred model.

One of the primary holdouts in the Senate was Peter Galbraith, a Democratic senator with a strong libertarian orientation, who was drawn to the standard-of-practice model. According to Ellen Pennybaker, Senator Galbraith was strongly influenced by a Compassion & Choices representative with whom he had a private meeting early in 2013. This representative purportedly persuaded Galbraith that the hoops were unnecessary. Galbraith himself was an influential political figure who could sway the remaining swing voters. In order to pass the Senate, compromise was necessary.

The compromise was a provision in which the legislative safeguards would "sunset," or expire, three years after the law took effect, at which time the standard-of-practice model would take hold. Although many of the proponents in the House disapproved of this plan, which lacked the reassurances of the Oregon approach they had been sold on, time was running out. It was already May by the time this compromise was reached, and there would be no time to go back to the drawing board before the session ended. Advocates were averse to postponing the process to the next session, an election year. The House proponents reluctantly agreed, but they did so with the understanding that the law would never sunset, as the House leadership promised there would be another legislative process in two years to make the safeguards permanent.

One year later, two of the crucial swing votes, including Senator Galbraith, were gone. "They had not run for reelection so dynamics changed a little," a House representative, who had opposed the legislation, explained to me. "There were a number of people who were very anxious to have a more protective version." In the 2015 legislative session, the legislature considered a bill that would remove the sunset provision, thereby making the safeguard measures permanent. Another series of hearings was held, and caregivers of individuals who had used medical aid in dying in the two years since Act 39 had passed offered testimony about what this option had meant for their loved ones. Despite a solid opposition group that attempted to repeal Act 39 in the House, the proponents were ultimately successful in solidifying aid in dying with the safeguards in place. Governor Shumlin signed Act 27, An Act Relating to Repealing the Sunset on Provisions Pertaining to Patient Choice at End of Life, on May 20, 2015, exactly two years after signing Act 39.

IMPLEMENTING UNCERTAINTY

To accommodate the compromise, the final text of Act 39 was written late at night, at the last minute. Claire Ruskin recalled, "It wasn't ideal. It was written as a compromise and it was written at 2:30 in the morning by leg counsel that was very tired and trying to accommodate this crazy man that had some crazy ideas in his mind about what he wanted." Leading up to this, Claire explained, she had sat with one of the holdout senators trying to get him to articulate what it would take for him to vote for the bill. "He said, 'There's just too many words.' I'm like, okay, well, all the words mean something, and they're all there for a reason. So maybe you can talk about which words you want to get rid of. . . . So that was sort of what we were trying to work with." Nevertheless, she continued, "It is solid and it works. If I was writing it, it would have been a lot clearer. There would be less confusion. It would have been more internally consistent. But that's just not the way that legislature works."

A prime example of this confusion involves the lack of clarity surrounding immunity for pharmacists. Where Oregon's law very explicitly stipulates immunity from both civil and criminal liability for the prescribing physician, the physician who confirms the patient's eligibility, and the pharmacist, the authors of Act 39, in their haste to write a passable version of the law, had neglected to extend these protections to pharmacists. Scott Connelly told me, "We've had to kind of make peace with a lot of oversights. I don't think anybody thought that that was an intentional omission. I think it was in a rush to get the bill written, they forgot to put that in." When concerns surfaced about this issue, the lobbyists went to the Vermont attorney general to request such protections for pharmacists. "And so, the AG did issue this sort of wishy washy opinion that said, 'You're fine,'" Claire Ruskin said. "The pharmacists would be fine if they practice the way that they normally would practice under this law." Nevertheless, this oversight provided ammunition to opponents, who claimed that Act 39 did not offer sufficient protections, and it likely contributed to the barriers that patients and physicians would go on to face in securing pharmacy participation.[16]

In addition to such omissions, there were concerns about wording. One of the key requirements of medical aid-in-dying laws in the United States is that physicians determine that patients are of sound mind and able to make informed decisions about their health. The bioethical term for this ability is *decision-making capacity*. The legislative text of Act 39, however, required patients to be "capable." Claire described this shift in language from an earlier version of the bill as "sloppy" but not a meaningful change: "That's definitely another example of how it's not really clear why that decision was made by the drafters and I don't even know where she came up with that. But it was frustrating for everybody. . . . Once the Senate passed it, our job was not to try and wordsmith it because we just needed the House to agree to these words."

Claire maintained that the law defined *capable* in a way that approximated the same point as *capacity*. The legislative text of Act 39 reads, "'Capable' means that a patient has the ability to make and communicate health care decisions to a physician, including communication through persons familiar with the patient's manner of communicating if those persons are available."[17] This definition supports Claire's contention, yet it also highlights another major concern for opponents: the possibility that the physician's verification of capability and other eligibility requirements might be mediated through third-party communication. Opponents felt that this possibility could make it difficult to ensure that the patient's choice was free and voluntary.

Although the definition of *capable* matched Oregon's Death with Dignity law almost exactly,[18] opponents saw this wording as an intentional shift designed to expand aid in dying to more constituents. As a hospice stakeholder averred, "A child may be capable of ingesting an ant, or dirt, or whatever it is, but have no idea whether it's good or not." When I probed as to whether this change had been intentional, she responded, "Oh yeah, yeah. I mean why would they change that language? Because the word capacity was in the House Bill, the word capable was not there. It got changed."

A related objection was that some key terms were not properly defined. Act 39 requires that the patient seeking life-ending medication be a Vermont resident but does not stipulate any criteria for state residency. In contrast, Oregon's Death with Dignity law specifies verifiable qualifications for residency, including possession of an Oregon driver's license, being registered to vote, owning or leasing property, or filing an Oregon tax return for the most recent year.[19] Act 39's silence on this issue set the stage for later uncertainty, when physicians realized they would be forced to determine who counts as a Vermont resident. Jeff Braswell, an employee of the Vermont Department of Health, explained to me that "there are other places in state law where residence means six months, or it means three months, or whatever it is. So, we just sort of said, 'We think residency means you pay taxes. It means you have a driver's license.' I mean, these go toward the idea of residency, but it's ultimately up to the physician to make the call which, I would say, it puts the physician in a very uncomfortable place. He or she is making a legal determination as to whether or not somebody's a resident."

When I interviewed him in 2016, Jeff estimated he was fielding between ten and twenty telephone calls per week from out-of-staters inquiring about how to establish Vermont residency in order to qualify for aid in dying. While he worked at the Department of Health, his background was in law, and he felt ill-prepared for these heart-wrenching conversations: "There's times when I have these calls, I'll close my door and say, 'I'm going to be in my office crying for a while. I'll be okay.' You have these awful conversations with people. They call, and they say, 'I have brain cancer.' 'My mother has ALS.' And the person is incredibly emotional and my response is like, 'Oh, well, let me give you some bureaucracy.'" Such comments demonstrate how the emotional dimensions of caring for dying persons can exceed the organizing frameworks for bureaucratically scripted death.

In recounting how one patient had moved to Vermont from a midwestern state to access aid in dying, the nurse coordinator of an ALS clinic lamented the residency requirement, saying, "They left [that] up to the discretion of the doctor. We didn't have any guidelines for it and we just didn't know, and since then we've had other people who have moved into the area because they have family, but they've also asked about Act 39, which makes me wonder, is that why you chose to come?" Several policy stakeholders I interviewed doubted legislators had envisioned people moving to Vermont to die, acknowledging that it puts a different kind of pressure on physicians.

Opponents also expressed concerns that the safeguards did not go far enough. One point of contention in this regard was Act 39's limited reporting requirements, particularly compared with Oregon. An activist who opposed aid in dying told me, "All that's reported is the prescriptions that are written. . . . So I guess our problem is how do you really expect to monitor something and know that it's working well when the only people who are telling you its working well are those who are in favor of this?" Act 39 stipulates that the Vermont Department of Health "make rules to facilitate the collection of information regarding compliance" with the law. Beyond that, however, the Department of Health has considerable latitude in developing regulations to monitor aid in dying.

The department faced an urgent timeline for doing so. The original version of the statute, based on the Oregon model and endorsed by Vermont's House of Representatives, had an effective date of September 15, which would have given the department several months to prepare. Yet another of Senator Galbraith's prerequisites for voting in favor of the bill was that it would be effective upon passage. "From the day the legislature adjourned, the governor had ten days to sign the law and once he signed the law, it was effective. And no one was ready to use it," Claire Ruskin recalled. She continued, "The law was only as good as the providers that were willing to use it. . . . Legally a doctor could have prescribed, but they would not have known the first thing to do."

Jeff Braswell recounted how the Department of Health responded to this accelerated implementation timeline. They convened a group of fifteen or so stakeholders, including representatives from the Vermont Medical Society, the Vermont Hospital Association, the Visiting Nurses

Association (Vermont's nonprofit hospice and home health agency), the Vermont Ethics Network, the University of Vermont Medical Center, and Compassion & Choices, which funded a part-time employee to assist with implementation efforts in Vermont. The stakeholder group wrote a "Frequently Asked Questions" document and created forms to collect information. Jeff explained that these steps were not mandated by law, yet the stakeholders viewed them as necessary for the law to function adequately: "It had to do with the clumsiness of the original law. It wasn't clear how people would—how physicians and patients would actually meet the obligations. So, we just sat down with the law and a blank piece of paper and created forms that, if you look at the forms and you look at the original law . . . they mirror each other. So, here's a checkmark for every step that the law requires that you take and we didn't add or subtract anything." According to Jeff, the Department of Health had the forms posted to its website within a month of the law's effective date.

Under Act 39, the only information the department collected was a form indicating the primary physician's intent to write a prescription. The department had no idea if the physician eventually wrote the prescription, let alone whether the patient filled and ingested it. In 2013, Jeff explained, the department understood the legislative intent of Act 39 as being disinterested in collecting comprehensive utilization statistics. However, Act 27, which repealed the sunset provisions in Act 39, also bolstered the reporting requirements for aid in dying by mandating the distribution of a biennial statistical report—provided that releasing this information did not conflict with privacy protections on confidential health information imposed by the federal Health Insurance Portability and Accountability Act of 1996.

Beginning in 2015, then, the Department of Health worked to strengthen the rules governing medical aid in dying. Jeff Braswell distinguished this process from the political process that led to legalization. "I like the rule-making process," he said. "This is, of course, a legislative process. I think it's more insulated from politics. There's more flexibility. You can do it faster. You can be more responsive to the needs of patients and doctors." For example, they wrote a brief rule explaining how to dispose of unused medication, which had been left out of the original law. They also wrote a rule asking physicians to report whether the patient died. While the department had wanted to impose a mandatory obligation for physicians to determine cause of death, the Vermont Medical Society objected that this would be unreasonably burdensome. Advocates on the proponent side also feared it would create an additional access barrier. Instead, the department created an optional form for the physician to indicate how the person had died, and included "I don't know" as an option.

Leading up to the Department of Health's first public report in 2018, there was a great deal of uncertainty about how much specific information about the deaths would be reported. Given Vermont's small size, there were ample concerns about confidentiality and the potential for individuals to be identified. In Oregon, information about the age, gender, race and ethnicity, educational attainment, diagnosis, hospice enrollment status, and motivating concerns of people using the Death with Dignity Act is publicly reported, as are details about psychiatric referrals, a provider's presence at the time of death, adverse events, and physician characteristics.[20] In Vermont, however, there were concerns that releasing information about race and ethnicity or a specific diagnosis could be identifying. When the first report was released in 2018, it offered minimal information regarding patient characteristics, stating only the broad disease categories—cancer, ALS, and "other"—the number of patients who had a death certificate on file, and the cause of death.[21] For skeptics hoping for substantial evidence that the law was working as intended, this level of generality offered little reassurance.

THE "NEW NORMAL"

In October 2013, several months after Act 39 took effect, the Vermont Ethics Network devoted its annual fall conference to practical and ethical issues in implementing medical aid in dying in Vermont, titling it "Vermont's New Normal: End-of-Life Care and Physician's Aid in Dying." Invited speakers included experienced physicians from Oregon, Compassion & Choices representatives, and local experts. Anita Clarke, an attendee who opposed aid in dying, challenged the normalization implied by this title. "No one had even used it yet and they were already trying to make it normal to take your own life," she suggested. The unfortunately named conference generated many unanswered questions, revealing a large number of lingering uncertainties about how the law would operate.

As the speakers and organizers prepared for this event, elsewhere in Vermont, the first prescriptions were being written, with physicians, patients, and caregivers encountering their own uncertainties about the bureaucratic scripting of death. In fact, the person publicly believed to have received the first lethal prescription under Act 39 died several weeks after the conference, though he did so before ingesting the medication.[22] As I will show in the chapters that follow, the events that unfolded over the next few years showed that—notwithstanding opponents' concerns— it would be a long time, if ever, before aid in dying would become "normal" in Vermont.

The early history of Act 39 in Vermont demonstrates that medical aid-in-dying laws are not made only through legislative processes or voter referenda. Instead, laws are produced through a series of interpretive acts, as institutional actors put their policies into practice. A law, in other words, gains meaning and power from how the legislative text is interpreted, deployed, and sometimes subverted in real-life situations.[23] Law is in this respect coproduced by various state agents and "street-level bureaucrats," who help to interpret and enact it.[24] This dynamic view of law unsettles the assumption that implementing law is a straightforward act of following established legislative scripts. As one of my respondents put it, "I think a good law is written with holes so that people can make it work." In this sense, the meaning of laws is always in flux and subject to further interpretation and negotiation; social scientists refer to this process as the social production of law.

Consider, for example, the self-administration requirement. Nothing in Act 39 or in other state laws expressly prohibits patients from ingesting medication through a gastrointestinal tube, an intervention that is routinely offered to people with ALS who lose the ability to swallow. In Oregon, the self-administration requirement has been interpreted as permitting caregivers to put medication into the patient's G-tube, as long as the patient commits the last act of ingesting it,[25] and similar interpretations have been applied in Vermont. In fact, one ALS clinic provider told me some patients have considered obtaining a G-tube in order to facilitate access to aid in dying; an acquaintance confirmed that at least one patient in Vermont had done so.

This understanding of the social production of law reveals how policy stakeholders, such as legislators, activists, lobbyists, and Department of Health officials, share control over scripting death with physicians and patients. In regimes of medical aid in dying, terminally ill people share the power to script their own deaths with a variety of state actors, who read and interpret the law and serve a critical gatekeeping function, assuming much of the social control over death that in earlier times was held by religious institutions.[26] Therefore, if medical aid in dying permits a new form of agency over death, it is necessarily constrained by certain social and political forces.

Proponents were ultimately successful in bringing aid in dying to Vermont, but the uneven path to legalization exposed some of the crucial differences between the legislative pathway and the ballot initiative process. Claire Ruskin explained,

> With a referendum, you put words on a paper and you say yes or no, vote on this, this is what you're voting on. There's no opportunity to debate or deliberate about the words on the paper. . . . What we did in Vermont was people actually debated and talked about it. So as much as we don't necessarily love the outcome, the outcome is a result of trying to find a middle ground, a place where enough people, the majority of the legislators could agree. And that's the legislative process. It's much messier. It's a lot cheaper than a referendum. It's not all the rhetoric; it's actual people talking. So that's a big difference and I'm glad that we don't have referendum in Vermont.

The democratic process that Claire alludes to here was a particular point of pride for the activists in Vermont, who worked tirelessly to make medical aid in dying a legally authorized option for residents of their state. They viewed this process as reflective of certain fundamental qualities of their state identity. To be sure, the legalization story demonstrates the privileged role of personal liberty and progressive values within the state's political sphere, as well as the Yankee tenacity to see the advocacy process through until they attained success. Yet the democratic process also reflects a softer side of Yankee grit, by illustrating the compromises necessary to achieve the final outcome. For proponents, therefore, the history of Act 39 showcases Vermont at its best.

Earlier in this chapter, I cited Anita Clarke's comments about the cheap price of purchasing political influence in Vermont. While Anita and other opponents viewed Vermont as a convenient forum for national organizations seeking to air debates on a local, low-cost stage, proponents insisted that the legalization of medical aid in dying was a homegrown issue, the success of which resulted from the determination of local advocates. The truth probably lies somewhere in between these positions. Funds from national groups undoubtedly played a critical role in the legalization of aid in dying in Vermont. Yet without the catalyzing efforts of the state-based advocacy group, the national groups would not have paid much attention to Vermont. Conditions on the ground had to be ripe for the movement to take off. The rest of the book picks up where many sociological accounts of legalization have left off. What happened once aid in dying was implemented?[27]

2 Making Death

The Northeast Kingdom, a mountainous region nestled in the northeast corner of Vermont, comprises Essex, Orleans, and Caledonia counties, and is one of the most remote and picturesque areas of the state. The writer Howard Frank Mosher, who immortalized the area in his novels, described the Northeast Kingdom as "a region of jumbled mountains, deep forests, glacial lakes, and scattered hill farms, where people still live close to the world of nature we were all once part of."[1] This lush and untouched landscape had lured Frances and Tim Sullivan with the promise of a tranquil retirement. The cabin they purchased, with its modest design and sweeping vistas, seemed like the perfect place to begin their next phase of life. Several years later, however, Frances, a retired nurse, was diagnosed with ALS, disrupting the Sullivans' plans for a quiet retirement.

I was apprehensive about our meeting because it would be the first time that I would meet someone who knew she was close to death. While working on my study, I had done much to confront my own mortality and was much more comfortable with death than I had been before beginning this research. Yet my feelings about death remained on an abstract, intellectual level. Driving to the Sullivans' cabin, I felt like I was going to confront death for the first time in a concrete, visceral sense; the prospect of meeting a woman who intentionally planned to die, and very soon, was oddly unsettling. Her awareness of death's proximity seemed to violate basic cultural norms about holding death in abeyance and preserving a space for uncertainty. To settle my nerves, I focused on the hills as my car rolled along the scenic drive.

Tim Sullivan, a burly man with a thick, white beard, greeted me at the door and welcomed me into the cabin. Frances was sitting on the sofa waiting for me, wearing a medical scrubs top and jeans. Aside from her slightly matted hair, she looked healthy and composed. As I took a seat next to her, Frances handed me a notebook in which she had written the following:

> I've been critical care RN 1975–2016. Seen many patients die on respira-
> tors, tied down, pleading eyes as I give meds to "settle" them but who know
> what they were thinking trapped like that. Families coming and going
> exhausted. In acute care, some patients would never go through what was
> going to happen to them if they had the choice. But once that starts in that
> setting there's no going back—they die attached to tubes, feedings, inconti-
> nent, no communication, tears sliding from corners of eyes. Many patients
> and families need to have this ~~choice~~ option. It's our bodies and lives and
> should ALWAYS be our choice. When and how we die is our right. I would
> advocate for my patients when no hope at all but would be endless discus-
> sions with "their team of doctors," then each specialist weighing in, then
> palliative care, then family meetings. On and on. But the person left out is
> the one dying slowly who was never given a choice.

By this point, the ALS had impacted Frances's speech, and she was communicating primarily through writing. Our interview settled into a plodding rhythm: I posed a question, Frances would begin typing a response on her iPad, Tim would fill in some details while she typed. Then I would read Frances's response aloud, so that it could be captured in the interview transcript. As we proceeded, I chose my questions carefully, acutely aware of not wanting to take up too much of Frances's quite precious time.

Frances's illness had begun with a pain in her hand five years previously. After a protracted, two-year diagnostic odyssey, during which she retired from nursing, Frances had finally been diagnosed with ALS. While the disease initially progressed slowly, Frances, now in her midsixties, had no speech, difficulty eating, and limited mobility, aside from the use of three fingers. When I asked Frances about her quality of life, Tim responded, "She struggles every day. She fights. She fights every single day with the smallest things, tying your shoes, getting dressed, take a shower. I mean it just gets to a certain point where this isn't any fun at all." Meanwhile, Frances typed, "Terrible. Can't do anything but stay in chair." Throughout our exchange, Frances's clipped responses underscored the extent to which ALS had limited her.

As a retired nurse, Frances knew enough about Vermont's aid-in-dying law to resolve to pursue it immediately after her diagnosis. After nearly fifty years of marriage, Tim was initially reluctant to support this desire. But eventually he came to accept Frances's wishes, recognizing that she was suffering terribly and declining more rapidly. He explained, "It's not going to get better, the ALS. It doesn't get better. It gets worse. So, today, tomorrow, it's going to be worse. It doesn't get any better. There's nothing you can do. You can't stop it. You can't slow it down. You take pills all the time, to relax or even when she has to go to the bathroom, is a problem. All these little things that people do every day. You don't think about them until something like this happens."

When Frances requested aid in dying from her ALS team, the initial response was discouraging. The nurse coordinator tried to dissuade Frances, citing the exorbitant cost, and the doctor was cold and unsupportive. So, Frances "fired" them (in her words) and sought care from a palliative care team at a different hospital. There, Frances encountered a much more compassionate response from two physicians, who came to her house for a consultation, agreed that Frances qualified for aid in dying, and started the necessary paperwork.

Tim had sent the Seconal prescription to the pharmacy the day before our interview, and the Sullivans were busy planning the details of Frances's death, which she had set for two and a half weeks later. (Seconal, a barbiturate, is the medication most commonly used for aid in dying in the United States.) On her doctors' advice, Frances had been practicing eating the amount of applesauce they figured she would need to mix with a hundred emptied Seconal capsules—the number required to form a lethal dose. Tim showed me the plastic spoon, wrapped in a red foam casing to make it easier to hold, and the individually packaged containers of applesauce that

Frances was using. Tim explained that the doctors wanted her to be able to consume the entire container in two minutes, but she was currently able to do it in one minute, fifteen seconds. Frances seemed a bit nervous about the reportedly bitter taste of Seconal, but I assured her that people said that, when mixed with applesauce and cinnamon, it is not too bad.

I asked Frances about her two children, and if she wanted them to be present when she took the medication. This was one of several times in the interview that she broke down crying. She did not want them there, perhaps to shield them from the pain of watching their mother die, but Tim was insistent. "I don't care if they're outside. I don't care where they go as long as they're here," he said. "This is their mother. And I just, I just won't, I wouldn't feel right about this." Frances also wanted two of her closest friends from her nursing days to be there, to help mix the medication and provide support. This was comforting to Tim, who doubted whether he could help Frances on his own. With support from hospice, the Sullivans had also put a lot of thought into Frances's postmortem care. Frances wanted to be cremated, and Tim had gone to the town clerk's office to obtain a burial transit permit, so that he could transport her to the crematorium himself, with the help of family and friends.

The planning undertaken by Frances and Tim Sullivan illustrates that, in an era of expanded medically assisted death, understandings of death and the kind of experience it might be have shifted dramatically. Scripting death through medical aid in dying can restore a sense of order and control to what might otherwise be seen as the ultimate uncontrollable experience. In this chapter, I analyze how actively producing death through medical aid in dying transforms death into a particular kind of event, in which humans have substantial agency to craft the dying process in an aesthetically pleasing way.

FROM "LETTING DIE" TO "MAKING DEATH"

During the course of my fieldwork, I heard about a woman who had consulted with her physician about accessing aid in dying. Apparently, she was in end-stage renal failure and felt like she could no longer endure dialysis. The physician was unwilling to participate and indicated that he did not know of anyone in the area who would prescribe life-ending medication; he advised her to stop dialysis and said that she would die within the week. Several weeks later, the woman was still very much alive and angry with her physician for—in her view—lying to her.

I was disconcerted by this story when I first heard it. Physicians are notoriously bad at determining terminal prognoses. Surely this undesired outcome was more a predictive error than an outright lie. Moreover, I was troubled that this woman framed being alive negatively. Particularly if her suffering was related to the grueling process of dialysis itself,[2] shouldn't she be grateful that she did not die right away? How did living beyond the anticipated time span come to be seen as a problematic result? And wouldn't she die soon, anyway?

Several years after hearing this story, however, I now understand this woman's anger and disappointment as reflecting a failed attempt at control. I call the desire for a particular type of death an *aspirational death*, a term that highlights the affects and attachments that inform orientations to dying as an object of choice, control, and careful choreography. The concept is also meant to signal the possibility that the desired form of death might not be possible. In this sense, aspirational deaths always contain the possibility of hope foreclosed.

The distance between the woman's aspirational death and the death she undoubtedly had (for one can live only so long in kidney failure) demonstrates a distinction between "making death" and "letting die" that is significant to contemporary scholarship on biopolitics.[3] Recent anthropological studies of life and death have used the framework of biopolitics to explore the role of the state and its associated regimes of knowledge, expertise, and power in governing human life processes. This body of work treats life and death as matters of political concern and contestation, addressing such topics as the distribution of antiretroviral treatment for HIV,[4] reproductive choice and genetic diagnosis,[5] and pharmaceutical development.[6]

For many contemporary scholars of biopolitics, the philosopher Michel Foucault's conceptualization of biopower as the power to "make live and let die" has served as a key point of departure.[7] Foucault observed that one of the most important shifts in political power during the nineteenth century was that the sovereign power to take life was gradually replaced, under liberalism, with the power to make live (for example, through public health interventions) and let die (by abandonment). Foucault called this power "biopower," and suggested that it was constituted through disciplining techniques that operated on individual bodies, as well as collectively on populations. From this perspective, contemporary biopolitics is often understood as "active with regard to life, and passive with regard to death. It *makes* populations live and *lets* portions of the population die."[8]

For example, consider the changes to Georgia's Emergency Medicaid program, which led in 2009 to the closure of a public outpatient dialysis center in Atlanta's Grady Hospital disproportionately populated by undocumented immigrants. After the closure, Grady medically repatriated some patients to their home countries, a legally and ethically contentious practice. Other patients were stuck waiting, several of whom died. This case reveals how state-level policies around the provision of public health insurance condemn some populations to death by failing to provide the care that keeps them alive.[9] Therefore, while life must be actively made, "death is neither made nor unmade, it just happens, as it were."[10]

From this perspective, aid in dying presents a challenge to Foucauldian biopolitics. Scholars of suicide have explicitly noted the limitations of the biopolitics framework for elucidating the specific forms of agency and power at stake in making death.[11] As the anthropologist Lisa Stevenson puts it, "Suicide, whatever else it may be, is the active usurpation of the individual's power over death—a power that biopolitics has foregone."[12] To counter these limitations, the literary theorist Stuart Murray has used the framework of thanatopolitics, an alternative politics of death that departs from the biopolitical logic of making live and letting die. Murray explains, "If biopolitics is a productive power that necessitates or silently calls for death as the consequence of 'making live,' then thanatopolitics is not merely the lethal underside of biopolitics but is itself a productive power in the voices of those who biopolitical power 'lets die.'"[13] For Murray, thanatopolitics draws attention to the power of certain deaths to speak back to neoliberal regimes that abandon them to death. Using the example of suicide bombing, he shows how actors may produce rhetorical effects by inducing their own deaths in ways that elude biopolitical logics foregrounding the passivity of death.[14] Protest suicides like hunger strikes or self-immolation entail similar political processes.[15]

If the Grady Hospital dialysis patients had engaged in protest suicides, rather than waiting to die, they might have exemplified a thanatopolitical logic. While something different was at stake for the Vermont dialysis patient I heard about—who I can only presume wanted aid in dying for personal reasons having little to do with speaking back to political power— I find the concept of thanatopolitics useful for underscoring the limits of biopolitics and the productive possibilities for theorizing human agency in "making death." The anthropologist Anita Hannig recently examined how the debates about the porous boundaries between suicide and physician- assisted death reflect understandings of agency, responsibility, and ration- ality in regard to hastened death.[16] She identifies a process of *agentive displacement*—that is, the idea that agency and responsibility over a spe- cific action, such as death, can be distributed among a range of actors. Hannig argues that agency over death in medical aid in dying demon- strates a dialectical tension between aid in dying as an autonomously authored act and aid in dying as authorized by medicine and the state. She explains this process as follows: "An aided death cannot be achieved autonomously but depends on other actors (physicians, psychiatrists, pharmacists, hospice staff, volunteers, and family members) sanctioning, facilitating, and sharing responsibility for such a death. While human agency is not wholly evacuated in aid-in-dying, it becomes distributed among entities that have the power to affect the moral and conceptual status of assisted deaths as something other than suicide."[17]

Here, I pursue a similar line of analysis by illustrating how terminally ill people exercise agency over death against a backdrop of existential uncertainty, bureaucratic regulation, and biomedicalization of end-of-life care. In doing so, I foreground how aid in dying permits certain people to script their own deaths and thus (re)claim agency over death from a dis- tributed set of actors. However, as others have noted, and as I will show in subsequent chapters, the opportunity to script one's death is not evenly distributed.[18] The legalization of aid in dying may offer an aspirational death, but it is not one that is equally available to all. How, then, does the emergence of an aspirational form of death transform understandings of death?

My particular interest here is in how aid in dying renders death an *event:* an anticipated occasion that may be painstakingly planned, staged, and produced. This possibility transforms death from an inchoate experience, which a terminally ill person awaits passively, to a carefully crafted event that is actively managed, shaped, and controlled. Aid in dying as an aspirational death is formed in reaction to a normative undesirable death—a "bad" death, in popular cultural terms. The normative death to be avoided through aid in dying transpires slowly and is experienced passively, in circumstances that lie largely outside personal choice and control. Even for the end-stage renal disease patient who is granted the option of actively hastening death by discontinuing dialysis (i.e., letting die), death may not come as quickly as desired; its timing is uncontainable and admits too much suffering (or even just the possibility of too much suffering). There is thus an important distinction between waiting to die and actively making death. In what follows, I illustrate how this distinction matters and how it results in a very different orientation to death and the kind of event it might be.

PRODUCING DEATH

In July 2015, I interviewed Bert Glaser, a chaplain and death-with-dignity advocate, at his weathered farmhouse in rural Vermont. Summer had been unseasonably warm, but at this early hour a chill still hung in the air. We sat on the lawn in a pair of metal rocking chairs, a verdant landscape of rolling hills and farmland stretched out before us.

Now retired, Bert had dabbled in several different professions, culminating with a role in the local volunteer fire department as a department chaplain, for which he had completed a certificate program in clinical pastoral education. Bert referred to himself as a community chaplain and explained that his pastoral work extended outside of the fire department. He had counseled many people in the final stages of life and had been around death and dying a lot. He had become interested in the assisted-death movement in Vermont when the law was being debated in the Vermont State House, and he had testified to the state legislature. To prepare for my arrival, he had printed out some of his testimony and letters to the editor, which he had prepared years ago. He told me he felt "very strongly that people should have the right to choose when their quality of life is such that they don't want to sustain it."

For Bert, "not lingering" was an essential component of a good death. He explained, "I don't want to be helpless in a bed where I can't get out and everything is—you've got to wash me, you've got to clean me, you've got to empty the bedpans. I don't want to live like that. I don't want to live like that, you know, for a day, let alone for an extended period of time." Bert's reasoning exemplifies why disability rights activists have been so opposed to aid in dying: they fear that Bert's motives devalue the lives of people who, every day, depend on others for precisely the kind of care that Bert wants to avoid.

Such preferences were not mere conjecture: Bert had developed a stubborn bacterial infection ten years prior, and he almost didn't recover. This episode, which Bert described to me as a "near-death experience," had cemented his end-of-life preferences. When it became apparent that he would survive, he left the hospital against his doctor's recommendations to go home and relay his wishes to his family. He recounted how he had told them, "When the day comes, if I get hit by a bus tomorrow, you need to know that from my perspective, life doesn't owe me a single more day. I'm not owed a single thing. I'm content with the opportunities I've had. I've lived five lifetimes in the time I've had. So, you know, be sad, miss me, love me, but don't regret that I went too soon and didn't have a chance. That's for the boys in war."

Because Bert preferred not to linger in a prolonged state of dying, he considered an assisted death an attractive option for scripting a swift exit. He explained,

Let's just figure out a good moment here and let's wrap this up in a bow. You know, I'm a planner, I've put on many exhibits, I've done lots of orchestration of things. Things have a beginning, a middle, and an end. Let's not, you know, drag this thing out to the point where the audience is going, "Shit, if they did ten less songs it would have been a better opera," you know. And I do think there's a virtue in timing and a virtue in giving people—well, my wife and I have talked about it and filled out advance directives. We'd come home, play some classical music, and choose the moment. What's wrong with that? It's comforting to think that I have that option. It would be terrifying to me if I was sick to think I didn't have that option, that I had to simply go with the whims of a disease that I hated.

"And just to be clear that option you're referring to is death with dignity?" I interjected. "Yes," Bert responded. "I'm absolutely referring to the opportunity to say, 'Tomorrow is gonna be the day. Get the kids. . . .' Planning when you're gonna choose to end your life because of the circumstances around you."

In Bert's account of hypothetical death, the theatrical imagery is striking: death is an event that one choreographs, a matter of careful timing. Choosing the right moment to die requires an appreciation for dramatic time. From this perspective, orchestrating the right time for death has not only an ethical but also an aesthetic quality.[19] Bert does not envision himself as being passive at the scene of his death, watching his life unravel. Instead, he is a producer, one with a moral charge to engage and release his audience at appropriate intervals through careful dramaturgical sequencing.

To call something an event is to mark it in time in a particular way.[20] Bert's vision of death as event contrasts with the way Julie Yip-Williams wrote about dying in her memoir about living with and dying from metastatic colon cancer after her diagnosis at age thirty-seven. In the last chapter of her book, in which she acknowledges that her body is finally failing her and grapples with the imminence of death, Yip-Williams muses over the prospect of witnessing her own death. She writes, "I was sad to be leaving my husband and my daughters, but I felt something else, too: awe at what was happening to my body. I couldn't watch myself be born, but with eyes open, I could watch myself die. And that is no less a miracle than any other. It is hard to find the beauty in dying but I've learned; I'm learning still."[21] In Yip-Williams's account, she is a passive observer, with no hand in shaping her end. She is an awe-filled spectator at the scene of her death, which she treats as a miracle. The contrast between these two imagined scenes illuminates just how the possibility of aid in dying transforms death from a boundless experience that one endures, whether with trepidation or wonder, to a staged event, concretely fixed in time, that one might actively shape, orchestrate, and produce.

Although Frances Sullivan wanted the group gathered for her death to be as small as possible—her husband, two friends from her nursing days, and her children (and them, under protest)—I heard many more stories about terminally ill people faced with the prospect of planning for death who viewed aid in dying as an opportunity to throw a final celebration. Rae Callo, a hospice nurse, described one assisted death she had attended: "She picked out the date, she threw a party. Very meaningful to her to have—be surrounded by certain people. And I feel very blessed that she asked me to be there and the chaplain as well. And so, it was a party atmosphere. . . . She had a performance of opening the capsules and making the milkshake.[22] And it was very sad, too, when she realized that the journey was ending."

The juxtaposition of sadness with joy is common in death rituals. What stands out in assisted death is the way in which the dying person actively crafts and cultivates this tension. Geoffrey Tomkins, an aid-in-dying advocate in his fifties living with a long-term cancer diagnosis, told me, "I've been through, personally, hell and back. I know I've endured screaming pain, crapping in a bag, peeing in my pants, all this stuff." He knew he would probably die of the cancer; when, he couldn't say. At the point at which he decided he did not want any more treatment, he said, he would plan a great party. "You go to funerals. They have great parties afterwards. Well, you don't get to go. So have it beforehand."

Geoffrey's comments raise another key dimension of how medical aid in dying transforms traditional American death rituals: the active presence of the guest of honor. In his classic work, *The Rites of Passage*, Arnold van Gennep identified a three-stage cross-cultural framework for rites of passage, including: *separation*, when people withdraw from normal social life and prepare for a shift in role or status; *transition*, a liminal period between two disparate states; and *incorporation*, during which the status shift is completed. For death and mortuary rites, transition often begins with the extended stay of the corpse or coffin in an area of the home or gathering place and culminates with the funeral and mourning rituals, which focus on the survivors. In contrast, aid in dying enables transition for the dying person as well, through a sort of living wake.

Leanne Ford, an oncology nurse practitioner, recalled another patient who had fixated on the party, yet never followed through with his plans for assisted death.

He knew who he was going to invite to his house. He was going to have a party. He was basically going to blow whatever he had left on sort of entertaining his friends, and then he was going to ask a couple of them to stay behind and he would take the medicine and that would be it. I mean, he had it very well thought out, but never could get himself to do it, even when things were sort of getting bad. So it's kind of interesting to have people sort of process it.

For this patient, and others like him whom I heard about, planning a party enabled him to establish a measure of control over death, even though he did not ultimately end his life as he thought he would.

Gloria Fleming, a woman in her sixties and one of the first individuals in Vermont to use medical aid in dying, gathered her closest friends, a group of eight or so women, and a beloved hospice nurse to surround her at the scene of death. Yet she saved the elaborate party, which she planned with painstaking detail, for after her death. Her dear friend Sheila recounted, "She didn't want a memorial service, she wanted a cocktail party." Gloria and Sheila had discussed the party on one of their long drives to Boston for treatment at the Dana Farber Cancer Center. Sheila explained how Gloria had told her:

> "I want you to take five thousand dollars out of my money and I want you to throw a great party. I want everyone to dress up, none of this Carhartt bullshit."[23] You know, cause we're in Vermont. And that's how we wrote it. In quotes: "none of this Carhartt bullshit." And I'll tell you, all of our Carhartt boys, they came dressed to the nines. They followed instructions. We rented out our local place downtown. And decorated it black and gold, which were her colors. Wore nothing but black and always had gold on. Classy lady. We did a slideshow on a laptop and then pictures and a few people spoke. But mostly it was just an opportunity to get together and drink and think of her.

Gloria's celebration of life highlights how aid in dying affords an opportunity to approach death as a final event to be thoughtfully produced. Her frank mention of cost, however, also emphasizes the financial dimensions of this sort of death planning. Not everyone has the socioeconomic means to carry out this sort of a vision. For some, death will be an occasion that squeezes their family's finances.[24] One's capacity to assume agency and attain an aspirational death thus depends in no small part on one's socioeconomic status.[25]

TO GO OUT SAILING

In July 2016, I sat on the porch of Clara Barnstable's home drinking tea. To get to her small Vermont town, I had traveled several miles over unmarked dirt roads, then over a one-lane wooded pathway to her secluded lot. Her father, Arthur Rivers, had died earlier that year, after a lung cancer diagnosis in his early nineties, and Clara was recounting his choice to end his life using medical aid in dying. Before his death, I had met and interviewed Arthur, a retired business executive, and his wife, Bea, about their activism for aid in dying. Together, they had helped to form the grassroots advocacy group discussed in the last chapter, which retained a political lobbyist and helped get Vermont's law enacted.

Clara explained that typically, with cancer, you had two choices: treating it aggressively or letting the disease take its course, relying on morphine for pain management. With the latter option, Clara said, "you're basically making a decision . . . to be out of it" because of the drugs. However, she continued, "If you have the alternative to, you know, choose the time of your death, then all the discussions are different. And it's really hard to put your finger on it until you've seen it. But the whole nature of the discussion is different. It's about, well, what are the key things you want to be doing in the last months of your life? And my dad said, 'I want to be sailing. I want to be sailing on Lake Champlain.' And he did."

According to Clara, choosing the time you die changes the stakes of how you live. Arthur Rivers embarked on his last sail one month before he died, taking a half day's sail from where his boat was moored to Malletts Bay, an inlet on the central Vermont side of Lake Champlain. In his last week, he entertained visits from scores of family, colleagues, and friends. Clara recounted, "And he said he had some of the deepest conversations of his whole life. The most meaningful conversations of his whole life in the last week. Well that doesn't happen if you're all drugged up."

In her moving ethnography of hospital death, *A Time to Die*, Sharon Kaufman asked, What happens when waiting to die becomes an active practice, not merely passive waiting, but an experience to be structured, managed, and controlled?[26] Her response to this question was subsequently extended and complicated in *Ordinary Medicine*, in which she showed how the modern deathwatch has been transformed yet again through a chain of health care drivers that includes scientific advancement, industrial complexes, and policy apparatus.[27] Together, these works highlight how advances in contemporary medicine can prompt us to rethink human agency over death and view the time of death as not just a moment that happens but as one that physicians, patients, and caregivers actively shape through individual decision making, institutional structures, and systems-level policies.

The expansion of aid in dying in the United States in the early twenty-first century provides an opening for another decisive shift in human agency over death and the temporality of dying. Here, death is not simply a moment in time but an event that is actively made through human choice and control. Through aid in dying, we may not only influence the general timing of death but also choose precisely *when*, as well as how, and with whom.

For Clara and Arthur, a key tenet of this new way of orienting to death was that making death changes the end of life. For Arthur, it was imperative to "go out sailing," to continue to experience a desired quality of life until the very end. In fact, he surprised his family and friends by choosing a date much earlier than they expected because he feared he might become incapacitated and unable to swallow the medication. Arthur's aspirations to be sailing in the last months of his life were quite literal. An avid outdoorsman, he enjoyed sailing throughout his retirement, even as he slowly gave up more intensive forms of physical activity.

Yet sailing also offers an apt metaphor for agency over death. On the surface, it may appear that the wind is carrying the boat. But sailors are not simply "moved along," Sharon Kaufman's term for how dying people are driven by hospital bureaucracy as they approach death.[28] Sailing demands careful control of the sails and the rudder. Sailing, like dying, can be slow and unpredictable. Sailors are always acting, with intentional movements and subtle corrections, even when they seem not to be. At the same time, the person sailing the boat never acts alone. The boat must be in good working order, and the wind and weather conditions must be right. Moreover, a properly rigged sail leads to better control of the boat. In other words, the structural conditions must also be suitable.

Arthur Rivers exemplifies the structures of power and privilege that made it possible for him to help launch a grassroots social movement in

Vermont to legalize medical aid in dying. The ultimate success of this movement eventually made it possible for him to attain a particular kind of aspirational death. Arthur had begun his efforts one winter, when he needed to get his knee replaced. He told Clara, "I have to have my knee replaced. So we're not going to be able to go out West and go skiing all winter. Can you help me draft this law, I've talked to some legislators and we'll get it passed this year, and then next year, Mom and I will go skiing out West." Arthur's confidence and optimistic timeline amused Clara in retrospect. The law did pass, but it took twelve years. Several years after that, Arthur completed the paperwork to avail himself of this option.

Arthur also benefited from the privilege of having the kind of terminal diagnosis that made it possible to "go out sailing." This sort of active end-of-life stage would not have been possible for Frances Sullivan, whose ALS had already led to a drastic reduction in mobility by the time she seriously began to consider assisted dying. People with neurological disorders often experience significant impacts on daily activities and quality of life long before they seriously contemplate hastening death. Many of my research participants commented that Vermont's aid-in-dying law seemed tailor-made for cancer patients, who are more likely to experience a predictable decline and terminal trajectory, making it possible to pinpoint an ideal time to die.

Arthur chose the day of his death for a practical reason—the availability of a physician he'd asked to attend. In his last week, Clara said, "He got more and more directive—he wanted to have his last stamp on things." He dispensed advice to family members and people he had mentored, and helped to craft a press release about his death. He and Bea hosted a final dinner with friends. On his final morning, Arthur attended to a number of practical issues, signing paperwork regarding his plans to donate his body to the medical school and dealing with administrative tasks. Before taking the medication, at home, in a hospital bed, Clara recalled, they toasted with bourbon and "sent him off with lots of sailing analogies. Setting out to sea, that sort of thing . . . this was joyful, and peaceful, and it's exactly what he wanted."

Clara's recollection of her father's last day reveals a transformation in how we understand death: as event. By carefully scripting his death, Arthur was able to live the way he wanted to for his last days and take care of his final arrangements. The day of his death involved a curious combination of the joyful (gathering family, toasts, and stories) and the mundane (paperwork and bureaucracy), with Arthur maintaining constant control of his environment and the people surrounding him. What was at stake for Arthur was not simply a desire to tame uncertainty but a new way of reckoning with mortality and envisioning death in an aging and increasingly technocratic society. Ultimately, attaining an aspirational death marked the culmination of Arthur's years of advocacy and hard work.

PLANNING FOR DEATH

In April 2017, I was invited to attend a death-planning workshop in Vermont, organized by some attendees of one of the Death Cafes I attended regularly over the course of my fieldwork. Early on, I attended Death Cafes in a handful of towns across Vermont as a way of familiarizing myself with the culture of death in Vermont. Death Cafe is an international phenomenon founded by Jon Underwood in London in 2011, in which people, often strangers, meet in various public venues (e.g., churches, community centers, libraries) to discuss death over cake and tea. Over the years, I had continued attending one of these monthly meetings whenever I was in Vermont because I liked the ambiance of the group—boisterous, lighthearted, not taking itself too seriously or hewing too closely to the Death Cafe's many rules and regulations—and because I genuinely liked the regular attendees, mostly women, and a few men, in their fifties and sixties.

The workshop was organized by Susie Williams, one of the founding members of the Death Cafe in the small Vermont town where she lived. Susie, an artist and a nurse, was passionate about increasing awareness about death and dying. A deeply spiritual person, Susie was drawn to contemplative practices and had studied Vipassana meditation with a local teacher, through whom she had met her friend Adrienne Singleton. When Adrienne was diagnosed with metastatic breast cancer, they both started reading about death and performing death meditations. Adrienne eventually pursued aid in dying, and Susie was there when she died.

Adrienne's death was a painful experience for Susie because of tensions between Susie and Adrienne's family members, who made Susie feel unwelcome. Although Adrienne had carefully planned for her death, her advanced directives disappeared and her wishes—such as having Susie by her side, meditating and holding her hand—were not followed. It took everyone by surprise when Adrienne took nine hours to die, in part because she had sipped the medication slowly rather than gulping it down. She eventually died, but the atmosphere was strained and emotionally fraught for those in attendance. This protracted course of dying was not uncommon in my data; of the fourteen assisted deaths described to me by direct witnesses, four involved people who took longer than expected to die, causing some distress for caregivers.[29]

The experience left Susie wishing that anyone pursuing medical aid in dying would be better educated and better prepared. It also prompted her to develop a death-planning workbook, which she hoped would help prepare individuals and their families and friends for facing death. Susie held the workshop I attended to try out her workbook on a friendly audience. The workshop was held in a cabin owned by another Death Cafe member and was attended by several regular members of the Death Cafe. Susie had set out a lavish spread of cheese, crackers, cookies, and nuts, and big mugs of chamomile tea. There had been a late-season snow earlier that day, and I was quite content to take a seat near the fireplace.

I had not been looking forward to working on my death workbook. A part of me was somewhat resistant to planning for death, not because I was reluctant to think about it, but because I know that things often do not go according to plan, that there is a danger in trying to plan too much. When I was pregnant with my son, I did not write a birth plan, although many of my friends were doing this sort of thing. In fact, I was very resistant to planning at all, because I wanted to remain open to various possibilities: to having a "natural" childbirth, to getting an epidural, to needing an emergency caesarean section. I did not want to get attached to a particular plan because I wasn't sure how I would feel in the moment—or perhaps because of my medical anthropology training, I knew I might not even be in a position to choose. My feelings about death are similar.

Despite some initial skepticism, however, I found the death-planning exercise surprisingly enjoyable. I spent most of my time working on some questions that Susie had prepared. Do you have any tasks you would like to finish before you die? What unfinished business do you have? What are your passions? It made the idea of death planning much more approachable to break it down question by question, and I found myself answering them even though I did not have a terminal diagnosis and was decades younger than the others in attendance. For the "tasks" question, I wrote that I wanted to finish my book before I died. Susie had written "pay my taxes" as an example for this question, and I jokingly asked who would feel committed to doing that before death. But she noted that Renee Long, another woman who had used Vermont's medical aid-in-dying law, did her taxes on Saturday and died on Monday.

Susie's death-planning workbook illustrates the extent to which planning for death has infiltrated the popular culture. If aid in dying is an extreme example of exercising control over death, there are many more ways that contemporary middle-class Americans approach death in a planful manner and attempt to achieve agency over death. At one end of the spectrum are those who invest in cryonics—the practice of deep-freezing the bodies of the recently dead—with the hope that future biotechnological advances will enable them to restore their bodies to life.[30] At the other end of the spectrum are more ordinary ways of planning for death, such as by completing advance directives, which I discuss in the next chapter, or by completing Susie's workbook. Although many of Susie's prompts focused on planning for time left, rather than on planning for death itself, they reveal the way in which life and death are always entangled. Planning for death often entails planning for how our loved ones will continue on living after we die. Those who plan are often motivated by a desire to reduce the mess and confusion for those they leave behind.

Making death through aid in dying is another way of aspiring to reduce the unruliness of slow and passive deaths. Imposing temporal boundaries on death transforms not only the experience of dying (and the final stages of living) but also the cultural meanings of death itself. Aid in dying renders death a bounded, staged event with a well-timed and carefully crafted ending, as Bert Glaser alluded to: "Let's not, you know, drag this thing out to the point where the audience is going, 'Shit, if they did ten less songs it would have been a better opera.'" As we will see in chapter 6, orienting to death as a staged event incites the dying person to carefully choreograph the scene of death. If there is a "virtue in timing," as Bert maintained, such virtues are inflected with aesthetic as well as moral values.

From the perspective of aid-in-dying advocates, a well-timed death is good because it avoids the unsightliness of lingering.

Orienting to death as a staged event also creates a space for new forms of human agency over death. As I have shown in this chapter, legalized aid in dying, as an emergent form of death, permits terminally ill people to conquer uncertainty by choosing a particular place and moment to die. Yet it is not only a matter of timing but also of maintaining coherence with life as lived, through engaging in favorite pastimes and celebrating with loved ones. As Brian Nelson, a palliative care physician, put it, "The people who have requested physician-assisted suicide from me don't want to lie still in bed and die. They want to be walking along and controlling their bank account and then not existing the next day."

Scripting death in this way is empowering, as Clara Barnstable suggests, and changes the terms of how dying people spend their remaining time, permitting them to "go out sailing," as it were, for Arthur Rivers, or to avoid the mortal terror of respiratory failure, as would have been likely in Frances Sullivan's case. From this perspective, the production of death is more than a ritual event: it is an opportunity to create continuity in the face of a biologically imposed rupture. Death becomes part and parcel of the good life, an extension of a life that has meaningfully reached its end. Foregrounding human agency in making death through aid in dying thus requires us to rethink dominant frameworks on the biopolitics of death, which flatten human experience and cast people like Frances and Arthur as passive in the face of death.

At the same time, the emergence of such aspirational deaths also has a darker side. Aspirational deaths entail the possibility of failure—that is, the possibility that such deaths will not be attained, as was the case for the dialysis patient in Vermont who was unable to find a physician to prescribe a lethal dose of medication. Scripting death also entails considerable pressure for dying persons and their caregivers to get things right. This grim pressure was demonstrated poignantly by Frances Sullivan, who practiced eating applesauce as quickly as possible with a foam-encased spoon for several weeks until she died.

If making death through aid in dying is a way of speaking back to organizing frameworks for biopolitical power, it is critical to point out that individuals who pursue assisted death do not exercise absolute autonomy.

Instead, the patient's power to make death is mediated by the state's power to permit death by medical aid in dying and the physician's power to grant (or deny) a request for a lethal prescription. This configuration of agency over death as distributed between the individual, medicine, and the state belies the simple framing of "making live" and "letting die."[31] As I show in subsequent chapters, the patient's capacity to attain an aspirational death always depends on prior actions by others—the physicians, who must agree to write the prescription and complete the associated paperwork, and the family members and caregivers, who provide practical and emotional support throughout the process. Aid in dying thus demands a relational perspective on biopower, one that attends to how agency over death is distributed, in nuanced fashion, among a variety of stakeholders, permitting specific deaths to be crafted and produced for select members of society. In the next two chapters, I turn my focus to the physicians and explore their roles in scripting death.

3 Starting the Conversation

During my first two summers of fieldwork, I volunteered with the Wake Up to Dying Project, a Vermont-based awareness and action campaign aimed at fostering public conversations about dying through storytelling, art, and a traveling multimedia exhibit.[1] The goal, in the words of the project's founder, Nina Thompson, was to "take death out of the closet." In an interview with a Burlington newspaper, Thompson said, "We think this awareness campaign will help people be more prepared, practically and emotionally, for this shared human experience. We also think if we pay more attention to the way we die, we'll pay more attention to the way we choose to live."[2]

In July 2016, the third and final year that the project set up tents on the lawn of the Burlington Public Library as part of the traveling exhibit, I attended a workshop on "Death, Documents, and 'The Conversation'" held on a Sunday afternoon. It was the last day of the exhibit, and I couldn't help but think that this timeslot had been strategically chosen. This topic seemed less likely to draw a crowd than some of the other events—such as a workshop on exploring dying through poetry and prose and a live performance from a choral group—and in that respect, it would minimize competition with the host of lakefront activities and street performers that make downtown Burlington so enticing on a summer afternoon. But I was a death "junkie," or so the volunteer coordinator playfully dubbed me when she saw me ducking into yet another of the weekend's workshops on the second floor of the library, and I was happy to take a reprieve from the sun to talk about death.

The audience was almost entirely women, nearly all of them white haired. The expert panel included a nurse case manager from a Vermont-based health insurance company, who served as moderator; an end-of-life hospice educator; a critical care physician; and an estate attorney. After some brief introductions, the moderator invited the panelists to address myths or misconceptions about planning for death. One of the hospice educator's contributions—"if you talk about it, it's going to happen"—garnered a few chuckles from the audience, who almost certainly had not fallen prey to this fallacy, if they were willing to give up a pleasant Sunday afternoon to talk about death. "I've been doing this for four years, and I haven't heard about anyone dying after one of these workshops," she quipped.

While this joke was designed to poke fun at a seemingly irrational notion, the superstitious belief that planning for death can cause it to happen is surprisingly commonplace in American society. A colleague recently admitted that she and her husband had not created a will because she was afraid it would lead to her imminent demise. Variations on such views are widespread, even among physicians. In *Death Foretold*, the sociologist and physician Nicholas Christakis observed that many American physicians adhere to an implicit norm of not communicating terminal prognoses unless asked because they believe that doing so can affect therapeutic outcomes through a type of self-fulfilling prophecy. One young general internist in Christakis's study reported, "The words coming out of my mouth feel like a proclamation. They can make things happen."[3] This concern—that talking about death can make it happen—is my point of departure for the issues explored in this chapter regarding the social, ethical, and legal stakes of starting a conversation about death.

Start the Conversation is the name of a public education initiative created by Vermont's Visiting Nurses Association (VNA), an organization of nine not-for-profit member agencies that deliver home health and hospice services in every Vermont county. Established in 2009, the goal of this initiative is to help people have conversations with loved ones about how they want to be cared for at the end of life. The idea was that "starting the conversation" would culminate with people writing their advance directives for end-of-life care. The initiative produced a flashy conversation guide, complete with definitions of common terms; a checklist for preparing to speak with one's doctor; and worksheets to clarify values and preferences. It also hosted local events across the state to increase public awareness.

This initiative reflects an ongoing, nationwide public health effort to engage Americans in advance care planning, a broad term that encompasses multiple forms of planning for death, including talking with one's loved ones and medical care providers, anticipating future care needs, appointing a surrogate decision maker in case of future incapacity, and recording end-of-life preferences in writing. While the focus of advance care planning is often on instrumental tasks like completing written advance directive forms, patients have indicated that the process of communicating with caregivers about values and preferences can also be extraordinarily valuable. Preparing for death and dying and relieving loved ones of the burden of substitute decision making are important ancillary goals.[4]

Despite these laudable goals, advance care planning has been met with a great deal of contentiousness. In the early 1990s, the SUPPORT study, a controlled trial funded by the National Institutes of Health (NIH) to improve care for seriously ill hospitalized patients, found that a robust advance care planning intervention did not improve patient outcomes.[5] Furthermore, the intervention did not affect the proportion of patients or surrogates who reported having a conversation about cardiopulmonary resuscitation or change the likelihood of a patient having a conversation about prognosis with a physician. The bleak results of this high-caliber, carefully designed study, whose principal investigators were among the most prominent palliative care researchers in the country, underscored how difficult it is to improve care for dying patients by targeting clinical communication. In an article published in the *Journal of the American Medical Association,* the investigators concluded, "The study certainly casts a pall over any claim that, if the health care system is given additional resources for collaborative decision making in the form of skilled professional time, improvements will occur. In phase II of SUPPORT, improved information, enhanced conversation, and an explicit effort to encourage use of outcome data and preferences in decision making were completely ineffectual, despite the fact that the study had enough power to detect small effects."[6]

In 2009, another significant setback occurred when then governor of Alaska Sarah Palin coined the term *death panel* to refer to proposed legislation that would provide reimbursement to clinicians for time spent in advance care planning with Medicare patients. The issue became a flashpoint of political controversy surrounding President Obama's proposed health reform legislation, and public education efforts were unsuccessful in correcting Palin's erroneous claims that the Medicare proposal would permit government officials to make decisions about end-of-life care for Medicare recipients. The provision was withdrawn in 2011, under heightened political scrutiny.[7]

Finally, in 2016, the policy to reimburse clinicians for advance care planning conversations quietly went into effect.[8] However, many end-of-life researchers have remained skeptical about the potential of advance care planning to improve end-of-life care. A growing body of evidence suggests that values and preferences are susceptible to a range of external influences and do not remain stable over time.[9] Social scientists have criticized both the emphasis on the physical document (over the communication processes that produce it) and the assumption that people always want a voice in decisions about their care.[10] Furthermore, even when advance care planning is performed, it does not always point to a clear decision in specific circumstances, and it is unclear whether patients' wishes will be followed. Perhaps most importantly, the health care context limits the capacity to choose. Emphasizing advance care planning may distract from necessary systems-level improvements. As the legal scholar and bioethicist Rebecca Dresser puts it, "People can make only the choices that the health system makes available to them."[11] In this respect, advance directives may instill false promise by suggesting more control over end-of-life care than should be expected.[12]

I begin this chapter with a discussion of advance care planning because it highlights how talking about dying is not only culturally but also politically fraught. We may think of "starting the conversation" about medical aid in dying as a highly particularized version of advance care planning, insofar as both practices are fundamentally concerned with expressing one's values and preferences for end-of-life care. As with advance care planning, starting the conversation about aid in dying in Vermont came with unexpected political consequences. And, as with advance care planning and referrals to hospice, part of the hesitancy surrounding talk about aid in dying is that it requires acknowledging the inevitability (and sometimes proximity) of death. Therefore, one of my goals is to reflect on what my research on aid in dying might tell us about the way that Americans talk about death more generally, and the place of such conversations within the clinical encounter.

In this chapter, I explore cultural norms and assumptions that govern talk about dying, and starting the conversation, more specifically. One of the consequences of legalizing assisted death is the necessity of a new set of communication norms to support the emergent clinical practice. I describe these norms, as articulated by health care providers in my study, and discuss a dominant clinical and bioethical assumption regarding clinical communication about aid in dying: that talk be patient initiated. For physicians and bioethicists who subscribe to this view, concern that a physician's words could be powerful enough to either damage the patient-physician relationship or influence a patient to hasten her death is a potent deterrent against recommending that physicians ever discuss aid in dying unless a patient requests it. For others, however, merely informing patients about aid in dying cannot move them to act against their own values and preferences. In what follows, I analyze these divergent perspectives and reveal how they were mobilized in a lawsuit that challenged the constitutionality of Vermont's aid-in-dying law.

STARTING THE CONVERSATION ABOUT ASSISTED DEATH

The practice of physicians assisting patients to alleviate suffering and end their lives peacefully through medical intervention is as old as the practice of medicine itself. It was only through the political struggle over euthanasia that emerged in the twentieth-century United States that such practices became covert.[13] In 1991, the palliative care physician Timothy Quill broke the silence surrounding physician-assisted death when he published a personal account in the *New England Journal of Medicine* of prescribing medication to help a terminally ill patient end her life.[14] In his candid essay, Quill described how "Diane's" request for aid in dying unfolded as her leukemia progressed:

> A week later she phoned me with a request for barbiturates for sleep. Since I knew that this was an essential ingredient in a Hemlock Society suicide, I asked her to come to the office to talk things over.[15] She was more than willing to protect me by participating in a superficial conversation about her insomnia, but it was important to me to know how she planned to use the drugs and to be sure that she was not in despair or overwhelmed in a way that might color her judgment. In our discussion, it was apparent that she was having trouble sleeping, but it was also evident that the security of having enough barbiturates available to commit suicide when and if the time came would leave her secure enough to live fully and concentrate on the present. It was clear that she was not despondent and that in fact she was making deep, personal connections with her family and close friends. I made sure that she knew how to use the barbiturates for sleep, and also that she knew the amount needed to commit suicide.[16]

Quill's account demonstrates several points regarding clinical communication about assisted death. First, in a context in which medical aid in dying is illegal, physicians may prescribe large doses of barbiturates with a wink and a nod to seriously ill patients, ostensibly to address sleeping problems, while knowing that a large dose could be lethal. Second, in such scenarios, communication may be coded and oblique because a direct request for assistance would implicate physicians in a potentially illicit act. Finally, Quill himself was, and remains, deeply committed to open and honest communication with patients.

What is less self-evident was just how radical it was for Quill to publish this account in a prestigious medical journal. Responses to the essay ranged from shock and disapproval to praise for his moral courage, but people across the spectrum of beliefs could agree that Quill had addressed a frankly unspeakable topic. Once medical aid in dying is legalized, however, it ceases to be an unspeakable act. How, then, does one start the conversation? What assumptions and norms guide patients and practitioners as they enter this morally fraught terrain? What clinical scripts are available for shaping clinical talk?

Starting the conversation about aid in dying is generally seen by health care providers as the patient's responsibility. Many physicians and bioethicists worry that informing patients about this end-of-life option can signal a loss of hope or abandonment or damage the patient-provider relationship. Consequently, patients must bridge tremendous power asymmetries and communicative norms (e.g., that clinicians guide the encounter) to meet clinical expectations for talk about assisted death.

Neil Lewis was present when his best friend Tom broached the subject with the oncologist, who agreed to serve as the certifying physician.[17] Neil relayed the events to me as follows:

> We had never met her. But we knew that she had to sign off on Act 39 for Tom. So he went in there. He was already weaker and weaker and weaker. It was hard enough getting him out of his apartment to drive him forty-five minutes to the hospital. So we're sitting in the doctor's office waiting for her to come in. You know, there's tension in the room. I'm feeling—I don't know what I was feeling, just kind of numb. And wanting to help him if I had to describe things to the doctor. But Tom, as articulate as he is, he knew he had to make a pitch. It was like making a Hollywood pitch to movie directors. You have five minutes, you know, make your pitch.
>
> So as soon as the doctor walked in, introduced herself, Tom didn't even let her start talking. He went right into his pitch. Really impressive. I was thinking, this guy is dying, and here he is, being so articulate. I took a lot of notes. I wrote down things that Tom said, and basically the gist of it was, he said to her, "The most important thing in my life, as an older man, is the conversations, the deep conversations I have with people about literature, about science, about art, about music, about film." And he said, "The most important thing is having those conversations with people. And if I start to be so diminished that I can't communicate, I can't have conversations, and not only physically but mentally, if I start to see that that's happening, and there's no turning back, that's it. That's when I would make the decision to take 'the drink,'" as we call it. And he was very clear about it. And he went on a little further in his pitch. And the doctor was really impressed, that he was so articulate in understanding what he wanted, what he didn't want, and his understanding of what Act 39 was. Those are three important points that were very impressive.

Neil's account reveals how making a Hollywood-style pitch for medical aid in dying constitutes an important first step in scripting one's death. Just as a movie cannot be produced without the backing of a film studio, an assisted death cannot be attained without buy-in from two physicians. By Neil's recounting, even in his debilitated, cancer-ridden state, Tom had the foresight and presence of mind to treat his doctor's appointment as a critical sales opportunity, in which he must promote his vision for an aspirational death. Tom had fine-tuned his pitch to persuade the doctor that he was pursuing aid in dying for morally worthy reasons. He was clear about what he wanted and, correspondingly, what he wanted to avoid. And he conveyed that he was educated and informed about the law's parameters.

A request like Tom's may launch physicians into uncharted clinical terrain. Because legalized aid in dying is still in its infancy in the United States, there are few established clinical scripts to guide such conversations. Medical students are not explicitly trained in responding to such requests, and the few guidelines that exist have been published largely in the past few years;[18] physicians may not be familiar with them at the time they become pertinent.

Nevertheless, many of the health care providers in my study had participated in such conversations many times over, developing practical wisdom and expertise along the way. Providers emphasized that reassuring patients they would be there for them and exploring their reasons for requesting medical aid in dying were important first steps. "If someone says, 'I want you to help me die, I want Act 39,' the first question is, tell me more," said Amanda Townshend, a palliative care physician. "And we deepen the conversation." Providers were particularly attuned to concerns about finances or being a burden on others due to terminal illness, which were widely considered invalid reasons because they raised the possibility that pursuing aid in dying might not be a voluntary choice.[19] They also explored whether the patient's concerns could be addressed through alternative means (for example, pain relief through medication); sought to address untreated symptoms, such as depression; and discussed alternative options for end-of-life care, including hospice, palliative care, and voluntary stopping of eating and drinking. Willa Redmond, a palliative care nurse, observed that, after a patient brings up Act 39, "I feel a little bit freer to discuss with people the ways that they can maybe hasten or allow the dying process to occur without involving medical assistance."

Many providers indicated that a request for aid in dying could lead to conversations about other end-of-life concerns. Kim Treadway, a palliative care physician, reflected, "So many times, it's a proxy for, 'I am really scared of what's ahead. I don't think anybody is going to be able to control my symptoms and I think I'm going to be abandoned because I'm a person with a terminal illness.'" The ability for such requests to "open the door" to critical conversations, as several providers put it, was sometimes seen by those opposing the practice to be an unexpected benefit of medical aid in dying. Brian Nelson, a palliative care physician, explained,

> I think there is a serious silver lining because people do not have the vocabu-lary in our society and in our medical system to talk about death and dying, right? So, I actually brought my office note from a patient I saw yesterday. He was sent to me with a request for a physician-assisted suicide. He comes in saying he wants the shot. Really, all he is saying is he wants to talk about what happens when he dies. All he really wanted to know was, is he going to have to be in a nursing home in the last two weeks of his life? . . . So it is a major shortcut for talking about death and dying.

For Brian, whose views on the topic were ambivalent, starting a conver-sation about aid in dying could be valuable for its ability to facilitate other forms of advance care planning—which would likely be more appropriate and useful for many patients. Many providers agreed that starting a con-versation could be beneficial for end-of-life care, irrespective of whether the patient ultimately pursued assisted death. Other observers have made similar points when interpreting data from Oregon indicating that hos-pice referral rates increased after the passage of its Death with Dignity Act.[20] Such patterns may suggest broader social spillover effects of "open-ing the door" to deeper clinical conversations about death and dying and various forms of advance care planning.

But what happens when a patient does not start the conversation? Do physicians ever inform patients that aid in dying is an option? And how do they understand their moral responsibilities with respect to clinical com-munication? I turn to these questions next.

PHYSICIAN-INITIATED CONVERSATIONS

The dominant clinical script for communication about medical aid in dying begins with a patient's request. This built-in assumption is evident in the professional medical guidelines, which focus on responding to requests, rather than communicating about aid in dying more generally.[21] At a nursing conference I attended, the moderator began a session on aid in dying by announcing, "We are not here to decide right and wrong—it's about figuring out how to respond when people make a request." Such comments reveal how patient requests are treated as an implicit starting point of ethical reflection. The conventional bioethical rationale for avoiding informing patients about aid in dying is that patients may view this information as communicating the physician's endorsement of this option, or signaling a loss of hope or abandonment, and may cause patients who hold conflicting values to lose trust in their physician. In addition, some worry that simply introducing the option could constitute undue influence on patients' decisions. From this perspective, informing patients about aid in dying may not be in the patient's best interest, despite widely shared views in the United States about patients' rights to health-related information.

Physicians and nurses in my study articulated a range of reasons for avoiding such discussions, unless they were initiated by a patient, yet most of their concerns focused on the potential for harm to the patient-provider relationship or the potential to influence the patient's decision-making process. Ruby Cooper, an oncology clinic nurse coordinator, explained to me, "We never bring it up. It's something that somebody else brings up with you." When I asked her why, she elaborated,

> I think you have to be careful about how people feel about this. And let's say, for example, that you have a relationship with the patient and the family, and it's a comforting, trusting relationship and they happen to be individuals who are completely against this. If I bring that up and it's something that they wouldn't even consider, that could create a huge scar in that relationship. And so, again, they can bring it up and then you know that the door is open to that conversation. But unless that door was opened, I would not bring it up to a patient.

Ruby suggested that mentioning medical aid in dying as an end-of-life option with a patient who opposed the practice could irreparably damage the patient-provider relationship. If the effect of this conversation would be to open the door to a new stage of end-of-life counseling, Ruby would not step over the threshold unless the patient first welcomed her in.

Alanna Reynolds, a hospice physician who had prescribed medication for assisted death and described herself as an advocate for the practice, was more ambivalent than Ruby. Ultimately, however, she came down on the side of not informing patients, pointing to concerns about her potential influence: "I'll think to myself, 'Should I bring up Act 39?' And then I feel conflicted about it because I feel like it's a really patient-driven thing, and so I don't want to bring it up to them. I don't want them to feel like what they're going through isn't valuable. So, I don't typically—I will bring it up if people are asking questions that kind of indicate that they've reached a point—I try not to bring it up directly, actually, because I don't want to influence people." Here, Alanna suggests that bringing up medical aid in dying could implicitly suggest that the process of natural dying is not valuable in itself, or that living with serious illness is not worth it because of a reduced quality of life.

Both Ruby and Alanna were committed advocates; their objections were not to the practice itself but rather to informing patients about it. While Ruby focused on the relational implications of introducing a culturally and morally contested topic, Alanna worried about potentially contaminating the decision-making process. Although she stopped short of describing such conversations as coercive, the specter of coercion nevertheless looms over her remarks. In both cases, concerns about the performative effects of clinical language—the notion that language is a form of action that can have powerful social effects[22]—and the possibility for harm animate their moral reasoning and their stance on informing.

On the other hand, the assumption that clinical communication about aid in dying should begin with a patient's request at times came into conflict with other clinical scripts, particularly those regarding patients' rights to information. Of the twenty physicians and nurse practitioners I interviewed who discussed their informing practices with me, twelve indicated that there were at least some circumstances in which they might initiate a discussion of aid in dying as an option in the absence of a patient's request.[23] While some indicated that these circumstances would be somewhat unusual (for example, a patient threatening to shoot himself), others brought it up more regularly, as part of the "slate of options," as one physician put it. In justifying this approach, several providers specifically mentioned concerns about patients' access to information. Terri Nichols, a neurologist, said, "I think I want my patients to understand everything that's available, and I don't think it's fair to leave a patient in the dark. Whether or not they want to do it or ethically agree with it is not the issue. I want them to be informed."

Similarly, Greg Wright, a hospice and internal medicine physician, noted, "I've talked to people when we've made a diagnosis of some terminal illness, saying, 'Here are your options and here are, how things can go, and here is an option under state law which is relatively new in recent years, and this is how it would work.' Just to inform people, because I think a lot of people are very misguided." Ken Greene, an oncologist, downplayed the common worry that a provider-initiated discussion could influence the patient to pursue aid in dying: "It's a certain type of patient who's going to follow through on this. It's not going to be the patient for whom it's the physician's agenda to do this. It has to become or start off as the patient's agenda. A physician is not going to convince a patient to do this."

The physicians who did sometimes inform patients about the option were emphatic that context mattered. The particular patient's circumstances were important for deciding whether or not to inform a particular patient about Vermont's law, as well as *how* to initiate such a discussion. Here, knowledge of patients' values and preferences was critical. James Loftin, a primary care physician, suggested he would have ample opportunity to learn about the patient's potential interest by such time as medical aid in dying might become a relevant option: "I might talk to them about their beliefs or how do they feel God feels about them doing this. Usually by that time we've talked about palliative care and they'd have opportunities to tell me, 'Well, I don't want to stop taking my medicines because that would be a sin,' kind of thing. If someone had told me that that they were not willing to stop taking their Digoxin for fear of committing a sin I certainly wouldn't go into Act 39 with them."[24] This comment suggests that patients communicate their religiosity to physicians in subtle ways leading up to the discussion of end-of-life options.

Providers stressed the need to be thoughtful about when and how the conversation occurs, and, in particular, stressed that patients must have come to grips with their terminal prognoses. They also emphasized the importance of being nondirective in their counsel to avoid giving the impression of endorsing medical aid in dying as an option. Terri Nichols recalled one such patient, to whom she said, "'So you need to also understand that in Vermont we have a law, that should you feel that you want to access this law, it's there for you. And here is what the law is, right.' I didn't say, 'I think you should do this,' I didn't say, 'This is what I want you to do,' I didn't say, 'This is the right thing to do.' I said, 'You could get hospice, but this is where we're headed.'" Ken Greene indicated that it is reasonable to "mention it and leave it out there," then move on to other discussions. This approach would presumably give patients space to discuss it further if desired.

These divergent perspectives on informing patients about medical aid in dying are tied to competing language ideologies surrounding clinical communication. The term *language ideology* refers to culturally informed, beliefs and assumptions about language use within a particular context.[25] Some clinicians, like Terri Nichols, focus on the content of clinical communication, emphasizing their responsibility to convey information to patients so that they can make informed decisions about their care. This perspective regards language as a relatively neutral vehicle for transmitting health-related information. Others, like Ruby Cooper and Alanna Reynolds, view clinical communication as an arena for a dynamic, performative act (i.e., informing), expressing legitimate concerns about the possibility of harm.

That these divergent perspectives denote distinct ideologies of clinical speech is underscored by the different language employed by representatives of each viewpoint. In defending the view that physicians cannot inform patients about aid in dying, the bioethicist Raphael Cohen-Almogar poses the question of "whether a physician should *suggest* euthanasia to his or her patients" (emphasis added):

> With respect to professional ethics, talking about euthanasia upon a patient's request is different from suggesting it to the patient. By suggesting euthanasia to a patient, the physician implicitly includes euthanasia in the canon of proffered rational treatment options. In light of the professional authority that she is offering, she thereby establishes euthanasia as a rule, and not as an exception. This conduct conflicts much more with the role of the physician as a healer than is the case if the physician talks about euthanasia upon the patient's request.[26]

In this account, Cohen-Almogar casts "informing" as "suggesting" and concludes that "suggesting" communicates an implicit endorsement, thereby changing the scope of the physician's role as healer. At the same time, it appears that discussing euthanasia "upon a patient's request" is morally uncomplicated for him.

Yet Cohen-Almogar does not address the power dynamics that might constrain the patient's capacity to initiate such a request. Professional authority is not "offered" by the physician, as Cohen-Almogar proposes. Instead, it is structured into the power dynamics of the clinical encounter, in which a terminally ill patient is inescapably vulnerable. Such dynamics can make it very challenging for a patient to make such a sensitive and potentially stigmatizing request. When physicians are concerned about the relational fallout of introducing the option of medical aid in dying, such consequences can easily cut both ways; a patient's request might ultimately be just as damaging to the patient-provider relationship as a physician's introducing the topic. Several activists commented to me that they had broached the topic with their primary care physicians, although they were not currently ill, and knew that they would eventually need to find new physicians because of their physicians' opposition. Such examples make clear that asking about aid in dying is morally loaded, with potentially powerful consequences.

Moreover, informing and suggesting are distinct speech acts that differentially construe the speaker's agency and intentions with respect to the information being conveyed. While a physician may inform patients about an option on which she remains neutral, to suggest something implies a preference for a certain outcome. The selection of these terms thus encodes implicit ideas about the social function of clinical language. In other words, to speak of suggesting medical aid in dying implies that the physician can never merely inform because of her social influence.

On the other hand, if we accept that clinical communication about aid in dying must begin with a patient's request, we must acknowledge that a request, too, is a specific kind of speech act, the production or reception of which may be more or less effective in certain circumstances and among certain kinds of actors. Waiting for patients to initiate the conversation makes sense only within a context in which patients feel empowered to make such requests of their health care providers—and one in which providers are willing to listen and respond.

A DUTY TO INFORM?

In Vermont, debates about this issue culminated in a July 2016 lawsuit by the Vermont Alliance for Ethical Healthcare, an advocacy organization that opposes medical aid-in-dying death in Vermont, and the Tennessee-based Christian Medical & Dental Associations, which provides a public voice for Christian health care professionals, against the Vermont Board of Medical Practice and Office of Professional Regulation. The plaintiffs were represented by the Alliance Defending Freedom, a conservative Christian legal advocacy organization, whose platform focuses on religious freedom, the sanctity of life, and marriage and family. The plaintiffs alleged that the Patient Choice and Control at End of Life Act (Act 39) required physicians to inform terminally ill patients that aid in dying was a legal option in Vermont, and that this violated their constitutionally protected right to free speech. In their complaint, the plaintiffs asked the court to enter a declaratory judgment saying the law was unconstitutional and requested protection from professional disciplinary action or civil or criminal proceedings for physicians neglecting to comply with this provision.

The basis for this claim was a specific clause of the law that refers to a preexisting mandate to inform patients of all options for end-of-life care and treatment under the Vermont's Palliative Care Bill of Rights.[27] The plaintiffs claimed that the Vermont Department of Health had interpreted this mandate as requiring physicians to inform all terminally ill patients about the availability of aid in dying under Act 39. Here, the plaintiffs drew from a "Frequently Asked Questions" document posted on the Department of Health website, which included the following:

> Do doctors have to tell patients about this option?
> Under Act 39 and the Patient's Bill of Rights, a patient has the right to be informed of all options for care and treatment in order to make a fully-informed choice. If a doctor is unwilling to inform a patient, he or she must make a referral or otherwise arrange for the patient to receive all relevant information.[28]

Therefore, while Act 39 does not require physicians to write a life-ending prescription or otherwise assist, the plaintiffs argued that the state had imposed an affirmative duty to inform terminally ill patients about this option, which violated the constitutional rights of physicians with religious or moral opposition to it.

I had been hearing debates on the ground about this issue since the beginning of my fieldwork the previous summer. Advocates on both sides of the debate agreed that Act 39 entailed an affirmative duty to inform, although many health care providers were unaware of this stipulation. Overall, participants were divided on the moral stakes of this issue and on whether informing was justified. The lawsuit crystallized an incipient focal point in my research by confirming that the duty to inform was a key point of controversy surrounding Act 39. The entwining of legal and ethical questions particularly piqued my interest: how the suit was resolved would offer a referendum on what the law actually required while furthering debate about what was ethical.

The lawsuit intrigued me for another reason, however. The questions it raised about physicians' rights to free speech and the limits of state power reflected familiar debates from my earlier research on scripted abortion counseling. Poring over the legal documents associated with the case, I realized that many of the relevant legal precedents were borrowed from case law regarding abortion. In my previous work, I had proposed scripting as a metaphor for representing efforts undertaken by lawmakers to regulate clinical speech. Here, abortion providers perceived themselves to be "scripted" by the state, even though their words were neither chosen by lawmakers nor dictated by law.[29]

It seemed that a similar process was at stake for the plaintiffs in the Vermont lawsuit. According to the plaintiffs, the provisions of Act 39 in question required them to "promote the State's views" and "deprived Plaintiffs' members of their right *not* to speak the State's message on the subject of assisted suicide" (emphases added).[30] In a memorandum of law supporting their request for a preliminary injunction (a judicial order that would, in this case, have temporarily overturned the law), the plaintiffs' attorney explained, "Because being forced by the State to counsel and refer for a procedure they do not believe provides any medical benefit and which they ethically oppose is the essence of coerced speech in violation of the First Amendment, Plaintiffs have had to bring this lawsuit."[31] Ironically, in the context of abortion, conservative physicians' groups typically support laws that require counseling with state-prescribed content and mandate ultrasound viewing, both of which raise concerns about compelled professional speech for reproductive rights advocates. Therefore, in the Vermont case, the antichoice plaintiffs drew on some of the same legal arguments that have been used to oppose restrictive abortion legislation in the contest between state power and biomedical authority.

In response, the defendants filed a motion to dismiss the lawsuit, stating that the plaintiffs' interpretation of Act 39 was incorrect, and that the law did not in fact stipulate an affirmative duty to inform. At most, the defendants argued, the law requires physicians to ensure that patients who inquire about medical aid in dying or the Act 39 process receive accurate information. If physicians objected to providing this information directly, they could arrange for the patient to receive it elsewhere—from another physician, organization, or online materials. Moreover, the defendants denied that the law was ideological, or that the state had a particular "message" to convey: "Act 39 is designed not to promote a particular viewpoint but to remove legal obstacles that prevented terminally ill patients from having this end-of-life choice. Without Act 39, a physician who intentionally prescribed medication for a patient to use to hasten death (as opposed to use for easing pain) risked liability, criminal charges, or professional sanctions. Contrary to plaintiffs' allegations, the Act does not suggest that 'assisted suicide is indicated' for terminally ill patients nor does it require any 'ideological' statements."[32]

After the state's motion to dismiss was filed, several patients and advocacy organizations that were supportive of aid in dying, including Compassion & Choices, filed a motion to intervene in the lawsuit on the grounds that they had a legitimate interest in the outcome of the case. They objected to the state's position that the minimum responsibility for physicians was to respond to questions about aid in dying. Instead, the intervenors concurred with the plaintiffs (to whom they were otherwise ideologically opposed) that the law entailed an affirmative duty to inform.

A hearing regarding the lawsuit took place on November 8, 2016. It was Election Day, and the tight presidential race between Hillary Clinton and Donald Trump distracted me from my normal fieldwork jitters as I drove to the federal courthouse in Rutland. Unseasonably warm temperatures had extended the peak of fall foliage, and my drive afforded sweeping views of the brilliant yellow, orange, and scarlet landscape. After walking through the metal detector and leaving my laptop at the security checkpoint, I took a seat at the back of the courtroom.

The hearing proceeded along familiar terrain for those who had followed the legal documents. Bridget Asay, the solicitor general of the State of Vermont, who represented the defense, argued that the law had been in effect for three and a half years with no harms, no threats of adverse action, and no evidence of a chilling effect. The plaintiffs did not allege that they had changed their practice in response to their interpretation of the law, nor did the regulatory boards interpret the statute in the way the plaintiffs suggested. Therefore, the defense maintained that the plaintiffs had no jurisdictional standing for the suit.

Steven Aden, the plaintiffs' attorney, defended his clients' request for a preliminary injunction on the grounds that it would be impossible for many of his clients to participate in counseling because their belief that medical aid in dying provides no benefits flies in the face of Act 39. Moreover, they could not discuss risks and benefits because they did not have adequate knowledge of the procedure. "They want the right to control the conversation," he asserted. Picking up on this point, Assay responded that "controlling" the conversation was a step further than the state was willing to go: it raised the question of whether patients' rights would be respected.

The hearing concluded with a promise from the judge to try to make a decision soon. On my way out of the courtroom, the bailiff, a member of the US armed forces, asked me what the conflict was about, wanting to know whether it was about whether patients have a right to receive information about the law. I corrected him and explained that it was actually about whether the physician had a duty to *provide* this information. He looked at me incredulously, and said that he could not believe it could be something so simple. In his opinion, he told me, the patient's rights are fundamental to the Hippocratic oath. The doctor and her emotions were irrelevant; the doctor should act only in the patient's interests.

The lawsuit was dismissed five months after the hearing. In his opinion, Judge Geoffrey W. Crawford acknowledged the common ground between the two sides: both agreed that referral to a website was sufficient to satisfy disclosure obligations to patients inquiring about aid in dying. Crawford explained, "It is critical to an understanding of the standing

issue to recognize at the outset that the parties agree on at least one potential solution to their shared dilemma of answering patients' questions
without violating the physicians' beliefs. Not all such conflicts between
conscience and the state have lent themselves to such a compromise."[33]

After this decision, both sides signed a consent agreement that more
clearly spelled out the terms of their common ground. It stated that there
was no professional obligation to counsel or refer patients for medical aid
in dying. There was, however, an obligation to provide accurate information upon a patient's request or to otherwise ensure that the patient could
obtain such information. The defendants agreed to revise all state-owned
websites to reflect this understanding, and plaintiffs waived their rights to
an appeal.

The decision and resulting agreement put the onus of responsibility on
patients to start the conversation about medical aid in dying. Importantly,
several providers I interviewed subsequent to this decision indicated that
there were circumstances in which they might proactively inform patients.
The legal decision did not seem to hold tremendous sway over clinical
practice—in fact, many providers were unaware that the lawsuit had even
taken place. At the same time, the decision also rejected the view that physicians had an unqualified right to control the conversation. While clinical
speech would not be scripted in a direct literal sense—that is, with the
state choosing words for physicians or requiring verbatim disclosures—it
was nevertheless scripted in a broader metaphorical sense. This process
was similar to what I had documented in my research on abortion.

If scripting is a metaphor for representing state control over aspects of
clinical speech, the lawsuit showcases certain fault lines of responsibility
in the management of medical aid in dying. For the bailiff I met at the
hearing, patients' rights are preeminent. Yet interpreting and ensuring
such rights are necessarily subjective and contested processes that depend
on the physician's own moral worldview. Moreover, physicians have relevant rights as well. A robust set of legal precedents protects their rights of
conscientious objection—that is, their right to abstain from participating
in health care services that violate moral or religious beliefs.[34] The plaintiffs' perceived threat of harm illustrates that aid in dying is more than a
personal choice for fulfilling an aspirational death. However, what is at
stake here is not simply competing values—for example, the physician's

and the patient's—but different visions for the proper intersection between law and medicine and the state's role in the clinical encounter. Scripting death through medical aid in dying thus requires acknowledging that the state's interest in governing clinical speech is legitimate. In this respect, scripting is a potent metaphor for thinking through how physicians share biomedical authority with the state.

Finally, the lawsuit reveals how laws are always open to revision. Despite their tremendous social and political power and authoritative tone, legislative scripts are actually quite malleable. They are continually subject to new interpretations as their meanings are negotiated, contested, and interactionally produced.

OPENING THE DOOR TO TALK ABOUT DYING

In March 2017, I attended a nursing ethics conference and participated in a small-group discussion session entitled "When Patients Want to Die Sooner Rather than Later." The first case we considered was that of "Carol," an eighty-three-year-old widow with cancer. Carol had repeatedly refused to discuss advance care planning, and her physician did not think she understood the gravity of her situation. Then she started giving small cues that she was ready, like telling her daughter she would like her to have her diamond necklace when she died. Finally, Carol said to her nurse, "I'm ready to talk. Can you please give me a shot to end it?" Our charge, in our small groups, was to discuss our personal values, professional values, and professional obligations in relation to this case.

A young woman in my group immediately said she would "call in palliative." Another woman agreed, reasoning that we would need to call someone else because nurses could not assist in this manner. Then an older woman interjected that she did not think we were there yet with Carol— we first needed to explore her request. The discussion foregrounded tensions between talking and acting in response to a patient's suffering. Many people, especially the young nurse, jumped immediately to action: connecting Carol to resources, calling for additional support, and so on. Talking with patients about their fears is much less intuitive for some. Of course, part of the challenge lies in talking to patients who may not want to talk. In Carol's case, talk was hampered by her initial reluctance to discuss advance care planning. Someone noted that, when patients do not want to talk, you can't offer them certain options, and then there is a sense of depriving them of possibilities. Once again, the assumption that starting the conversation belonged in the patient's domain was strong.

This perspective resonated with other health care providers over the course of my study. In a symposium on aging in Vermont, a social worker described a patient she had worked with early in her career, who talked about being tired of going into the hospital. She was afraid to tell him that he had options, such as stopping treatment. In affirming someone's options, she explained, you have to be careful not to be too prescriptive. Another provider described this as a tenuous boundary between assisting and advocacy—or, put differently, between informing and influencing.

Yet Carol's request for "a shot to end it" cut through such tensions and opened the door to another sort of conversation. In this respect, it echoed the comments of Brian Nelson, who had observed that patients sometimes requested "the shot" because they lacked a richer vocabulary for talking about dying. My conversation with the nurses underscores that health care providers will respond to these requests in different ways. Not everyone will view them as opening the door to another sort of conversation about advance care planning, as Brian Nelson, a board-certified palliative care physician, had done.

In this chapter, I have described how many medical professionals who support medical aid in dying argue that communication should always be initiated by patients, because they believe that informing patients may communicate an implicit endorsement or signal a loss of hope or abandonment, leading to a loss of trust. Others worry that simply introducing the option could influence patients to pursue it, thereby compromising the voluntariness of the procedure. On the other hand, the accounts and experiences of health care providers in my study suggest that many believe there are at least certain circumstances in which proactively informing patients about aid in dying is advisable. Reasons for sometimes informing include the view that patients ought to be informed of all available options, as well as the beliefs that such information could be communicated in a contextually sensitive manner and that concerns about undue influence are overblown.

My own view is that the presumption of patient-initiated communication about medical aid in dying at least partially evades clinical responsibility for difficult conversations about death and dying. As I will describe
in the chapters that follow, my research has demonstrated stark inequalities in access, including different levels of awareness of this legally authorized option. Having had multiple opportunities to explain to strangers or
acquaintances with no connection to aid in dying just what I was doing in
Vermont over the course of my fieldwork, I know that the general public is
not well informed about Act 39's requirements or affordances. As a medical anthropologist, I also know that power imbalances in the patient-
physician relationship might make some patients feel uncomfortable ini-
tiating such requests. For these reasons, it seems likely to me that waiting
for a patient to request aid in dying could reinforce access disparities by
making it more available to affluent, well-educated patients. This is not to
deny that informing patients about aid in dying carries serious risk of
harm or that it could go terribly awry in the hands of poorly trained clinicians. Such conversations clearly must be handled with tremendous care
and sensitivity. However, I think that providers misjudge the moral stakes
of the situation in assuming they must wait for a patient's request.

Medical professionals have been largely resistant to my position. In
February 2018, I participated in a workshop at the National Academies of
Science, Engineering, and Medicine designed to explore the evidence base
and research gaps pertaining to the clinical implementation of medically
assisted death in the United States. A key message of my brief presenta-
tion was to challenge the conventional view that communication about
assisted dying must always begin with a patient's request. I recognized
that my ideas would be controversial, not only because American physicians are notorious for avoiding death talk, but also because the notion of
mitigating access barriers for the poor challenges the logic of long-standing concerns that socioeconomically marginalized groups may be vulnerable to coercion in the context of aid in dying. Nevertheless, I was surprised when a member of the planning committee said, as part of his
summary remarks, "It was clear from the presentations . . . that patients
must opt in rather than be offered these services by providers."[35] I understood his point about "offering" to mean that physicians should not inform
qualifying patients about aid in dying but should rather wait for them to

"opt in," presumably by making a request. This comment seemed to disregard the central thrust of my remarks, quoted in the summary report for the meeting, that "we need to be thinking about 'circumstances in which it might be ethically permissible for physicians and nurses to inform qualifying patients about aid in dying.'"[36] Communication norms around medical aid in dying, it appears, are quite tenacious.[37]

These tenacious beliefs underscore why, if it was difficult for the nurses to envision how to respond to Carol, it is all the more challenging when patients do not first open the door. The dilemmas facing health care providers regarding whether, when, and how to initiate a conversation about aid in dying mirror larger gaps and silences in the culture of US medicine. Studies of clinical communication about "do not resuscitate" orders, hospice referrals, and other key elements of advance care planning have revealed concerns similar to those discussed in this chapter about how "starting the conversation" may cause emotional distress or extinguish hope for recovery.[38] Insofar as both the Medicare hospice benefit and US aid-in-dying statutes require a six-month prognosis in order for patients to qualify, introducing these options requires acknowledging, whether implicitly or explicitly, that death is expected within six months. Yet many health care providers remain reluctant to discuss prognoses with patients or assign specific time frames.[39]

One woman I interviewed shared the story of her mother's death from dementia several years earlier. The woman was surprised to learn that her mother's physician was unwilling to mention hospice until she, as surrogate decision maker, directly inquired about it:

> I was kind of expecting, or fishing for him to suggest hospice, and he didn't. And then in the seventh month, she started really going kind of crazy. She was hollering "help, help" all the time and couldn't say what she wanted help with. The dementia was really becoming more pronounced and she was pretty weak. She got some kind of respiratory infection and they were going to start antibiotics and I called the doctor again and I said, "Why are we doing this? Isn't it time for us to be thinking about hospice?" He said, "Oh, yes, that would be a good idea. Would you like me to recommend hospice?" It was like it couldn't come from him. It had to come from me, which was very frustrating.

As this story suggests, physicians and other health care providers may be very willing to have the conversation, as long as they don't have to start it.

However, the moral and relational stakes of opening the door can often seem insurmountable.

Despite these challenges, there is greater recognition in medicine today of the importance of having these conversations. Physicians like Atul Gawande, Ira Byock, and Jessica Zitter have gained national acclaim by advocating for difficult conversations about what matters most at the end of life and popularizing their arguments through best-selling books.[40] Even during the conservative Trump presidency, advance care planning is no longer as politically fraught as it was a decade ago. The cultural significance of aid in dying must therefore be interpreted as part of a growing national movement to get people talking about death and bring it "out of the closet," as Nina Thompson put it. If medical aid in dying offers an accessible vocabulary for patients to "start the conversation" about what matters to them in end-of-life care, it does so within a context in which very few people will ultimately choose to have an assisted death.[41] From this perspective, the social, cultural, and ethical force of starting the conversation is far greater than it may seem on the surface.

4 Reconciling Assistance with the Physician's Professional Role

In the spring of 2017, I attended a palliative care conference in southern Vermont. The plenary speaker, a palliative care physician who was a prominent critic of medical aid in dying, had been asked by the conference organizers to talk about suffering and the physician's role in end-of-life care but to avoid talking about aid in dying. This did not stop him from interjecting his views into his talk, however. He cautioned that physicians err in thinking that the only clinical response to suffering is to eliminate it, and quipped, "I know what state I'm in." Moreover, he averred, when palliative medicine professionals assist patients to die, they set themselves up for distrust from patients who are opposed.

When the floor opened for questions, Lena Rhodes, another palliative care physician, rose to challenge the speaker. "I don't recognize what you're saying as the work that we do," she said boldly. She had received three requests for aid in dying in the time since the law was passed, and, each time, she felt that she would be abandoning the patient if she did not help them pursue it. She went on to tell the speaker about a patient who had recently chosen aid in dying: he lived alone, had no family, hated doctors, had stage IV cancer, and did not want anyone with him at the time of death. All this was very much in keeping with how he had lived his life.

The patient had threatened to hang or shoot himself if she did not help him, which would be far more distressing for everyone.

The speaker responded, "I think it's a false dichotomy to think that you'll either go there with patients or abandon them. What if you had promised to take care of him to the end?" "He'd shoot himself," Dr. Rhodes retorted. "He was not impulsive or depressed. He was very clear about what he was going to do." The speaker demurred, "This is an ongoing contention in our society. Many people agree with you. My question is: is this congruent with the purpose of medicine? You say this allowed him to die in a way that was consistent with his story. I think it still may be asking a physician to do what a physician shouldn't be doing."

The tense exchange between these two physicians raises a fundamental question that I grapple with in this chapter: To what extent does the act of writing a script for lethal medication align with the physician's professional role? Or, as the plenary speaker put it: Is this congruent with the purpose of medicine? Historically, organized medicine has had a contentious relationship with medical aid in dying. The American Medical Association opposed early legalization efforts out of fear that it would lead to government-sanctioned active euthanasia, potentially under involuntary circumstances. In Oregon, the opposition movement was led by the state's medical societies, with the financial backing of the Catholic Church.[1] Even today, when many more physicians have shifted their views, ethics subcommittees of the American Medical Association and the American College of Physicians have maintained opposition.[2]

Those who oppose medical aid in dying agree with supporters that patient autonomy should be respected, but they also argue that it is not absolute and medicine cannot relieve all suffering. Writing on behalf of the Ethics, Professionalism and Human Rights Committee of the American College of Physicians, Lois Snyder Sulmasy and Paul Mueller maintain that physicians are more than merely service providers working to fulfill patients' wishes—they are members of a profession with corresponding social and moral responsibilities.[3] They argue that aid in dying (or physician-assisted suicide, in their terms) requires physicians to breach prohibitions on intentionally ending a person's life dating back to Hippocrates, and violates commitments to the moral principles of beneficence (doing good) and nonmaleficence ("do no harm"). The American

Medical Association puts it succinctly in declaring that aid in dying is "fundamentally incompatible with the physician's role as healer."[4]

The invocation of professionalism and the physician's role by the American College of Physicians and the American Medical Association underscores that physicians who participate in aid in dying do not act only as individuals, weighing personal moral and religious beliefs against the circumstances at hand. Rather, they also act as representatives of a larger community of practice. Professionalism encompasses implicit and explicit codes of conduct for members of an occupational sphere. In medicine, professionalism is derived from moral principles and social norms that are applied to clinical practices, relationships with colleagues and patients, and broader aspects of public life.[5]

However, medicine is not a monolith, and views regarding whether or not aid in dying aligns with the physician's professional role vary widely. By 2018, many professional medical associations—including the American Academy of Hospice and Palliative Medicine, the Washington Academy of Family Physicians, the Oncology Nursing Association, and state medical societies in California, Colorado, Maine, Maryland, Massachusetts, Washington, DC, and Minnesota—had moved from a position of opposition to one of neutrality. Several additional groups—including the American Medical Student Association, the American Medical Women's Association, and the American Public Health Association—have taken a more affirmative position in endorsing medical aid in dying.[6]

In palliative care, in particular, there have been long-standing debates about whether or not medical aid in dying is "congruent with the purpose of medicine," as the plenary speaker put it.[7] At stake in such debates are divergent understandings about the professional role, including what it means to "do no harm." For some, assisting a patient to end their life directly conflicts with the Hippocratic oath, which explicitly states, "I will not give a lethal drug to anyone if I am asked, nor will I advise such a plan; and similarly I will not give a woman a pessary to cause an abortion."[8] Others see this edict as hopelessly dated, arguing that, precisely because palliative care is concerned with the relief of existential suffering, aid in dying falls squarely in its domain.

Debates about medical aid in dying also reflect different understandings of "nonabandonment" with respect to the professional role. The physicians and medical ethicists Timothy Quill and Christine Cassel argued that nonabandonment means a continuous caring partnership between physician and patient and a commitment to facing an uncertain future together.[9] Abandoning patients is clearly harmful, they acknowledged, but requests for assisted death can create conflicts between two competing harms. While physicians should not violate their own values in upholding nonabandonment, "the 'bright line' between 'allowing to die' and 'causing death' can become indistinct when physicians are faced with real patients who are suffering intolerably and to whom they have made the commitment not to abandon."[10] Here, Quill and Cassel invoke legal precedents and ethical norms that permit physicians in the United States to withhold or withdraw life-sustaining medical treatment and maintain a distinction between such acts and writing a lethal prescription or administering lethal medication.

In a response to this essay, the physician and medical ethicist Edmund Pellegrino argued that Quill and Cassel's definition of nonabandonment is too expansive. For Pellegrino, nonabandonment meant simply withdrawing from a patient's care without first transferring care to another qualified physician—that is, leaving a patient without any care at all.[11] Quill and Cassel's definition was so broad, he maintained, that it dilutes the moral power of the concept. In their formulation, he suggested, "Abandonment would become one end of a spectrum of moral infractions of varying degrees of seriousness. What part of the spectrum would be morally obligatory, what part optional? Where would the line be drawn between the legal and the ethical obligations and culpability?"[12]

How physicians understand their professional roles with respect to nonmaleficence, relief of suffering, and nonabandonment is also shaped by clinical specialty. While it may seem intuitive that physicians should be committed to relieving patients' suffering, those trained in palliative care may be more sensitive to apprehending psychological or existential suffering. Similarly, abandonment is much more common in specialties like oncology, for which physicians are socialized more intensely to save lives at any cost and may feel their job is complete when the chemotherapy options have run out.

Of the twenty-nine physicians I interviewed for my research, nineteen had participated in medical aid in dying in some capacity—twelve as prescribing physicians. The remainder had initiated but not completed the protocol (3); participated as a second physician to confirm the patient's diagnosis, prognosis, and decisional capacity (3); or counseled patients (1). Even this group of supporters, however, exhibited diverse views regarding the moral meanings of assistance in relation to their professional roles.

At one end of the spectrum lay those who viewed the practice as a professional obligation and even, at times, a privilege. Terri Nichols, a neurologist, exemplified this view in stating, "I don't think it's a burden at all. I think it's something that we're supposed to be doing for people." Lila Maupin, a primary care physician, added that it "strengthens your relationship because they really appreciate the support." Many physicians in this camp did not consider aid in dying a separate category from other forms of palliative medicine. Ted Crandall, a primary care physician, put it this way: "I feel like I have tools that can help them stay comfortable. So, my job is to try and figure out how best to use tools, whether it's the old-fashioned keeping somebody pain-free with morphine, or anti-nausea medicine . . . or the physician-assisted suicide." Ken Greene, an oncologist who firmly believed that all oncologists should be well versed in palliative care, said, "I don't look at Act 39 as something totally different from everything else we do. I look at it as another option of what we can offer to the right patient at the right time in the right setting." Janine Thiel, a family medicine doctor, noted that aid in dying was not the only case in which physicians make decisions that ultimately hasten death: "I think that we make a lot of decisions even without a law like this. We're constantly making decisions about how long people live. This is just saying it more clearly." Each of these physicians located medical aid in dying on a continuum of ordinary end-of-life care and concluded that participating lay well within the scope of their professional role.

For others, however, aid in dying was an exceptional case that came with a distinct set of emotional burdens. Eleanor Reilly, an oncologist, typified this view:

> It is emotionally exhausting to give someone a prescription that you know they may use to end their life. And there is an obligation to do everything you can to try to keep them from not feeling like they need to use that. You don't just give them the gun without the gun education, you know. . . . You just loaded the gun for them and you need to make sure that they

understand what they're doing, and that everything has been done to treat their distress. Are they depressed? Did you screen for depression? Is there financial distress? Have you gotten a social worker in there? Is their pain under control? You have an incredible burden to be sure that every t got crossed, every i got dotted. It's exhausting.

Here, Eleanor compares aid in dying to handing a patient a loaded gun, insinuating that she views this medical practice as a form of abetted suicide. In doing so, she suggests that the physician holds tremendous power over the patient's death (although the medication is self-administered) and expresses a professional responsibility to try to prevent such deaths. For physicians in this group, participating in aid in dying was fundamentally different from routine medicine and represented a dramatic departure from previous understandings of the physician's professional role. This view was not generally shared by patients and caregivers in my study, who saw the physician's power as important, yet ultimately subordinate to the patient's agency in deciding to ingest lethal medication.

Lying between these two poles of professional obligation and professional burden is a range of perspectives on the physician's role in medical aid in dying—perspectives that do not always map neatly onto social categories, such as physician specialty, political or religious affiliation, or gender. While oncologists collectively may be more reluctant to participate in aid in dying, it is noteworthy that my sample included several who viewed it as falling within the scope of their professional role. In what follows, I introduce four cases to illustrate this range of views. By focusing on those most intimately involved in the practice, I show how the significance of aid in dying for the physician's professional role varies considerably, even among those who agree to participate. I also consider whether and how the physician's ability to "script death" by writing a lethal prescription constitutes a radical break from professional medicine's business-as-usual.

The nuanced and varied responses to patients' requests for assistance demonstrate how physicians become lay philosophers of action in navigating such requests. Thirty years ago, the anthropologist Rayna Rapp proposed that women grappling with new reproductive technologies become "moral pioneers" who must engage in ethical decision making about pregnancy termination and childrearing under conditions of uncertainty, with limited authoritative knowledge to guide their way.[13] Physicians faced with requests for assisted death in this emergent medical frontier become moral pioneers of a similar sort, weighing distinctions between different forms of clinical action—such as writing prescriptions and administering medication, or writing a prescription and assisting in other ways—or between foreseen and intended effects. Like the women in Rapp's study, because they work in a new medical frontier, they typically engage in this moral reasoning without the benefit of accumulated wisdom and clinical experience from a professional community of practice.

Professional roles are socially constituted and one of this chapter's core contributions is to describe how medical aid in dying subtly threatens the relational aspects of medical practice. The conflict between professional colleagues with which I opened this chapter highlights one kind of relational threat that aid in dying manifests. The potential for rifts between physicians and patients is another. Such relational threats require care, attention, and, sometimes, repair work, which add to the moral and emotional weight that physicians who participate in aid in dying necessarily carry. By emphasizing these dimensions of physicians' experiences, I illustrate that aid in dying is a fraught relational practice that implicates medical providers and caregivers, in addition to the patient who suffers from terminal illness.

LENA RHODES: "A HUGE WEIGHT AND RESPONSIBILITY"

Several weeks after the palliative care conference where I first met her, I interviewed Lena Rhodes in her home on a rainy evening. She had suggested the time and place, so that we could talk without people recognizing her, and warned me that everyone in her small town knew where she lived, so, if I got lost along the way, I could ask anyone to direct me. This wasn't necessary, though; I easily located the rambling wood house with a dilapidated red barn adjacent to the driveway. Lena called to me from her front step and gestured for me to follow her into the house. "I'm sorry it's so cold in here," she called out, as I removed my wet shoes and raincoat by the front door. After offering me tea and wine, she led me to a comfortable sitting area, which offered a view of her flower garden. She pointed toward her coffee table, where there was a flyer for a narrative medicine workshop that she was attending in a few weeks. After majoring in English in college, she explained, she had initially planned to get a PhD in literature but was motivated to pursue medicine after working in a refugee camp when she was in her early twenties. Recognizing that our interview had already gotten started, I told her that I better turn on my recorder.

Lena had a no-nonsense style and blunt sense of humor that I took to immediately. She explained that she prefers the poor patients, the ones for whom you need to step over a hole in the floor when you make house calls; her partner did better with the wealthy ones. For the first hour of our interview, I asked very few questions, letting her talk about how she got pulled into hospice and palliative medicine after experiencing several significant deaths in her twenties. Eventually, the conversation turned to the four patients with whom she had explored medical aid in dying: one, early on, whose father could not bring himself to fill the prescription; one who did not follow through because of cost constraints; and two who completed the protocol and ultimately ingested the lethal medication.

The first time Lena prescribed medication for assisted death entailed the case of the solitary man she had mentioned at the palliative care conference. Jacob was a veteran who had lived alone after a brief marriage.[14] He had no relationships with family and did not want to pursue any oncology treatment because he did not want to become dependent on caregivers. Jacob had investigated various methods of suicide but determined that aid in dying would cause the least distress to others. Initially, Lena felt surprised by her ambivalence. She viewed prescribing as bearing a tremendous moral and emotional responsibility, and she did not take the decision lightly. Yet she understood Jacob's choice and saw it as rational because it reflected the way he had lived his entire life. Moreover, she did not want to abandon Jacob, which is how she viewed rejecting his request. She was also convinced that, if she did not write the prescription, Jacob would end his life in a more gruesome manner. Lena's response puts an interesting twist on the dynamics of suicide risk management: her willingness to mitigate the harm of violent suicide by providing assistance placed her in a more agentive role with respect to Jacob's death.

Lena consulted with experienced colleagues and a pharmacist about the protocol. "I had never found out how you write the script; I never found out what the script was for; I never knew where you could get it filled; I had to do all that homework," she explained. She checked with Jacob's hospice nurse, a religious woman, to make sure that she felt comfortable caring for him, which she did, because "it was so in keeping with the way he had led his entire life."

Jacob wanted to be alone for his death, which presented a logistical challenge: he would need someone to attend to his body and pronounce him dead. With Lena's help, he worked out an arrangement with his hospice nurse, by which she would drive by his home on a specified day; if he had decided to go ahead with it, he would leave a sign for her, signaling that she should enter. Lena drove to Jacob's house to deliver his prescription. She was about to leave on a three-week vacation, and she had a tight timeline to get it to him. She brought her daughter for moral support and asked her to wait in the car. "I felt sad," she recalled. "I felt sad that his whole life had been so isolated. And I felt sad that he didn't want someone to hold his hand."

Lena was also the prescribing physician for Frances Sullivan, the woman whose story I introduced at the start of chapter 2. Lena had connected me to Tim, Frances's husband, after we met at the palliative care conference, warning me, "Be nice to them or I'll kick your ass." (After hearing her chew out the plenary speaker, I had no doubt she would.) Lena liked Frances and Tim immediately: his smart-aleck demeanor reminded Lena of her family, and Frances seemed like someone with whom she might otherwise be friends. Lena saw Frances five or six times for palliative care before they initiated the aid-in-dying protocol; this made Lena much more comfortable participating than she had been when Jacob requested assistance at their first meeting.

Yet while Lena had become more comfortable with the practical aspects of medical aid in dying by the time Frances sought out her help, she had not acclimated to the moral and emotional dimensions of the practice. Lena spoke at length about the burden of writing a lethal prescription. She described her orientation as very much aligned with her approach to practicing medicine: "I'm a very emotional doctor," she explained. "I mean, that's my driving force and maybe that's why I love [this area of Vermont] because I probably would be laughed at if I were at . . . some very formal place where you're supposed to maintain your distance, and your boundaries, and not say swear words, and not make jokes. I could never do that."

Lena viewed participating in aid in dying as "a huge weight and responsibility." She compared it to her experience working in an abortion clinic earlier in her career. Although she was very pro-choice, she reported, "I still found every abortion really painful and sad because I feel everything." She recalled, "The first time I did an abortion you know I did it in residency to get training, but it was really hard. Fishing out the little foot, oh my God, hard. But just because it's hard doesn't mean that I won't do it if it's what the person really needs and wants. I mean . . . if I have a philosophy of medicine, [it's] I will never abandon a patient. I will never, as much as I possibly can, I will not."

Lena described an image she had seen in *Our Bodies, Ourselves* during her childhood, of a woman who had died after attempting a self-induced abortion.[15] The picture still haunted her, many years later, and had influenced her response to Jacob. "She was a mother of six, in her forties. I hold those images and repercussions very strongly in my mind and in my heart. And I was convinced that if I did not write that script, he would have done something, whether he hung himself, or did the carbon monoxide, or—I don't think he would have shot himself because he thinks it was too messy, but he would have probably done the carbon monoxide."

For Lena and some other physicians, the fact that medical aid in dying was emotionally burdensome was a critical part of the practice. She explained, "I was saying that to, I can't remember which one I was talking to, one of my mentor doctors, and I said, 'This is really hard,' and they said, 'And it better stay hard.' It's supposed to stay hard." The point subtly insinuated here is that this difficulty was an essential protection against abuse: if it became too easy to assist a patient's death, a physician might do so for the wrong reasons. This logic mirrors the pro-choice logic initially expressed by President Bill Clinton in his 1996 contention that abortion should be "safe, legal, and rare." Recently, reproductive rights activists have challenged this position, arguing that the pro-choice movement has erred by suggesting that abortion ought to be rare; instead it should be normalized as a reasonable and common response to predictable and irreducible rates of contraceptive failure, problem pregnancies, and social challenges that factor into abortion decisions.[16] Similarly, most supporters of aid in dying cast it as "last resort option."[17]

At the same time, the substantial emotional labor made Lena resentful of those who opposed aid in dying and viewed her participation as a denigration of her professional role. Referring back to the heated exchange that I had witnessed at the palliative care conference, she reflected, "I think it's an important law to have available. I think that there should be some kind of support group for doctors who choose to do it. I think that that was very hard on me the day that I stood up in that palliative care meeting, I mean people were very kind, but . . . I was sad for Jacob and sad for Frances, especially Frances because I loved her, to have it be so hard and then to be questioned, or to be told I'm not a good doctor." She continued, "I'm like, you don't know how much I put into this, and thought about it, and contemplated, and worked with the patient, and talked to them, and offered them options other than this."

GREG WRIGHT: "PROUD . . . THAT I'M ONE OF THE PEOPLE WHO WILL DO THIS"

If Lena Rhodes lay at one end of the spectrum in experiencing her participation in medical aid in dying as a significant moral and emotional burden, Greg Wright, a family physician and hospice medical director, lay at the other. I met Greg in his office at his community-based practice on an early spring evening. It was the end of the workday, and he had told me the front door would be locked and I should bang on the side door. When I did, he came out to greet me in stocking feet and a rumpled button-down shirt. He had a youthful face that made him look younger than his fifty-odd years.

Greg told me about a formative clinical experience he had undergone as a third-year medical student that had cemented his interest in end-of-life care. His patient was a woman in her forties, who had been admitted to the hospital comatose, dying of breast cancer.

I had to go into her darkened room. She was all by herself. There was no family or anyone there. And she was unconscious and I had to admit her, and she was just going to die. Basically, oncology said, "She's going to die. Put her in the hallway; I don't want her anymore." . . . I loved Prince, and I think *Sign o' the Times* had just come up. And there was this Prince song playing, and I remember thinking, this is fucked up. This is really fucked up. This is Prince in this room alone with a woman who's going to die at a very young age from a horrible disease all by herself. There's no one else there. And I'm not even going to examine her because I don't know what the hell that's going to do, and this is where she's going to end her life. And I remember thinking, even at that age in my 20s, this is so crazy.

Twenty years into his career, Greg became the medical director at his local home health and hospice agency, and, several years after that, obtained his second board certification in hospice and palliative medicine. More recently, he had dreamed about starting his own inpatient hospice facility, a daunting endeavor owing to the fiscal and regulatory challenges.

Throughout much of his thirty-year career in medicine, Greg had had mixed feelings about aid in dying. In recent years, however, he had become much more supportive of it, to the point of suggesting that the law ought to go further toward helping people with Alzheimer's disease (who would not meet the competency requirement by the time they had a six-month prognosis) or neurodegenerative disorders (who would sometimes be unable to self-administer medication). Greg explained to me, "I think probably the younger me just felt like that was not our role as physicians. And I think that might have been more of a kneejerk response to this. As dealing with the hospice [became] a bigger part of my job, I became much more sympathetic to the fact that it's a really fine line between what I do in aggressive palliative care for patients and actively giving them the medicine for which they can terminate their lives. And I felt that the distinction between those is very blurred, like a lot of things in medicine." Here, I take Greg to mean that "aggressive palliative care"—medicating patients for pain control and symptom management—is not appreciably different from giving medication (sometimes the very same medications) for the purpose of hastening death.

Such comments hint at long-standing debates within palliative medicine regarding pain control and the rule of double effect. The rule of double effect, originally formulated by Thomas Aquinas and often invoked in contemporary bioethics, suggests that an action with two possible effects, one good and one bad, is justified if the action is undertaken with the intention of achieving the good effect. This rule is important for some physicians who oppose medical aid in dying but want to provide adequate pain relief to dying patients. Some argue that morphine controls pain but also suppresses respiration and therefore contributes to hastening death. The rule of double effect suggests that prescribing a large dose of morphine is morally permissible if it is intended to relieve pain and not to hasten death.[18] Others, however, have argued that concerns about respiratory suppression have been greatly exaggerated, noting that pain acts as a natural antagonist to the respiratory effects of opioids, and citing a lack of evidence that opioid use contributes to hastened death.[19]

An additional factor for Greg was that he was not religious, and therefore did not have objections to aid in dying on that ground. Consequently, he felt some obligation to participate, given that some of his colleagues would abstain on religious grounds. Greg could not participate in his capacity as hospice medical director because his hospice agency (and most agencies in Vermont) had a policy prohibiting their physicians from prescribing medication for an assisted death to their own hospice patients.[20] Yet Greg *was* able to prescribe for primary care patients.

Several hospice physicians pointed out to me that hospice physicians wear multiple clinical hats, affording them considerable latitude in circumventing hospice restrictions on prescribing. For example, Lena Rhodes told me, "I do not write the script on a hospice script. It has to be a palliative care script." After prescribing Seconal for Frances Sullivan, she had signed a document, cosigned by Frances, that said, "In my responsibilities for writing this Seconal script I'm not acting as the hospice medical director." Because Frances had seen Lena for palliative care before enrolling in hospice, Lena's hospice agency viewed this approach as a legitimate workaround.[21] Alanna Reynolds, another hospice physician, noted that her agency had amended its policy after encountering a similar situation. She explained, "If this is someone who the doctor has had a prior relationship with and this person wants to pursue Act 39 so now our hospice medical director becomes the attending, but for that patient she's no longer the medical director. We will assign another doctor to be the medical director for that patient." These workarounds "work" because of the different duties associated with different professional roles. Yet they also demonstrate that professional roles can be malleable, and hospice and palliative care physicians often inhabit multiple roles that may intersect or conflict with each other.

Several of Greg's partners had approached him for help with patients because they felt uncomfortable participating in medical aid in dying, and Greg was happy to fill this gap. Because his practice was large, and he did not generally accept new patients, his aid-in-dying work was essentially restricted to preexisting clinic patients, either his own or his partner's. Greg found this reassuring, as it helped to put boundaries around the practice. He had only one patient from outside the practice come to him specifically to seek aid in dying, having heard through word-of-mouth in the community that he was open to prescribing aid-in-dying medication. He told me that one of his colleagues had people coming from out of state to see her, which seemed horrible to him because it added another layer of risk and liability.[22]

Greg described his clinical experiences with aid in dying as "universally good." Of the patients for whom he had prescribed medication, only half had actually ingested it. Those patients had positive experiences, and their families were happy with the outcomes. Others were happy to have aid in dying as an option, even if they did not ultimately use it. Greg explained, "People love that you'll sit and talk to them about this and provide them with the option, which I think is really a huge part of this, is the whole option part."

When I asked Greg about how he viewed his role in aid in dying, and whether he saw it as a moral or emotional burden, he responded, "I think I consider it part of medical care, on the spectrum of palliative care, providing relief at the end of life. We've already decided that your death is inevitable from this disease, and it's coming soon enough that you meet a federal guideline for hospice. We are assisting you in obtaining drugs, and getting proper instruction to choose the time and place of that ending. I don't have any moral problems with that at this point in my life. I think that that is a reasonable thing." For Greg, then, aid in dying was not morally distinct from other forms of palliative care. Once it was clear that death was inevitable, it simply enabled the dying person to choose the time and place of their death.

Greg harbored no resentment that he was performing a disproportionate share of this work in his practice. Instead, he was proud of the role he served in facilitating patients' end-of-life wishes. Furthermore, he was committed to educating colleagues about the practice and noted that he kept a folder with information about Act 39 on his desk, so that he could offer it to colleagues if people approached him with questions, which they sometimes did.

> I don't feel resentful. And I also know from Oregon, that there really is a limited number of people who do this. And they're known as people who do this. And at the beginning of this, the oncologist and I would talk about being known as the death doctors around here. And we said it jokingly, but as time goes on, it's just like, no, I'm actually kind of proud of that, that I'm one of the people who will do this. And you can talk to me about this, and I think that's okay if you disagree with me. That's another thing about being in your fifties. Like screw everyone. I don't give a shit what you think about me. I'll do whatever I want, and it's very liberating.

To summarize, participating in medical aid in dying was, for Greg, not terribly distinct from other aspects of his professional duties. It was "one more tool to help people at the end of life," on a spectrum with other palliative care services. Moreover, it was an aspect of his clinical work of which he felt quite proud. Greg's stance on participating was similar to that of other male physicians in my study. Of the four male physicians who had prescribed under Act 39, including Greg, all viewed participating in aid in dying as a logical extension of the physician's professional role, and none had considered it a substantial moral or emotional burden. In contrast, female physicians, including Lena, were more likely to hold nuanced positions on the physician's moral role and to report investing emotional labor that stretched beyond their preexisting professional obligations.

While I am reluctant to generalize from my admittedly small sample, this difference is worth noting, particularly because it aligns with feminist ethics scholarship suggesting that women and men exhibit gendered orientations to moral judgment.[23] (This is not to essentialize biological differences between men and women but rather to suggest that men and women are socialized differently in most societies.) The care perspective in feminist ethics proposes that women's moral reasoning and decision making are often embedded in social relationships rather than lodged within a singular, autonomous moral agent.[24] This theory of moral reasoning can help to explain why female physicians who view participating in aid in dying as a significant departure from the physician's professional role might nevertheless be willing to participate: they may feel compelled to do so because of their moral orientation to care. From this perspective, the salient gender difference here may not be that men are more likely to view aid in dying as more aligned with the physician's professional role. I know from my experiences and interactions at professional conferences that there are plenty of physicians, both men and women, who view participating in assisted death as anathema to the physician's professional role. Instead, *those men who perceive such a misalignment may be less willing to participate.* To state this differently, women may be more likely to participate in aid in dying, even if they view it as a departure from their professional role, because of the ways in which moral judgments about aid in dying are inextricably linked to their relational commitments to care.

SHELLY MARKHAM: "IT'S BECOME A PART OF THE JOB THAT I DON'T REALLY WANT TO DO"

Shelly Markham was an oncologist who had been in practice for more than twenty years. Shelly shared Lena's and Greg's view that participating in medical aid in dying is a professional obligation. However, she did not view it as a privilege to assist her patients in ending their lives, and she expressed a great deal of bitterness about her role in the practice. Shelly was one of the most experienced prescribers in the state; she estimated at the time we met that seven of her patients had ingested lethal medication prescribed under Act 39. Shelly's name surfaced early in my research, and I spent a year trying to pin her down for an interview. She had agreed initially, then asked whether we could do it by phone, and then stopped returning my emails. I emailed her again several times the following summer, and was somewhat taken aback when she wrote to me after several weeks of not responding and told me she would be in clinic the next Friday, and could we meet then?

Shelly suggested that we meet at eight o'clock in the morning outside the radiation oncology suite in her hospital, where there was a sofa and big comfortable armchairs. I had interpreted her curt emails as irritation with me and expected her to be standoffish. Instead, I could not get her to stop talking, even though she had patients waiting, and I ended up being an hour late for my next interview. Over the course of our discussion, it became clear that Shelly felt incredibly burdened by medical aid in dying, and, although she supports it philosophically, she was overwhelmed by its role in her clinical practice. Some of this frustration may have spilled over into her response to me in my initial overtures, but when we finally met she found the interview cathartic.

Like Greg Wright, Shelly had a specific origin story for her supportive views on medical aid in dying: during her oncology fellowship, she watched her mother die from cancer. She explained, "I dearly loved that woman and I watched this disease take her from an incredibly physically and emotionally strong person, to a very, very dependent, incapacitated person." Shelly's father, who was also a physician, undermedicated her mother's pain because he wanted her to be alert and awake. Shelly got in the habit of giving her mother more medication whenever her father left the room, and every time her mother thanked her. One day, while her father was taking a nap, Shelly recounted,

> My mom looked at me and said, "I think it's time to go. I'm trapped in this body that doesn't work anymore and I think it's just time to go." And she kind of then fell asleep. And I think we all have those lightbulb moments, and I just realized that if I really, really loved her, I wouldn't keep trying to hang on here to somebody who had already crossed that bridge and wanted to pass away. Because there are things that are worse than death. And I medicated the hell out of my mom, and she died that night. Would she have died that night if I wasn't there? Well, who will ever know?

Shelly's experience recalls the "fine line" Greg Wright referenced between "aggressive palliative care" and medical aid in dying. Over the course of my research, I heard many stories from people who had similar experiences while watching a loved one die. These underscore that using medication to alter the timing of death is not an entirely new phenomenon but instead builds on a long legacy of human efforts to gain control over the dying process. This personal experience fueled Shelly's comfort with legalized assisted death and eventually made her an accidental champion of the practice.

As an oncologist, Shelley was accustomed to having difficult conversations, but she viewed the kinds of conversations she had around medical aid in dying as emotionally draining in an entirely new way. She also found it burdensome to navigate the bureaucratic protocol and ensure that patients met the legislative requirements, and criticized the legislature and Department of Health for not providing more guidance about what medications to use. Finally, she resented performing work her colleagues did not want to do. More than anyone else I interviewed, Shelly seemed to experience this part of her clinical work as a kind of dirty work: work that is generally regarded as morally tainted and unpleasant to perform, yet nevertheless essential.[25]

Shelly told me about Renee Long, a woman in her sixties with metastatic cancer. After several years of treatment, Renee decided that she had had enough and asked her oncologist for aid in dying. When the oncologist sent Renee to Shelly, Shelly asked why he would not help his patient, whom he had known for many years. Shelly relayed their conversation: "And he said, 'I can't do this because I believe she has not exhausted all of the different potential treatments.' And I said, 'Well, where in the law does it say you [have to exhaust other treatments]? There's nothing that says that.'" Shelly felt her colleague had punted on an important professional obligation and resented the burden that it imposed on her, yet she agreed to participate. The process was labor intensive because there was a concern about whether an estranged family member would be on board with Renee's decision. Shelly also spent a huge amount of time fighting the insurance company to cover the medication, which it eventually agreed to do.

Then, when Renee took the medication, "I didn't even know that. No one notified me of that. I sort of found out about that three months, four months after her death. When I sort of said, 'Has anybody heard about Mrs. So-and-so?' 'Oh yeah, she's been dead three months.' That just didn't feel right." For Shelly, participating in medical aid in dying entailed a great deal of intimacy, and it felt like a serious affront that she was shut out of the process when the death finally occurred; writing the script for Shelly implied a social and emotional obligation for Renee and her caregivers to keep her informed. Her comments also suggest that concerns related to patient abandonment, which had been raised by Lena Rhodes and others as reasons that support participating in aid in dying, can cut both ways: physicians may feel similarly abandoned by patients if there is not adequate closure after an assisted death. This point recalls Quill and Cassell's suggestion that nonabandonment as a continuous caring partnership between physician and patient is a two-way street.

As a result of experiences like these, Shelly indicated that because her participation in medical aid in dying was leading to burnout, she did not want to keep doing this part of her job. She had come to dread going into a clinical encounter when she knew the conversation would be about aid in dying. She explained, "It's one of those things where you know that you're now turning the knob on a door and you're going into this room—that's really emotionally draining." She resented colleagues with convenient excuses for not participating, and she resented families who did not bother to inform her when a patient had died, which made her feel exploited.

Moreover, Shelly worried about how her involvement would affect her relationship with colleagues who were opposed to the practice: "Some of our colleagues are terribly opposed to this, and, you know, is that going to affect my relationship with them? I don't know. If they have really strong views on this, will they say, 'Oh, she's Dr. Death, she's going to knock everybody off, so I'm not referring anybody to her?' These are things that doctors do think about. I don't think real hard about them, but they are things [I think about]." Working in oncology, a specialty largely committed to curing and saving lives at any cost, likely heightened Shelly's concerns about how her participation would affect her standing in her professional community.

Shelly maintained that no one understands the kind of impact that medical aid in dying has on physicians. "Having these discussions about taking one's life actively and working to actively help people to do that, it's not just one chunk of flesh, it's more than one," she told me. "And I realized that it's become a part of the job that I don't really want to do. I don't think that any of the legislators or anybody, really, understands what that chunk of flesh out of the person is." Here, Shelly expressed a subtle critique of medical aid in dying: it is not just the life and livelihood of one person that is at stake. Instead, the practice also demands a large "chunk of flesh" of the physician who is called on to assist. Shelly felt aggrieved that policy makers did not account for the burden aid in dying places on participating physicians.

Given these sentiments, I was not surprised when I heard several years after our interview that Shelly had retired early. This drastic outcome raises the question of why Shelly chose to participate in the first place. It may be that she found it too difficult to say no when confronted with an individual suffering patient, but taking early retirement still seems like an extreme response to this predicament. There very well may have been other factors contributing to her decision. Nevertheless, Shelly's experience provides an important foil to that of Greg Wright, and even Lena Rhodes, when the clinical significance of participating in medical aid in dying is considered. Her point about the "chunk of flesh" that aid in dying cost her is also an instructive reminder of the limits of bioethical frameworks for autonomy in explaining the moral dimensions of aid in dying. Aid in dying is a deeply relational practice that enlists medical providers and caregivers to buttress the patient's autonomy.

BRENDA JONES: "FOR ME PERSONALLY, IT CROSSES THE LINE TO ACTUALLY WRITE THE PRESCRIPTION"

The last case I consider concerns a physician who ultimately chose not to prescribe medication but was nevertheless committed to supporting patients pursuing medical aid in dying. I met Brenda Jones at a small coffee shop in the town where she works, the kind of place where one could, in 2017, buy an Americano for less than two dollars, which I found rather shocking. Brenda was a hospice and palliative care physician, whose clinical work was split between primary care and hospice and palliative care consultations.

Brenda had gone to medical school after spending a decade working as an emergency medical technician and discovering that she was surprisingly comfortable talking about death and being with patients who were dying. She became the go-to person for end-of-life conversations during her internal medicine residency, and eventually she decided to pursue a palliative care fellowship. Brenda liked making house calls, freed from the constraints of the fifteen-minute office visit, and she found that she lived her life differently as a result of working with dying patients. "I don't push off everything I've ever wanted to do until I'm sixty-five plus," she explained. "So yeah, I travel now; I'd like to travel later if I'm lucky enough to live to seventy, eighty, ninety."

Much of our conversation focused on Brenda's experience with Mary Llewelyn, a longtime primary care patient who asked Brenda, many years after she was diagnosed with cancer, if she would be willing to provide medical aid in dying.[26] Brenda felt conflicted. On the one hand, because she strongly believed in the capacity of local hospice and palliative care services to alleviate suffering and provide excellent care for dying patients, she was at least partially inclined to view such requests as a "cop-out" pursued by patients who had not truly exhausted all of their options. On the other hand, she was committed to the ethos of patient choice and did not want to abandon Mary (whom she sincerely liked and admired) during this difficult time. That aid in dying was a legal option made Brenda feel responsible to help Mary pursue this choice, despite her own objections.

It would have been possible for Brenda to support Mary's wishes without becoming deeply entangled—for example, by remaining involved in Mary's medical care for the remainder of her life. However, much like Lena Rhodes, Brenda felt obligated to do more. Ultimately, she decided that the best way to navigate her conflicting values was to do everything possible to help Mary, short of writing the lethal prescription. For Brenda, writing a prescription was a morally decisive action that she was unwilling to undertake, even though she was willing to support Mary throughout the process.

When Brenda initially informed Mary that she did not feel comfortable being the prescribing physician, Mary was extremely disappointed. "Nobody likes that answer coming out of their provider that they've had an ongoing relationship with," Brenda recalled. "She and I navigated it, but it was not always pleasant for either one of us." Brenda did assist Mary in identifying another physician willing to write the prescription, reaching out to an advocacy organization when she was unable to find anyone local. She also agreed to be the second physician certifying that Mary met the legal requirements, researched the medication protocol, and worked with the prescribing physician to make sure that contingency plans were in place for the day of Mary's death. In these ways, Brenda identified a middle path that allowed her to reconcile her opposition to Mary's choice with her deeply felt personal and professional obligation to help Mary receive the kind of care she wanted.

Overall, Brenda expressed a strong commitment to making sure that things went according to plan. To that end, she reported spending "a lot of time thinking ahead of all the unexpected things that can happen." Her worries included Mary losing consciousness before taking the full dose, vomiting after ingesting the medication, or simply not dying. Brenda and the prescribing physician decided what other medications Mary should have available in the house to treat pain or agitation, should they occur; who would give these medications to her and under what circumstances; and who would be responsible for calling Brenda if further assistance were necessary. Brenda also helped to prepare a palliative care nurse, who planned to attend Mary's death. For Brenda, then, the decision not to write the pharmaceutical script resulted in increased cooperation with other clinicians, highlighting how the collaborative scripting at stake in assisted death stretches beyond prescribing.

I asked Brenda whether it felt like a burden to perform such clinical labor in the service of a practice she opposed. She reflected, "I do all sorts of crazy logistical stuff for people, so this doesn't seem more burdensome perhaps than other things that were done. I mean, it was still important to me for her to get what she wanted even though I didn't agree with it. And so, the way you sort of show that commitment is by doing crazy things I guess—hopping on the phone and emailing around and understanding what the medication cocktail is."

I also asked why she drew the line at writing the prescription, pointing out that the prescriber may be less intimately involved than the person working out all of the logistics. (It certainly seemed that way in Mary's case.) Brenda acknowledged that she sometimes felt this way, too. This was the part of her that seemed to be "of two minds" about medical aid in dying. Yet she nevertheless continued to feel that the act of writing the prescription was morally significant in a way that gave her pause. She reasoned,

Is it really any different if you do everything else? You say, "I'm going to help you find a prescriber. I'm going to sort of script with all these people to make sure everything goes okay. We're going to make sure you have all these medicines. We're going to talk about the date. I'm going to do everything but sort of that final step." And I guess, you know, I sort of settle with the idea that I still think for me personally, it crosses a line to actually write a prescription that I know with certainty the purpose of it is for someone to die. It feels very different to me than when I write sort of comfort med orders or even palliative sedation orders. I feel like I'm sort of being used for something that just doesn't quite sit right with me. Because without the prescription it can't be done.

Brenda saw writing a prescription for medical aid in dying as categorically different from prescribing large doses of morphine to dying patients. It was also different from palliative sedation, the practice of continuously administering medication so that the patient is rendered unconscious until death.[27] (This may be what Greg Wright had in mind when he referred to "aggressive palliative care.") Brenda's position relied on a distinction between indirectly helping Mary to end her life and directly contributing to her death—a distinction that she recognized was a bit tenuous.[28] Yet it allowed her to reconcile her opposition to this choice with her deeply felt personal and professional obligation to help her patient receive the kind of care that she wanted.

THE PHYSICIAN'S ROLE IN ASSISTED DEATH

The four cases described in this chapter present a variety of perspectives on the question posed at the beginning of the chapter: To what extent does the act of writing a script for lethal medication align with the physician's professional role? Greg Wright was the physician who most perceived medical aid in dying as aligned with the physician's professional role. For him, there was not a significant moral distinction between, on the one hand, prescribing medication to alleviate pain, an action that might simultaneously hasten death, and, on the other, prescribing medication with the sole intent of enabling the patient to hasten death. He viewed both actions as following from the palliative care physician's obligation to treat patients' suffering and a commitment to patient-centered care.

While his supportive stance ingratiated Greg with some advocates, a physician perceived as being too accommodating could also raise suspicion. One acquaintance suggested to me that Greg might perhaps be *too* permissive, to the point of being encouraging. My own research did not substantiate this claim. In fact, quite to the contrary, Cora Tremblay, whose husband, Arnold, had been Greg's patient, praised Greg for prescribing medication for an assisted death, despite her religious objections to medical aid in dying.[29] Nevertheless, this gossip from the field provides an instructive reminder of the cultural expectations that aid in dying ought to be hard, and physicians who make it easy risk their clinical reputations.

Like Greg Wright, Lena Rhodes and Shelly Markham also viewed participating in medical aid in dying as a professional obligation, yet they differed from him in experiencing moral and emotional discomfort. Lena's comparison of aid in dying to abortion is quite revealing of her moral stance toward assisted death. In the United States, abortion is heavily stigmatized and cultural boundary work maintains its special status outside the realm of traditional medicine.[30] By comparing aid in dying to abortion, Lena set it apart from conventional medicine and treated it as an exceptional category of clinical work—one that is difficult but nevertheless important. Moreover, reflecting on Canada's aid in dying policy, which permits physician-administered medication, Lena indicated that she felt "psychologically protected" because "I write the script, but they have to do everything." For Lena, then, prescribing lethal medication was less morally fraught than actually *administering* such medication.

Shelly also found participating in aid in dying morally and emotionally taxing, noting the "chunk of flesh" that it took from her. However, unlike Lena, Shelly became embittered by her role in the process and acknowledged that it was a part of her job that she no longer wanted to do. Notably, some of Shelly's frustrations pertained to the procedural and bureaucratic dimensions of medical aid in dying. As I describe further in the next chapter, Shelly resented that it fell to her as the physician to research the best medication cocktails and determine whether patients met the state's residency requirement. Yet a big part of her grievance lay in having to conduct the clinical conversations, which she perceived included a strong obligation to dissuade patients from hastening death. Those clinical encounters were incredibly emotionally draining, because, as she put it, "you're not an automaton that's detached and you just go in and do this." Moreover, she found it increasingly difficult both to reconcile the conversations within the limits of the thirty-minute office visit and to bill for the appropriate time without incensing other waiting patients and hospital administrators.

It may be tempting to attribute Shelly's more negative experience to her status as a hospital-based oncologist. As hospice and palliative care providers, Lena, Greg, and Brenda enjoyed relatively more latitude in their daily schedules and were more capable of carving out time for extended patient visits. As an oncologist, however, Shelly may have found it more difficult to reconcile assisting patients who wanted aid in dying with her own practice, given oncology's prevailing ethos of cure at any cost. At the same time, I do not think that Shelly's clinical specialty fully accounts for why she struggled more than the other physicians I profiled here. Ken Greene, another oncologist I interviewed, maintained that palliative care was a critical component of oncology practice and viewed medical aid in dying as clearly aligned with his professional role. As he said in the passage I quoted earlier, "I don't look at Act 39 as something totally different from everything else we do." The differences between Shelly's and Ken's positions underscore the rich and subtly varied perspectives that physicians bring to this work. While professional norms matter to how physicians understand assisted death, reconciling this work with clinical practice is ultimately an individual moral process—one that casts physicians in the role of lay philosophers of action, as I suggested earlier in the chapter.

Finally, Brenda Jones represents a dissenting voice in her view that prescribing medication for an assisted death would cross a line that would threaten her role as a hospice and palliative care provider. There was something about prescribing medication with the sole intent of hastening death that Brenda could not accept. At the same time, other aspects of the practice were very much aligned with Brenda's commitment to patient choice and nonabandonment. For this reason, she could not imagine passing her patients off to physicians more comfortable with the practice.

Brenda's case offers a novel perspective on recent debates regarding the role of the physician's conscience in medicine. Broadly speaking, conscience refers to a mode of thought in which individuals consider how specific actions align or conflict with their commitment to core moral principles or values.[31] Much of the scholarly literature and public debate about the role of conscience in medicine have focused on the moral contours of refusal, considering whether health care professionals should be permitted to abstain from providing certain types of morally contested medical services, such as medical aid in dying, abortion, and emergency contraception.[32] Brenda's case challenges the stark and heavily politicized dichotomy between participation and refusal, however, by showing that conscientious objection does not necessarily mean abstaining from all forms of assistance.[33] Other studies have noted the highly contextualized nature of decisions to participate, suggesting that physicians may be more likely to prescribe for particular patients in particular circumstances.[34] Brenda also demonstrates the need for a relational concept of conscience, in which conscience claims in medicine may be motivated by a concern for maintaining and protecting relationships in addition to preserving an individual's moral integrity.[35]

Referral to another health care provider is often posed as a solution for navigating conflicts of conscience; the bioethicist Dan Brock has called this the "conventional compromise."[36] Yet this type of solution was ultimately unsatisfactory for Brenda. Even once she had found another physician to assist Mary, Brenda did not feel she had fulfilled her obligations to Mary's end-of-life care. Brenda's narrative reveals how referring a patient to another provider for morally contested care can feel like abandoning her: although it may satisfy a minimum threshold of professional responsibility, as Edmund Pellegrino suggests, it falls far short of a more robust vision of patient-centered care. Therefore, referral does not offer the neat solution to conflicts of conscience that the conventional compromise presumes.

Another problem with the conventional compromise is that we cannot guarantee that a conscientiously objecting physician will be able to identify a willing colleague for a referral, given how many physicians are uneasy with medical aid in dying, particularly absent a long-standing patient-physician relationship. A physician colleague of mine once told me she had asked her medical students what they would do if a patient asked for an abortion. After several students in a row indicated they would refer the patient elsewhere, she asked, "But to whom will you refer? How can you *all* refer?" Thus, while referral may seem like a middle ground between two poles of a moral dilemma, it can also come across as an evasion of responsibility.

Brenda's narrative shows striving toward an ethical middle ground can involve a different approach, one that is less fully explored in the bioethics literature. It emphasizes that there are multiple ways a physician can contribute to "scripting" death that do not involve a script pad. Other physicians followed this pathway when they were restricted from prescribing by institutional policies. For example, when her hospice agency's policy prohibited Alanna Reynolds, a hospice and palliative care physician, from prescribing medication under Act 39, she worked closely with another physician and contributed substantial on-the-ground clinical support work to assist with a patient's medically assisted death.

The cases explored in this chapter likewise hint at the gendered nature of physicians' moral reasoning about assisted death. To be clear, any assertions of gender differences in physicians' perspectives on medical aid in dying are necessarily provisional: my sample is too small and nonrepresentative to draw any definitive conclusions. Nevertheless, this pattern is evocative and worthy of this intellectual speculation, however provisional it may be. The Vermont Department of Health does not release any demographic data on the physicians who have participated in Act 39, yet a key policy stakeholder told me that women physicians were "stepping up" to participate much more frequently than their male counterparts. My data lend support to this observation: of the nineteen participating physicians I interviewed, only six were men. Similarly, only four of the twelve prescribers were men. Of course, caution must be taken in extrapolating larger patterns from my sample, but given the low utilization in the state (i.e., fifty-two cases between 2013 and 2017, at least some of which were treated by the same physicians),[37] I have reason to believe that my sample represents a generous cross-section of Vermont physicians who have participated. Therefore, my sample provides suggestive evidence that women have participated in larger numbers, and gender differences in moral reasoning offer one potential avenue for understanding and explaining this difference.

So does medical aid in dying align with the physician's professional role? The range of responses described here demonstrates that we cannot answer this question in absolute terms. Instead, it depends on the contextual and relational meanings that physicians (as well as patients and families) attach to this form of scripting death. Most physicians were not either starkly for or against aid in dying in the aftermath of legalization. As moral pioneers in a new zone of clinical practice, they harbored nuanced and ambivalent feelings on the subject that evolved over time through direct experiences with patients. This chapter has explored their views, which are not always represented in advocacy narratives and legislative testimony, and which receive much less attention in public dialogue.

Overall, this chapter has revealed that scripting death through medical aid in dying entails more than just writing a pharmaceutical script. Physicians may help to script death in multiple ways—by having intimate clinical conversations about patients' hopes and desires, advising on timing, planning for adverse events, and, of course, prescribing medication—all of which showcase physicians' agency and improvisation in scripting processes. The moral significance ascribed to these different forms of scripting depends on physicians' personal moral worldviews as much as on broader cultural values surrounding their role in end-of-life care. Public dialogue that reduces physicians' participation in aid in dying to the willingness to prescribe (or not) overlooks the diverse possibilities afforded by these different modes of assistance and care and how they construct the physician's agency with respect to scripting death.

5 Access and the Power to Choose

While I was preparing to return to Vermont for another summer of field-work in spring 2017, I received an unsolicited email from a woman named Margot Hadley.[1]

Hello,

My husband Rich died 1 year ago.

Rich suffered from a chronic disease for which there was no cure. He very much wished to have a dignified, pain free death on his terms and was hopeful that Act 39 would make that possible. We were shocked to learn that our local hospital prohibits its physicians from participating in Act 39. An exhaustive search elsewhere in VT was no less promising, as we were informed by several physicians that heightened scrutiny in VT made them reluctant to participate in Act 39.

At a time when I should have been comforting my dying husband I was desperately trying to navigate Act 39 on his behalf. I regret that it took me from his bedside.

I think Vermonters would be shocked if they knew how inaccessible Act 39 is.

Sadly,
Margot[2]

Margot's email captures a sobering fact: for some Vermonters, Act 39 offers the false promise of an aspirational though fundamentally unattainable type of death. This is rarely acknowledged in the advocacy rhetoric surrounding assisted dying and has led to profound disappointment for some patients and families. In this chapter, I turn to their stories and describe the various constraints that patients, families, and clinicians have confronted in navigating access to aid in dying. I show how their capacity to overcome such constraints has resulted in critical access inequalities that reflect larger patterns in US health care and belie the public narratives that cast aid in dying as, fundamentally, a matter of personal choice. If the legalization of aid in dying represents the opportunity to script death in new ways, this opportunity is not equally available to everyone. Here, I explore who has the power to enact and perform new medico-legal scripts for dying, and who is ultimately left out of such processes.

Just a few months after receiving Margot's email, I found myself in her living room listening to her story, as her doting dog vied for my attention. Margot was a professional woman in her early sixties with a warm demeanor and a soft Boston accent. She and Rich had met later in life, after her divorce from the father of her two daughters. Rich was a Vietnam veteran and a confirmed bachelor, who traveled the world for thrill-seeking adventures: bungee jumping in New Zealand, skiing in the Alps. He was also the love of Margot's life. "I don't think he ever said an unkind word about anybody," she told me. "He was just really a very good man. And everybody who met him liked him. He was not judgmental. He never brought any ego into any interactions and he was just really confident about who he was."

Rich was diagnosed with Parkinson's disease a year after he and Margot married and died four and a half years later. They were together for fifteen years. Because Agent Orange is known to cause Parkinson's disease,[3] Rich received excellent disability and health benefits from the Veterans Health Administration, although the nearest VA hospital was over an hour away from Rich and Margot's home. Still, none of the medications seemed to help Rich. He experienced constant nausea, persistent discomfort, and terrible constipation. Toward the end of his life, his only respite was sleep. "In the last six months I had to spoon-feed him and change his diapers, and he couldn't walk, and we would have to, you know, figure out ways to ambulate him," Margot recalled. "And he never once complained. He would simply say, 'I've had a really good life.'"

When Vermont's aid-in-dying law passed, Rich knew immediately that he wanted to pursue it. At his behest, Margot had investigated various ways for him to end his life over the course of his long illness, yet none of them seemed promising. "You can't do it with carbon monoxide in the garage anymore because of the emission controls on the cars," she explained matter-of-factly. "You'll end up with brain damage, but not death, so that's out." They stockpiled pills, but the possibility of Rich surviving a drug overdose worried them. Margot had also researched helium, but the thought of watching Rich asphyxiate under a big plastic hood terrified her. "I just said, 'I don't think I could possibly participate,'" she told me.

Initially, Margot had been concerned about the requirement in the law for a six-month prognosis because Parkinson's disease entails a slow, progressive decline. Eventually, however, one of Rich's physicians pointed out that he was on hospice, which also requires a six-month prognosis, so he should definitely qualify. Margot contacted a local advocacy group for more information. She recalled this conversation as follows: "So they said I would just have to find two doctors in Vermont to prescribe. So, I said, 'Okay, great. Could you tell me what doctors have been prescribing?' 'No, we can't tell you that.' So, I said, 'Well, how am I supposed to find two doctors? One, I just can't go knocking on their doors. I have to transfer all the—they're not going to meet with me or Rich without all of our records being transferred. I can't do that times thirty, forty, fifty times.'"

After many conversations, Margot was finally told that doctors in a nearby town might be willing to help. This narrowed the field considerably: "I could knock on those six or eight doors," she acknowledged. In the meantime, one of her daughters mentioned the ordeal to her father, whose parents lived in that town. Margot's former in-laws, it turned out, were dear friends of one of the doctors. With their help, Margot connected with the doctor, who suggested they meet in his office at four o'clock on a Sunday. Margot understood this covert meeting as necessary to conceal the conditions of the visit from the receptionist and other clinic staff. At first, the doctor was incredibly supportive. He not only agreed to prescribe but also offered to connect Rich and Margot to a second doctor. He told the couple that his colleague would contact them within a week, and he would come to their house for the consultation. At this point, Rich's Parkinson's had advanced to a stage at which he experienced violent shaking and constant nausea, so traveling to a doctor's office had become an excruciating ordeal. When they left the office, Rich was elated. "He was so happy that he could have relief from his suffering," Margot said.

After a week went by, however, Margot received a call from the first doctor, who apologized and said, "We can't prescribe. The scrutiny in Vermont has gone through the ceiling." Margot continued, "He basically said, 'I am so, so sorry. People are going to think that you're doctor shopping.' And I said, 'I am doctor shopping. That's the truth. Of course, I am because Rich has no choice.' So, he apologized profusely, but he said he and the other doctor would not prescribe." While these physicians were concerned that Rich was not a preexisting patient, Margot had done her research and knew that this was irrelevant: "I know the law. There's nothing in the law that says you have to have a preexisting relationship with the patient. That is not a part of the law." Because Rich had been receiving all of his health care from the VA system, requesting a prescription from one of his preexisting doctors was not an option.[4] Rich and Margot considered approaching their primary care physician from many years prior, but she had moved out of state.

For the first time since his diagnosis, Margot saw Rich truly despair. She offered to take him to Switzerland, but he did not want to die in a hotel.[5] Moreover, they both knew it would be incredibly burdensome to get Rich to Switzerland in his condition. "He could feel every internal organ shaking," Margot recalled. "It was just brutal." Margot asked her daughter and a Spanish-speaking friend to accompany her to Mexico to purchase Nembutal, a barbiturate used to euthanize animals that is not commercially available in the United States, but both refused; her daughter advised her that breaking the law could jeopardize her ability to care for Rich if she got caught. Margot had also told Rich that she did not want him to end his life violently by shooting himself because she could not bear to find him afterward. "So, the only thing left for him was to stop eating and drinking," she said. "And that's what he decided to do."

Rich decided to stop eating and drinking about a week after realizing that aid in dying was not going to be an option he could access. That he made this decision so quickly took Margot by surprise. Rich, an "optimistic

and contented soul," had squeezed as much joy out of life as he could mus-
ter. "For him to throw in the towel was just really shocking to me, and that
spoke volumes," Margot said. "It really made me think that he was suffering far more than I could even gauge."

The six days and six nights that Rich took to die were excruciating for
Margot. Besides the Parkinson's disease, he was physically healthy, with
no cardiac problems or major organ dysfunction. Even though Rich was
ready to die, his body clung to life. He was agitated and gasping for air. "It
was really painful to watch," Margot said. Her daughters came home to
support her, and they took turns getting up every hour to dose him with
morphine. Margot kept hoping the morphine would kill him, but it did
not. She begged the hospice nurse to accelerate the process but was told
that would be euthanasia, which is against the law.

A year after Rich's death, Margot harbored many regrets about Rich's
end-of-life suffering and his long, protracted death: "People say that I should
feel good that I gave Rich, you know, what he wanted, which was to die at
home, but I really felt like, no, he didn't get what he wanted. This is a man
who never really asked anybody [for] anything. And served his country and
died because of serving his country, and he wanted Act 39. He couldn't have
it, and that really, really—it really bothers me." Margot had since promised
her daughters that they would never see her die that way. "I'll put a bullet in
my head before my daughters have to witness that," she said. She likewise
had many misgivings about the future of aid in dying in Vermont: "You have
to keep advocating and advocating. And when people say no, you have to
figure out where else to look. And so, I really worry about people who don't
have the personal resources or strength for that, or awareness."

THE ILLUSION OF ACCESS

Margot's story, I discovered, was not anomalous. As I learned more about
her local community, it became apparent that Margot and Rich had the
misfortune of living in one of the areas of Vermont where access to medical aid in dying was most severely constrained. The local hospital had not
developed an institutional policy for responding to patients' requests for
an assisted death, and the prevailing attitude among local physicians

ranged from adamant opposition to benign neglect. Nearly all were reluctant to participate in the stigmatized practice. Amanda Townshend, a palliative care physician and advocate who had lobbied for Vermont's law acknowledged that this community lagged behind other parts of the state in implementation efforts.

This situation was frustrating for local advocates. Penny Ginsberg, who had volunteered for one of the state-based advocacy groups that spearheaded the campaign in Vermont, had hoped to be a bedside volunteer with Compassion & Choices. (The organization ultimately decided not to develop a volunteer program similar to the one that it had developed in Oregon.) In June 2017, Penny emailed me and urged me to contact a local oncology nurse practitioner, Jacqueline Starks, whom she had seen in the audience for a talk Amanda Townshend gave on Act 39 at the local hospital. The talk was aimed at the general public, but many hospice workers, nursing home staff, and medical personnel also attended. Penny told me that near the end Jacqueline spoke about her disappointment in not being able to find a single physician, in all of her networks, willing to help the patients who requested medical aid in dying. Close to tears, Jacqueline said that her patients were lucky because they died relatively quickly from cancer, so their inability to access the law became a moot point. According to Penny, Jacqueline's testimony rattled the audience, and the session ended on a somber note.

Intrigued by Penny's recounting, I contacted Jacqueline and left her a voice message about my study. I was pleasantly surprised when she returned my call that night. I gave Jacqueline the same spiel that I always gave prospective participants, explaining that my research was focused on how aid in dying was being implemented. "Or not implemented," Jacqueline retorted, a sour note in her voice. She proceeded to tell me that she was neither strongly for nor against the law but found the way that it had been applied incredibly frustrating.

The next Friday afternoon, I drove several hours to meet Jacqueline in her office. She told me about how she had been an oncology nurse practitioner for twenty years, having started her career in HIV nursing and having been exposed to palliative care. Her current duties included a fair amount of end-of-life care, in addition to ongoing therapeutic coordination and toxicity management. She had received three direct requests for medical aid in dying, with additional patients raising the topic in a more oblique manner. When it came up, she said she would do her best to help, but the two oncologists she worked with were morally opposed, and she had been unable to identify others in the area willing to prescribe. It tended to come down to the patient's primary care provider—and many patients had nurse practitioners for primary care, which posed another problem, because nurse practitioners cannot prescribe under US statutes. "I think the perception amongst many patients is that it's the law. There must be a way to access it. It's a viable option for me," Jacqueline told me. Margot Hadley had echoed Jacqueline's sentiments regarding the public's misinformation: "I feel really badly that Vermonters are under the illusion that Act 39 is available to them, and it really isn't, was my experience."

Jacqueline told me about one patient who had asked about medical aid in dying. His sister found him dead after he shot himself in the head with a handgun he had hidden away. Jacqueline surmised that this patient would have been a good candidate for an assisted death, had it been more viable. Summing up her views on the law, Jacqueline said, "So it's very nice to have this, but I think you don't have equity. You know, if you're a patient who meets all the criteria, then is lucky enough to have a primary care physician who knows you, and then is willing to participate."

Jacqueline's comments highlight the substantial constraints on access to medical aid in dying in Vermont. In the remainder of this chapter, I describe a series of practical hurdles that patients and caregivers confronted in the pursuit of an assisted death: finding a supportive physician, identifying a pharmacy to fill the prescription and paying for the medication, obtaining social support to complete the bureaucratic protocol, accessing information about the law, and navigating legislative safeguards. As I will show, these structural constraints result in stratified access to aid in dying that favors patients from more privileged socioeconomic backgrounds and raises troubling questions about health care equity, justice, and the power to choose.

FINDING A PHYSICIAN

For patients seeking an assisted death, finding a physician to prescribe the life-ending medication often required a combination of gregariousness, grit, and good luck. Mary Llewelyn's story exemplifies the surprising routes that occasionally led patients to their prescribing physicians. Mary, an artist, was a single woman in her sixties, who had endured a long-term cancer diagnosis. Determined to live as fully as she could with whatever time she had left, Mary rarely complained about her illness. After many years of surgeries and treatments, however, her quality of life began to diminish, and she began to seriously consider medical aid in dying. Mary lived in the southern part of Vermont, and her oncology treatment was based in New Hampshire at the Dartmouth-Hitchcock Medical Center; therefore, her primary oncologist could not prescribe under Vermont's law. Mary's primary care physician, Brenda Jones, was conflicted about Mary's request. She agreed to support Mary throughout the process but ultimately did not feel comfortable prescribing.

Having for years attended a local cancer support group, Mary knew many seriously ill people, who might have connected her to a potential prescriber. Yet it was a chance meeting at a flea market in a neighboring town that provided the gateway to Mary's prescription. There, while waiting in line for the market to open, Mary struck up a conversation with Robin Staples, a palliative care nurse who noticed that Mary was ill and took an interest in her condition. The conversation went deep very quickly, when Mary learned about Robin's line of work. Mary told Robin that she was trying to find a doctor who would prescribe for medical aid in dying, and Robin connected Mary with an advocacy organization representative, who later told me that she had called in a favor from a physician in another part of the state to try to help Mary. What was most striking to me about this chain of events was the fortuitous meeting between Mary and Robin, without which Mary might never have been able to access assistance. There was something about this chance encounter that was so quintessential of small-town Vermont, where many health care providers have a hard time doing the grocery shopping without running into a patient.

Some patients' pathways to a prescribing physician were more circuitous than Mary's. Renee Long had found a primary care physician, who had assured her that he would sign for the prescription, and she planned to use that as leverage to get her oncologist on board as the second physician. Before he wrote the prescription, however, the first physician changed his mind and retired, and Renee had to scramble to find two new doctors. A friend of Renee's later recounted, "It was really down to the wire, finding them and then getting everything lined up for getting the prescription." Annika Gunters also had to scramble when her husband's oncologist, who had agreed to participate, stopped returning her telephone calls. Annika called the hospice nurse, who said that the hospice physician was willing to sign off if necessary; after receiving a lot of pressure, Annika's own doctor eventually agreed to prescribe.

In addition, the requirement that two physicians sign off on the six-month prognosis occasionally produced barriers. One particularly chilling case concerned a woman in her midfifties with a recurrent brain tumor. Although her primary care physician was on board with her request to use medical aid in dying, the neuro-oncologist they consulted to confirm a six-month prognosis required her to undergo consecutive MRIs, so that he could assess how fast her tumor was growing. Because she was bedbound, this required ambulance transport and was incredibly burdensome. Ultimately, the oncologist determined that the tumor was progressing but not fast enough to warrant a six-month prognosis. As Janine Thiel, the primary care physician, explained to me, "The patient was clearly dying. Do you know what I mean? I mean, the patient was just clearly *slowly* dying."

Patients living in certain counties had an easier time finding a physician willing to participate. These geographic patterns often, but not always, paralleled broader socioeconomic differences in access to care. For example, patients living closer to the University of Vermont Medical Center in Burlington, Vermont's biggest city and home to some of the state's more affluent communities, tended to have a relatively easier time accessing medical aid in dying. However, some relatively affluent areas—such as the county in which Margot and Rich lived—exhibited substantial access constraints. Meanwhile, certain rural and poorer areas of Vermont stood out for meeting patient demand successfully. Amanda Townshend was widely known in her rural community for being an advocate, and patients who lived in her town seemed to have an easier time than most accessing assisted dying. Several possible factors likely account for this trend. Because Amanda was well known, admired, and respected in the local medical community, her stance on aid in dying might have influenced other physicians in her area and helped to normalize her practice. She also may have been willing to advocate for patients and help connect them with prescribers. Finally, although she did not report this to me, it is also quite possible that she helped address the demand by serving as a prescriber herself.

Although policy makers and advocates had hoped to routinize the provision of medical aid in dying within standard pathways of clinical care, the model had several problems. First, the possibility of requesting assistance from one's primary care provider was simply unavailable to several groups of patients, including those who received their primary medical care in a neighboring state or from the Veterans Affairs system and the large number of Vermont residents who lacked a primary care provider at all due to the severe shortages in the state. Second, the expectation that a physician who was unwilling to prescribe would refer patients to someone else was possible only if the primary care physician was aware of which colleagues were willing to prescribe; aid in dying was still so stigmatized in Vermont, however, that many prescribers maintained a veil of secrecy around their participation. Furthermore, as I discussed in the last chapter, even among those who were willing to prescribe for their own patients, many were reluctant to accept referrals. As one physician put it, "You don't want to be like the drive-through Act 39er." Finally, the staunchest opponents would not consider referring because of concerns about moral complicity. Consequently, some patients resorted to extreme measures to identify a prescribing physician: one patient even took out an ad in a local newspaper for a physician who would help him.

Of the twenty patients represented in my study who obtained a prescription under Act 39, thirteen had done so through a physician who was already treating them. Four had resorted to "doctor shopping" for a willing prescriber, and two had moved to Vermont specifically to access aid in dying. (I do not know about the identity of the final patient's prescriber because the caregiver I interviewed, a close friend, did not know how her friend had acquired the prescription.) It would be a mistake to interpret these findings as suggesting that most patients were able to obtain a prescription from an existing provider; after all, patients like Rich, who could not use this pathway, were less likely to gain access at all. What my data do suggest, however, is that the expectation for aid in dying to be normalized as part of standard medical care has not at this point been realized: this option is simply unavailable to many Vermont patients who wish to pursue an assisted death. Moreover, to successfully doctor shop (or more dramatically, move across the country) to find a willing prescriber required persistence and ingenuity. What the six people who did so shared, beyond a strong desire for assisted death, was social support, connections in the medical community (two were health care providers themselves), and socioeconomic privilege.

MEDICATION

Once a prescriber had been identified, the logistical hurdles were far from over. Unless the physician already had experience with medical aid in dying, they had to determine what medication and dose to prescribe, identify a pharmacy to fill the script, and determine cost and insurance coverage. Several physicians told me they were surprised to learn that neither the legislative text of Act 39 nor the informational resources offered by the Department of Health scripted the medication protocol, and physicians were left on their own to determine what, and how, to prescribe. Some physicians sought guidance from local experienced colleagues. Many utilized Compassion & Choices' Doc2Doc program, which connects prescribers in permissive states with experienced physicians in Washington or Oregon, who can advise them about medication protocols and dosing. Still, many physicians, particularly those in private practice, felt isolated and longed for a more robust clinical support network to help them work through the challenges of implementing medical aid in dying.

When the law first passed, pentobarbital, the generic name for Nembutal, the drug that Margot Hadley contemplated purchasing in Mexico, was the first-line drug. Only a few people in Vermont were prescribed pentobarbital before it became unavailable for commercial use in the United States, because it is used in executions.[6] Sarabeth Grady, a community-based primary care physician, obtained one of the last doses for a patient in Vermont, but the prescription was accidentally given away. She told me,

> I called them to find out if they had the medicine because I knew it was getting hard to get and they said, "Yep, we've got one dose left." And somebody got it first. They brought in a script that morning and they thought it was my patient and they filled it. And then my script arrived in the afternoon mail and they called me and said, "We've given away your drugs." And so, then

that started a scramble for an alternate way of invoking the law. And I talked to a bunch of different doctors out in Oregon. And one of them gave me a protocol that involved Ativan and morphine and Zofran.

After this, secobarbital, another inexpensive, short-acting barbiturate, replaced pentobarbital as the drug of choice, but this came with its own challenges. In 2015, a month after California proposed aid-in-dying legislation, the Canadian pharmaceutical company Valeant bought the rights to Seconal, the trade name for secobarbital, and raised the prices dramatically.[7] A standard lethal dose now costs approximately three thousand US dollars. Although some insurance companies have agreed to pay for Seconal, others will not, and federal funding, including Medicare, cannot be used for aid-in-dying medications or services. While the California state legislature budgeted for Seconal to be covered by the state's Medicaid program (Medi-Cal),[8] Vermont has not done so.

To address these cost barriers, a multistate team of physicians and pharmacists began to develop alternative drug protocols, including a combination of phenobarbital, chloral hydrate, and morphine sulfate.[9] The drawback of this protocol, according to several physicians and one pharmacist I interviewed, was that it sometimes caused a burning sensation after ingestion and had a shorter half-life after dispensing. Morphine was also an option, but the primary disadvantage, a big one, was that if the patient had been using morphine for pain, the correct lethal dose could be very difficult to determine. James Loftin, a private-practice primary care provider, offered this option to a patient who had hoped to avoid the cost of Seconal, and the patient woke up after ingesting a 1,200-mg dose, which James thought "should have killed a grizzly bear." The patient obtained a Seconal prescription several days later and died.

Consequently, many physicians continued to view Seconal as the most effective choice—that is, the most likely to result in a quick and peaceful death, without unexpected complications or side effects. Shelly Markham explained,

So then doctors are looking, okay, what else can we use? What's the other cocktail? What won't cost as much? So, what, if you're privileged and have a lot of money, you can find the Seconal and pay for it? But if you're the poor guy, you can't? So, it's created a whole other division. And I had a patient who has Medicaid, and Medicaid wouldn't fund the money for the Seconal. So it's like, wait a minute here, you know, the state legislature says this is a legal thing to do; why is it any different than any other prescription I've written for this patient?

Shelly's comments underscore the sense of resentment she and other physicians felt for having to look for what they considered a second-class option for less privileged patients.

Even if physicians and patients were willing to pursue such alternatives, they did not always know about them. Lena Rhodes told me about a patient of hers, "a very funny eighty-five-year-old quirky guy," from a poor family, who was very interested in medical aid in dying but chose not to do it once he found out how much it cost. Lena explained, "He and his family both thought it was a pill. Like, I just give you one. You get your pill, you take it, you die in like ten minutes, and you're fine. And so, when he started getting all the information and then he heard the price he's like, I'm not doing that, we're not, this is ridiculous.'" Interestingly, Lena surmised that her patient was probably glad he had not pursued it because he ended up having a really good summer: "He actually was really sick when he first came on hospice because of the chemotherapy. As the chemotherapy was getting out of his system, he's felt better and better. He's back to driving. He goes to the VFW to drink Kahlua and milks, he's really enjoying himself right now."

Identifying a pharmacy to fill the prescription was a related challenge. None of the chain pharmacies in the state would have anything to do with medical aid in dying. For most of my study, a single independent pharmacy in central Vermont was the only pharmacy known to be filling Seconal prescriptions. Only two pharmacists who worked there were willing to fill the script for Seconal, because of concerns about inadequate protections in the law for pharmacists' immunity. The pharmacist I interviewed described this as a legal concern more than a moral concern. This pharmacy was not identified as a provider in any of the informational resources provided by the state, or on the pharmacy's website, so prescribing physicians had to find out about it through their professional networks. Shelly Markham reflected on her efforts to shield patients from these access challenges:

The other issue is once you've figured out the recipe, you can't get it. You have to find a pharmacy. And a pharmacist that will participate. . . . In some of the patients that I've dealt with, I'm trying to find them a pharmacy, I'm trying to figure out, you know how are we going to pay for this, and, I mean, those are two really awful things. Now, you *can* just write out the script and hand it to the patient and say, "Hey, good luck," but I would tell you that putting patients through that and their family through that, at a time that everything else is so upside down, is cruel.

Once the prescription was filled, patients or their surrogates sometimes traveled many hours by car to pick it up from the pharmacy. Some patients opted for mail-order prescriptions, which the pharmacy was willing to accommodate, but this depended on careful timing. In one case, a prescription arrived in the mail the day after a patient died of natural causes. For many caregivers, a long car ride was a reasonable cost to pay for the peace of mind that came from obtaining the medication directly.

SOCIAL SUPPORT

Access to physicians and access to medication both depended on social support from family and friends. All of the patients who had to look beyond their existing physicians to find a prescriber had substantial assistance from caregivers or, in Mary Llewelyn's case, a fortuitous encounter with a well-connected acquaintance. And most patients who utilized medical aid in dying had substantial help from loved ones in navigating the bureaucratic protocol and obtaining the medication. Ken Greene, an oncologist, noted, "They need a good advocate for them, if that's what they really want."

Health care providers reported that family members sometimes dropped the ball on helping patients complete the paperwork because they did not support a loved one's desire to hasten death. The uncertainty of how illness time would be reconciled with the bureaucratic process could work to the advantage of caregivers who were reluctant to assist, enabling them to pay lip service to a dying person's wishes while simultaneously avoiding participation in a morally contested act. Such hedging might offer a dying patient some final comfort, but it could also result in new forms of loss or pain—such as the foreclosure of an aspirational death. This was the case for several patients, whose caregivers reported that they died extremely disappointed that they had not been able to avail themselves of medical aid in dying.

Lena Rhodes told me about a patient for whom she had prescribed Seconal but who never completed the process because her father could not bring himself to fill the prescription. She explained, "He could never fill it. She ended up dying, you know, within days after the script was written, so it would only have hastened her death by two or three days, but he psychologically could not do it."

Jennifer Nichols, a hospice nurse who worked at the only inpatient hospice residence in the state, told me about a similar case involving a patient who wanted to pursue medical aid in dying but had not completed the paperwork in time. When he was admitted to the facility, his goal had been to improve symptom management so that he could be discharged and die at home. The nursing staff thought that the man's adult sons had taken care of the paperwork, but he died before the process was complete. When the staff members were cleaning out the patient's room, however, they found the forms, still blank. Jennifer did not know whether the sons had deferred on the paperwork because they were afraid to have their father come home to die or because they did not agree with his decision. While such instances were rare, they indicate the importance of robust social support in navigating the protocol, a process I describe further in chapter 6. Just as prescribing can impose a heavy moral burden on physicians, assisting with the practical aspects of navigating access proved to be an insurmountable barrier for some caregivers.

ACCESS TO INFORMATION

Access to medical aid in dying was also shaped by patients' differential access to information on the basis of variation in physicians' communication preferences and institutional policies. Many physicians will not discuss aid in dying with terminally ill patients unless a patient initiates such a discussion, and hospice policies likewise vary in the extent to which they permit staff to provide information. While physicians and bioethicists may view such practices as an important safeguard to ensure that an assisted death is voluntary and not influenced by a health care provider, patients may not know enough about aid in dying to inquire about it. Because better-educated patients are more likely to be informed and to initiate a conversation about it with a physician, access is further stratified along socioeconomic lines.

Craig Lawson, an affable man in his sixties, told me about his friend and neighbor, Ron, a single man whom Craig had helped care for when Ron was dying of cancer. Ron first heard about Vermont's aid in dying law from his hospice nurse, who had cared for two other patients who used it and whose agency was fairly receptive to caring for such patients. When Ron tried calling his oncologist to inquire about aid in dying, she wouldn't return his phone calls. At that point, it was too late to try to find another physician. "What we learned was that you need to have two," Craig said. "But, you know, if his oncologist—if he can't get his oncologist to agree, it's extremely difficult to find some stranger." Ron was disappointed, but he resigned himself to the fact that it was not going to happen. "I don't think it created any mental anguish," Craig said. "I think it was more like, 'Oh, shit, I could have done that if I had started sooner,' maybe." In reflecting on his friend's experience, Craig indicated, "I felt like there was two things that were wrong. One was the knowledge that it existed. It was like a secret. And then the other thing I thought was not right was that—because apparently, his oncologist was not for it, she didn't really pursue it aggressively." Craig compared the situation to that of abortion, where legal status did not ensure that one could find access to a provider: "It's like the law that you could have an abortion, but you can't find anybody so you have to go in the alley. Right. It's the same idea."

Two years after I met Craig, he responded to an email I had circulated to study participants with a copy of an article I had recently published describing some of the barriers to accessing aid in dying I had identified in my research.[10] His email stated,

> Thank you for sharing this. As a so called savvy health care consumer with reasonable intelligence I contend that most Vermont physicians keep the new legal aid-in-dying legislation secret so they do not have to be involved with such a contentious ethical matter . . . one which takes inordinate time/energy. And the time/wherewithal to get this approved deemed it not

available before his very undignified death. In talking to others after Ron's death most had no idea aid-in-dying was available in Vermont. And I believe you are correct in asserting those from the very top socio/economic population segment have much better access. . . . Hopefully your study will help (but, sadly, I doubt it).

While Craig blamed physicians for his friend's experience, uneven access to information also applied to physicians. As Lena Rhodes's lack of awareness of alternatives to Seconal suggests, physician knowledge about different medication options and the protocol itself varied. In one case, a patient was dismayed to have to begin the process anew because the physician had not documented the patient's request by completing the required paperwork. The patient ultimately died before completing the protocol.

LEGISLATIVE SAFEGUARDS

Pursuing medical aid in dying under Act 39, as in all permissive jurisdictions in the United States except for Montana, requires patients to clear several regulatory hurdles. The requirement that patients self-administer and ingest the lethal medication, a safeguard designed to ensure that participation is voluntary, was a major barrier for some patients who hoped to pursue an assisted death. Such obstacles were most pronounced for patients with neurologic conditions, such as ALS, which results in progressively declining mobility and often entails swallowing difficulties in its later stages. Nathan Christman, a neurologist, lamented, "Why can't a hospice nurse administer the medicine for the patients if they can't do it themselves? That doesn't make sense to me. It seems like it puts undue stress on my patients and it also prevents a patient who really needs this program from being able to access it. I feel like it was designed with the cancer patients in mind." On the other hand, cancer patients may also have difficulties swallowing medication in the final stages of illness. Candace Twomey had hoped to use aid in dying, completed the protocol, and spent five thousand dollars on the prescription. In the end, however, Candace was unable to ingest the medication because she had a type of cancer that gradually obstructs the intestines, making it impossible to eat or drink.

Caregivers and health care providers indicated that the self-administration requirement sometimes motivated patients to hasten death sooner than they otherwise would have, as waiting longer might risk losing the capacity to ingest the medication.[11] Lynn Tandewitz, a hospice physician, spoke of one patient with a neurological condition: "What really breaks my heart is that I don't think she was really ready but she was afraid she was gonna lose the ability to swallow it. And she wanted to do it before she would lose the ability to swallow it." While all people who pursue an assisted death must make complicated decisions about timing, what felt particularly tragic to Lynn was the way in which the legislative script forced her patient to say goodbye to family and friends before she was truly ready. In an interview a year after her death, Candace Twomey's brother Bill reflected on the paradoxical way in which being *able* to utilize medical aid in dying was for some people precisely what made it too soon to use it: "Oh, sure she could have taken it when she could swallow. Or pass food, yeah, but are you going to do it then? Because there's days when you feel pretty good." According to Bill, Candace might have taken the medication when she could still keep food and liquids down, but it would have been hard for her to accept the proximity of death until that capacity diminished.

Another set of barriers came from the legislative requirement that the patient be a resident of Vermont. While it may seem self-evident that state residency would serve as a constraint on a medical service that was only authorized by state law, less obvious is the fact that patients from more privileged backgrounds were more able to work around this residency requirement. Brittany Maynard—the twenty-nine-year-old California woman who helped to revitalize the movement for assisted death in the United States—was able to utilize aid in dying in part because her family had the economic means to purchase a home in Oregon.

Similarly, I learned about a handful of patients who moved to Vermont to access medical aid in dying and successfully did so—even though health department officials and representatives from state-based advocacy groups discouraged them from doing so, if asked, because of access challenges. Most of these patients came from higher status socioeconomic backgrounds, and many had connections within the medical field. Shelly Markham told me, "I've had two wealthy patients. . . . They came up to Vermont, they scheduled an appointment, and the only thing they want to see me about is Act 39. And they're establishing some sort of residency in Vermont, that you know, some lawyer has told them has all the legality, and they want access to Act 39." Such "thanatological tourism" demonstrates the stratification of access to aid in dying particularly clearly because most patients do not have the social or economic capital to take up residence in a new state for the last few months of life.[12]

A more mundane example of constraints related to legislative safeguards concerns the requirement that witnesses cosign the paperwork and attest that the patient's participation is voluntary. Sarabeth Grady spoke about how challenging it can be for dying patients in their nineties to identify witnesses who are not relatives or health professionals: "This woman who did invoke the law said to me, 'I'm in my nineties; all of my friends are dead. So basically, what you're saying is, I need to go up to some random person on the street, two random people on the street, and say, 'Hey, could you witness this for me 'cause I want to kill myself?'" Sarabeth acknowledged that this safeguard made sense to protect against coercion, because people who might stand to gain from the death would have a conflict of interest, but it nevertheless made for some awkward interactions.

Taken together, these constraints show how the bureaucratic scripting of legislative safeguards writes certain people out of access to aid in dying. They also demonstrate the multiple forms of assistance necessary to achieve a "self-determined" death. Alanna Reynolds, a hospice physician, observed, "I really believe it's a really important tool for a certain subset of the patients. But again, I think there are lots of barriers, and I think it's a little misleading because people see it as like this path of utter control. But it's challenging. It doesn't always work out that way. And there's lots of steps and lots of interdependence." Alanna's comments highlight how the possibility of aid in dying offered an illusion of personal control over death that, for many patients, was belied by numerous obstacles and dependence on others for support and practical assistance.

STRATIFIED ACCESS TO AID

The health care providers I interviewed regularly commented on the inequalities inherent in medical aid in dying and described the access barriers as patently unfair. "There's a lot of stuff that's sort of inherently unfair, so to speak, on a sort of societal level about the law," Brenda Jones told me.

> You need to be a certain kind of person who will follow the steps to make an oral request and go back and do a written request and kind of manage all of that. That's a certain kind of person, sort of inherently. Someone who plans ahead, someone who thinks ahead. People who are sort of, like, "I just live for today," they're not going to follow all these rules. They're not going to research it, they're not going to go find two prescribers, they're not going to make multiple appointments. We've had a couple patients who couldn't get it done because no one would do a home visit and they couldn't go to the office. One of whom put a gun in his head and killed himself. So that seems unfair to me. I mean, you can say I'm being unfair because I don't prescribe. I get it. But I think there's just—how the law is written makes it inaccessible to a lot of people that otherwise might choose that option, and so I think that's a pretty big flaw.

For Brenda, it was clear that differential access to medical aid in dying was socially patterned. Yet her remark about a "certain kind of person" more likely to access it does not quite capture the full extent of such patterning. Where Brenda conjures a personality type predisposed to gain access—the type who "plans ahead" and does her research—some providers more explicitly tied such personal characteristics to socioeconomic privilege. In the following excerpt from my interview with Jacqueline Starks, I asked her specifically about this possibility.

MB: Given that you've sort of framed this as an equity issue, do you see this differentiating along like socioeconomic lines? I mean—

JS: Yeah.

MB: Okay.

JS: The people who did it were connected enough to know who to go to.

MB: Mm hm. The people that you know of that did it, yeah.

JS: Yeah.

MB: Okay. Okay.

JS: They were of a social strata which was just higher than some of my others.

MB: Got it.

JS: And they knew how to find out who was the physician who may support that.

Jacqueline's comments demonstrate how ideas about personality types predisposed to succeed at accessing assisted death may elide the fact that one's position within the social structure can shape one's ability to "plan ahead" for death, insofar as someone well connected to physician networks will have a much better chance of carrying out plans for aid in dying. Cultural scripts for dying that emphasize the importance of planning ahead are also more prevalent among those from wealthier class backgrounds.[13] Jacqueline's comments also help to reveal why attributing success solely to personal characteristics can be limiting and even dangerous. Anthropologists have long observed that explanatory frameworks tying illness to individual psychology may obscure the social and structural determinants of health.[14] In a similar way, a focus on personal habits and traits may mask the role of social status and socioeconomic privilege in determining access to aid in dying. Moreover, misrecognizing the source of access barriers can make it difficult to fix the problem: it may be tempting to dismiss challenges resulting from personality differences, yet structural barriers merit structural solutions.

These findings suggest that access to medical aid in dying depends on what the sociologist Janet Shim calls "cultural health capital," the cultural knowledge, resources, and behaviors that predispose certain patients to more optimal health care encounters.[15] Shim's concept builds on Pierre Bourdieu's concept of cultural capital, which emphasizes the stratified nature of human social life and treats a range of cultural practices (e.g., knowledge, habits, styles of dress) as forms of capital which, like economic capital, may be strategically or tacitly deployed to maintain inequalities and class-based hierarchies. While the concept of cultural health capital is similar to concepts such as health literacy, it also recognizes the transactional and dynamic nature of displaying clinical knowledge. In other words, the concept acknowledges that physicians' responses to their perceptions of patients' cultural health capital exact a cumulative effect on clinical interactions. This dynamic process helps to explain why cultural health capital is largely shaped by racial and class inequalities, though not determined by them. As Shim explains, "Since access to and acquisition of clinically valuable cultural resources are often shaped by social hierarchy, the distribution of CHC often follows racial and socioeconomic lines, reinforcing providers' existing beliefs about minority patients, and, in turn, providers' interpretations of health-related information and interpersonal behaviors."[16]

The concept of cultural health capital resonates with the ways that many of my interlocutors spoke about access as dependent on both tangible and tacit forms of socioeconomic privilege. As Ken Greene put it, "There is a savviness that is also necessary. There's almost a doggedness on a patient's perspective that is necessary because they need to put their own request in, they need to get to a second physician who will attest to yes, this person is informed, yes, they have a poor prognosis, yes, they're aware of their poor prognosis. Yes, they are voluntarily requesting without any pressure. Those sorts of things." Insofar as referring to patient "savvy" may be a coded way of speaking about cultural health capital—in signaling knowledge, behaviors, and resources that often escape social awareness— Ken's statement suggests an implicit stratification in patients' access to assisted death. It is quite telling that Bea Rivers—who, along with her husband, formed one of the grassroots advocacy groups that successfully lobbied for passage of Vermont's aid in dying law—was the only person who described the process of accessing assistance as easy and smooth. As eminent advocates and fixtures in their local community, they were well connected to the professional networks necessary to navigate access.

For William Neace, a hospice physician who opposed medical aid in dying, this stratification meant that Vermont's law did not constitute an authentic public option: "It almost doesn't even rise to the level of public policy. It's sort of an adjunctive choice for people with sufficient education and resources and connections, or something like that." Here William seems to suggest that aid in dying did not constitute public policy because it was not actually publicly available.

For other providers morally opposed to the practice, stratification was a specific source of discontent. Claudia Richards, a hospice nurse, lamented, "I guess I feel that, again, there's a lot of wasted money that went into the passage of Act 39, that it's kind of a middle-class, upper middle-class project. The cost of the drugs, if you're gonna use Seconal and the drugs that actually are effective, are out of the range of many people." Willa Redmond, a palliative care nurse, reflected similarly:

> I feel like in some ways the situation is very elitist. I mean, someone has to have the intellectual wherewithal to track down a physician who's willing to prescribe and follow through with that. They have to be able to track down a pharmacy that's willing to dispense medication, and they have to be able to afford it, and most people who are in the last six months of life who meet the criteria to go through with this, don't have the resources, you know, intellectually, cognitively, emotionally, financially. So it limits it to a very, very small group of people. It seems not fair that way, too.

As these comments suggest, providers with moral or professional reservations about medical aid in dying were not generally mollified by low utilization resulting from patients' access difficulties. Instead, they viewed such constraints as creating new ethical challenges, beyond the question of whether or not assisted dying is ethical. That is, stratified access to aid in dying raises thorny questions about health care justice, which has historically been neglected in bioethical conversations about aid in dying.[17]

FROM RIGHTS TO JUSTICE

To consider the role of justice in aid in dying, we can take some helpful cues from recent scholarship on reproductive justice.[18] This framework has been proposed as a critical response to the reproductive rights framework, which is grounded in concepts of individual choice and autonomy that do not adequately account for the structural forces that shape women's reproductive lives, particularly low-income women and women of color.[19] Reproductive justice scholars have issued a call to look beyond the "right to choose," noting that choice itself is often a privilege, one that is unevenly and unjustly distributed.[20] Although justice encompasses rights, the presumed universality of certain core rights masks critical disparities associated with race, class, and other key social identifiers. Thus, while American women ostensibly have a "right" to abortion, the ability of any individual woman to access a desired abortion hinges on a host of social factors, including geography, money, employment status, child care, and social support—factors that are themselves compounded by other social determinants of health, like race, ethnicity, and education. In making this connection to reproductive justice, I want to emphasize that the legalization of medical aid in dying does not guarantee practical access, and well-intentioned policies designed to protect vulnerable groups may at times have unexpected and paradoxical effects.

Considering justice in relation to aid-in-dying access is rife with conceptual challenges. When unequal access to health care raises concerns about justice, it typically does so because health care is seen as a social good to which all members of society ought to have access.[21] In the context of aid in dying, the relationship between justice and access is more complicated because aid in dying is not universally viewed as positive. Even among those who *do* believe that aid in dying should be a legal end-of-life option, many believe that access to it should not be too easy. According to this view, safeguards and legislative protocols that impede access are necessary to ensure that the choice is voluntary.

A second conceptual challenge is that aid-in-dying advocates tend to invert standard arguments about health inequalities, justice, and access to medical services by socioeconomically marginalized groups. Historically, socioeconomically marginalized groups—along with women, the elderly, and people with disabilities—have been viewed as vulnerable to coercion in the context of aid in dying. Advocates have countered such claims with data showing that utilization is actually highest among the socioeconomically privileged.[22] However, such utilization patterns might plausibly reflect unequal access rather than a stronger preference for aid in dying among those with higher socioeconomic status. In the absence of better data on how terminally ill patients from a wide range of socioeconomic and racial/ethnic backgrounds think about aid in dying, including whether or not they seek it out in permissive jurisdictions, it is difficult to draw definitive conclusions about patient preferences from utilization differences between sociodemographic groups.

Third, interpreting the failure to access aid in dying is a difficult endeavor. Margot Hadley clearly saw Rich's pursuit of assisted death as an unassailable failure that resulted in unnecessary suffering at the end of his life, and Craig Lawson felt similarly about Ron. Yet what does it mean when the "failure" means a longer life that is unexpectedly pleasurable?

Recall Lena Rhodes's patient who declined medical aid in dying because of the cost of Seconal. Lena surmised that he was glad he had not pursued it further. When he enrolled in hospice, everyone expected he would die within weeks, but more than three months in, he was having an excellent summer. Having regained his strength after ceasing chemotherapy, he was once again able to drive and was drinking Kahlua and milk at the VFW, a favorite pastime. Of course, there is no guarantee that he would have ingested the medication had he obtained it; many patients who get medication do not end up taking it yet find it reassuring to have it on hand.[23] Yet stories like these complicate how we understand failures of health care access in this context, as do stories of patients dying of natural causes while navigating the aid-in-dying protocol, which I consider further in the next chapter. Whether such events are understood as misfortunes or happy accidents depends entirely on the context in which they unfold, and the meanings that caregivers and loved ones attach to them in their retellings.

How should we think about health care justice with respect to a clinical practice that many people believe should be difficult to access—a practice of last resort? What should we do with the fact that aid-in-dying policy in the United States seems to favor people with higher socioeconomic status? And more generally, how do we foster health care justice when it comes to assisted dying? These are vexing questions without simple answers, yet they offer some helpful starting points for shifting the rights-based paradigms that dominate current scholarly and public conversations. As an anthropologist, I see my role as not to offer conclusive answers but rather to reframe conventional ways of approaching the problem and unsettle master narratives.

One point that is clear is that increasing access to aid in dying without ensuring access to other end-of-life options, including hospice and palliative care, is problematic. Clearly, hastening death is ethically unpalatable if a dearth of good end-of-life care makes it the most attractive option. Equally concerning for justice would be a situation in which health insurance programs authorize reimbursement for aid in dying while rejecting coverage of life-prolonging treatment, as was the case for Oregon resident Randy Stroup—a patient featured in the popular documentary film *How to Die in Oregon*—until the Oregon Health Plan reversed its decision.[24]

For this reason, addressing health care justice in aid in dying cannot be isolated from broader considerations of access to high-quality end-of-life care.[25]

SCRIPTING DEATH AND THE POWER TO CHOOSE

The stories explored in this chapter offer a cautionary tale regarding the advocacy narratives suggesting medical aid in dying legislation offers a right to self-determination in end-of-life decision making. In some ways, access to aid in dying in Vermont mirrors the way that abortion care has evolved in certain parts of the United States, insofar as there is a two-tiered system, with the socioeconomically advantaged able to travel and access care, while others cannot, despite both having the "right to choose." While my focus has been on Vermont, recent media reports in other states have established that these access barriers are not unique to Vermont.[26] In the fall of 2017, a member of a Facebook group to which I belong posted a poignant plea for assistance in identifying a prescribing physician for a patient in Colorado, who desperately wanted medical aid in dying.

To address these access barriers, some alternative models of health service delivery have evolved in California. There, taking a cue from abortion care, several physicians have opened private end-of-life clinics that focus solely on aid-in-dying provision.[27] This model does not address cost constraints or help to normalize aid in dying within mainstream medical practice. It also makes some critical observers uncomfortable, in that the physician owners of these clinics appear to be monetizing death. Nevertheless, it is clear that these clinics fill an important gap for patients in California. They also provide a transparent, easy-to-navigate process that minimizes stress for patients and families. As Margot Hadley put it, "It shouldn't have to be like an underground endeavor to try to access this service that is legal in Vermont."

Although medical aid in dying offers a new script for controlling one's death, this chapter has demonstrated how many aspects of the procedure were relatively unscripted, including, for patients, how to identify a physician prescriber. More successful patients had greater experience innovating solutions to constraints on health care access. This point reflects the fact that scripting is always deeply tied to processes of improvisation, insofar as the script can only serve as a guide, and ultimately social actors must be authors of their own experiences. Similarly, the medication protocol itself was essentially unscripted, requiring substantial improvisation from physicians, particularly because they were operating in an entirely new domain of clinical practice. Such improvisation processes elucidate the relationship between scripting and stratification by showing how the ability to work around constraints is socially patterned in ways that reflect long-standing social hierarchies and inequalities. From this perspective, scripting death through aid in dying appears to be largely an "upper middle-class project," as hospice nurse Claudia Richards put it.

Nevertheless, the patients who successfully navigated the process were faced with a new set of questions regarding scripting death. Specifically, how do terminally ill people approach the tasks of timing and choreographing death when given the opportunity to do so? How do they determine the right time for dying, and whom do they choose to be at their side? I turn to these issues next.

6 Choreographing Death

Gloria Fleming sat on a couch in her living room, surrounded by six of her closest friends, mostly neighbors in her small Vermont town, two of their teenage daughters, and a hospice nurse she had grown close to in the preceding weeks, while she was dying from cancer. A collective sense of nervous anticipation had settled over the room. The women were so "intensely present," as one later described to me, that time appeared to stand still. Someone asked Gloria how she was feeling, and she said, "I'm scared and I don't want to go." Others were scared, too—no one had participated in something like this, not even the hospice nurse—and some were crying. But soon Gloria lifted a cup to her mouth, and, using a drinking straw, gulped down a slurry of pentobarbital and water. Within a few minutes, she fell asleep peacefully. Sixteen minutes later, she was dead. (Fall 2014)

While I was working on this book, I attended a public debate about medical aid in dying at a university featuring two prominent physician bioethicists.[1] In making his case against assisted death, the second speaker projected an image of Brittany Maynard, the young Compassion & Choices advocate who reinvigorated the assisted-death movement before her untimely death in 2015. In the photograph, Maynard stood in a California vineyard in a wedding dress of cascading ruffles, the perfect portrait of youth, beauty, and vitality. "Brittany Maynard illustrates a pattern," the speaker explained.

"Those who seek assisted suicide are rarely driven by concerns about pain. She was not experiencing symptoms beyond the reach of palliative medicine. She chose to end her life on her own terms to avoid debility, decline, and diminishment." Several minutes later, the speaker presented another photograph promoting a talent show being held the same night by a local organization serving people with developmental disabilities. "This performance will display a truth that Brittany Maynard could not see," he explained. "Debility does not render our lives not worth living. Dignity does not require living or dying on one's own terms."

For terminally ill people like Gloria Fleming and Brittany Maynard, the primary reasons to pursue medical aid in dying are to control the circumstances and timing of death and to avoid being a burden on others as their physical capacities decline. However, one common objection to aid in dying among disability rights activists is that such concerns reveal as much about cultural assumptions regarding what kinds of lives are worth living as they do about death and dying.[2] Therefore, many opponents portray aid in dying as a misguided expression of cultural fears of dependency that threatens to devalue the lives of people with disabilities, as the physician in the public debate suggested. And yet, Gloria Fleming's death scene subtly reveals how aid in dying is forging new forms of sociality and dependency, even as terminally ill patients seek to escape dependency on others. This showcases a critical disconnect between advocacy portrayals and lived experiences of aid in dying.

As a single woman in her sixties, Gloria Fleming had often worried about what might happen if she should fall ill. Who would take care of her? How would she manage? However, while it was true that she was hoping to avoid dependency in her final weeks of life, and that these concerns had particular salience for a terminally ill person living alone, this fact captures only a partial truth about the role of dependency in aid in dying. Gloria's best friend, Sheila, told me that Gloria had said to her, many years before, "'Please don't let me die alone.'" Sheila later recalled, "That was in my mind the whole time, that she couldn't have been further from that, that she had this beautiful, loving, community of people around her." These comments have helped me to rethink advocacy discourses on aid in dying that emphasize its ability to offer an escape from dependency in the final stages of terminal illness.

In the United States, one thing that sets medical aid in dying apart from ordinary suicide is that the person does not have to die alone to protect caregivers from potential legal consequences. Aid in dying presumes assistance, which may come in various forms. Yet the role of assistance in aid in dying—as a bureaucratic, social, and moral practice hinging on intimate dependencies—remains largely underacknowledged in both public and scholarly discourses. Certain forms of dependency are built into the medicolegal protocol, which invites robust social support at multiple points: completing the bureaucratic paperwork; identifying willing physicians; coordinating with the pharmacy; and planning for, attending, and assisting with the death. Therefore, while patients pursuing assisted death may avoid certain types of dependency—such as requiring assistance with eating, toileting, and other bodily care—the process requires them to affirm and strengthen other bureaucratic, material, and affective forms. In this chapter, I show how aid in dying results in specific forms of sociality and dependency that require terminally ill people and their caregivers to embrace a collaborative stance toward choreographing death.

The sociality emerging around assisted dying is distinctive in several ways. First, aid in dying does not present the same threat to normative middle-class American conceptions of personhood—which stress independence, productivity, and bodily mastery—that other forms of dying do.[3] Although proponents may wish to avoid being a burden on others, when they are so debilitated that they can no longer fulfill existing social roles, many will accept and even embrace assistance in navigating aid in dying. They assume such assistance will enable them to die before the slow decline of terminal illness renders them unrecognizable as the vital person they once were. In other words, aid in dying enables people to avoid a situation in which social death precedes biological death. It thus invites a culturally preferable type of dependency—one that allows dying people themselves to choreograph and participate in the social relations leading up to the scene of death in ways that render them unavoidably vulnerable, while caregivers play a supporting role. To be clear, I do not mean to suggest that the relational aspects of end-of-life care are in themselves new, or to deny that caring for a loved one through a natural death might have similar effects. Rather, I propose that legalized assisted dying generates opportunities for *some* dying people and caregivers to jointly produce and choreograph death. In doing so, aid in dying fosters social connections that challenge its public image as a radically independent practice.

In what follows, I describe the deaths of six people, as recounted to me by their friends and family members, who used Vermont's aid in dying law. The first three cases draw particular attention to the central role loved ones play in providing assistance and to the specific forms of dependency and care that emerge around this new end-of-life practice. If the dying person scripts and produces an aspirational death as a final vital performance, the caregiver is a stage manager who performs essential bureaucratic and emotional labor and provides the critical support the dying person needs.[4] The subsequent three cases, however, involve assisted deaths that did not go according to plan, highlighting the many ways in which dying persons may stray from the script of aspirational deaths.

TOM JARVIS

Tom Jarvis and Neil Lewis had developed an unusually close relationship during their many years as neighbors. They acknowledged that men their age (both were in their sixties) rarely found this kind of intimacy in friendships, yet their close physical proximity, free time (both were semiretired), and shared interests (in games, theater, literature, and film) had fostered an easy rapport that intensified over time. When Tom suddenly collapsed after playing tennis with Neil, it was Neil whom he called and Neil who insisted on taking Tom to the hospital, even though Tom hadn't seen a doctor in years.

After Tom was diagnosed with metastatic cancer and given six months to live, he decided quite quickly that he didn't want treatment (which wasn't likely to be effective) and instead wanted to pursue medical aid in dying. As Neil recounted, Tom had told the consulting physician, "The most important thing in my life, as an older man, are the deep conversations I have with people." If he started to feel so diminished by his disease that he couldn't communicate, that would be it, his "line in the sand." Although Tom was clear that he wanted to maintain his independence until his death, he expressed his wishes to his physician in fundamentally social terms.

Tom slowly put his plan into place, making official requests, completing the requisite paperwork, and having long telephone conversations with his son, who lived out of state. Tom's son initially opposed the idea but eventually came around. More than anyone, Neil was instrumental in Tom's planning. He assembled a support team of five of Tom's friends: a cook supplied Tom with soup, and an administrator helped with the paperwork, such as advanced directives and a will. Neil knew, however, that picking up the prescription would fall to him, and it did not occur to him to ask anyone from the support team to accompany him on this ominous errand.

Neil drove more than an hour to the pharmacy. Once there, he was unable to enter the building, instead idling for hours in a used bookshop, buying books he would never read. The pharmacy encounter itself was discomfiting because of an incongruously cheery pharmacist, and Neil's credit card was initially declined because of the exorbitant thirty-five-hundred-dollar charge. He finally got back in the car and drove home, a jumble of nerves, thinking, "This is a bag of death sitting on this seat. It should have been a big cloaked figure with a black hood, carrying a scythe. Instead it was this little bag."

As Tom grew weaker and weaker, he worried about Neil. "Death didn't worry him," Neil said. But Tom did worry about its effect on his best friend. Neil recalled, "I said to him, 'First of all, don't worry about me. This is not about me.' And then he just looked at me, and I realized, well, yeah, it is *also* about me. Because I have to deal with it after the fact. You know, losing my best friend and helping him die." During his last few weeks, Tom's social life contracted, and Neil became the buffer between Tom and the outside world. Finally, Tom decided it was time. He asked Neil not to tell his support team or his son, wanting only Neil by his side. "I remember thinking very strongly that I had one foot in the other world with him," Neil told me. "Because I was helping him intimately."

Tom chose the day of his death according to the weather forecast. It was winter in Vermont, and he did not want to inconvenience his friends, who would come to pay their respects after his death. When Neil arrived at Tom's apartment at the appointed time, he was struck by Tom's calm, almost serene presence. Neil himself had been unable to sleep the night before. He told Tom, "For me it was like the last night of a closing show that had been on Broadway for years and years successfully. But it's the last show and all the cast members are nervous because of the tension of the last show." Tom liked Neil's analogy and told Neil that for him going to sleep had been "like a dress rehearsal."

Tom shared some meaningful stories, how he wanted to be remembered. Together, they emptied a hundred capsules, twisting the two halves apart and dumping the powder out, which Neil described as laborious, though somewhat comedic, work. For many, this task represented a final opportunity to display care for a loved one and took on sacred, ritualistic properties. When the moment arrived, Neil said to Tom, "I'm not going to let you drink alone." Though Neil was not a drinker, he poured himself a glass of whiskey. They shared some final words, clinked glasses, and drank. Neil described this moment as follows:

> How to describe the tension in the room? The atmosphere in the room was surreal. I'm sort of in a state of shock watching him, wondering how's this going to play out. You know, is he going to slump over, is he going to throw up? What happens when he dies? They didn't really tell us that. They said, correctly, "Well, drink it all up because he'll fall asleep, quickly, then slide into a coma, then his heart will stop. Within two minutes." So that's what happened. He's sitting up like you're sitting up. I put a pillow behind his head. He put his head back, closed his eyes, sitting like you are, legs crossed, he had his arm on the arm of the couch. Sitting there relaxed. And sure enough, you know, breathing slowed down, and it stopped. Within two minutes. And I'm studying him, I'm watching him, kind of disbelieving that we did this. . . . And I got up, and I know I'm in a state of kind of euphoric shock. Euphoric because he did it, and he did it smoothly, and shock at what we did. Relief, and numbness, and everything else swirling around me. And there's nobody there with me.

After twenty minutes, Neil called the hospice nurse, as she had advised him to do. Together, they shared a moment of comic relief, finding amusement in the fact that Tom had died sitting up, with his legs crossed and his arm stretched out across the back of the sofa. Neil found this incongruous pose a fitting end to his friend's life. "It wasn't a religious ceremony, it wasn't chanting, it wasn't angels singing. It was his dying process was part of his life," he said.

Neil and Tom had shared a background in the theatrical arts. If Tom had approached his death like an actor giving his final performance, Neil was the stage manager, performing work essential for implementing Tom's vision. On one level, the aid-in-dying protocol engaged Neil in forms of bureaucratic dependency specific to legalized assisted death: helping with paperwork, picking up the prescription, preparing the pills. None of these tasks, or the dependencies they entail, is as physically taxing as caring for a loved one throughout a prolonged "natural" death. At the same time, the emotional labor necessary to carry out this work, as well as the personal, relational, and moral implications of Neil's assistance, had profound existential consequences for Neil himself, which he acknowledged in his revelation that his friend's looming death was "*also* about me." Moreover, the particularities of Tom's wishes—to pick up the medication, to keep the date of his death a secret, to bear witness alone—made Neil complicit in an act that was, if not morally dubious, at least highly secretive. Neil's account of Tom's death thus offers a different perspective on the public perception of an individually controlled death: in this case, the social practice of aid in dying among intimate friends heightened interdependence as well as dependency.

GLORIA FLEMING

Gloria Fleming was among the first people in Vermont to die using the state's aid-in-dying law. Gloria had been married twice, both for brief periods, but in her sixties, her strongest social ties were to female friends. "Gloria loved women," her best friend, Sheila, explained. "She loved men, too, but there weren't many that she had a lot of respect for." Gloria had no children and had not been interested in them until she started befriending younger women, many of them mothers in need of extra support. She became the "fun auntie" to Sheila's daughter and other neighborhood kids, teaching them how to read and to cook and later bringing them on weekend trips to Boston to stay in fancy hotels.

Sheila described her friendship with Gloria as "all about intimacy." They traveled together and had conversations that began in the car and stretched over entire plane rides, growing deeper when they were picked up weeks or months later. Before Gloria was diagnosed with cancer, Sheila's father was dying from Alzheimer's disease, and they talked about being each other's wingman should either suffer a similar fate. Sheila told me, "I said to her, even though she was twenty-five years older, 'If I end up with early onset, like my dad did, this is what I need you to do for me.' We had lots of conversations about that. And her, too. Being a single woman and living alone, even though she was young and healthy and vibrant, and so physically fit, she worried."

Gloria started talking about medical aid in dying immediately after her diagnosis. She had watched her mother die from the same kind of cancer twenty years earlier. "She wanted no part of that," Sheila said. "It was just an awful, slow, painful death. She'd be the first person to say, 'I have no tolerance for pain, I'm a wuss, I want no part of it.'" Initially, Gloria sought treatment at the renowned Dana Farber Cancer Institute in Boston, but soon after she learned her cancer had metastasized, and she transferred her care to a physician close to her hometown in Vermont. Her new oncologist was liberal, open minded, and compassionate: she spent almost three hours with Gloria and Sheila at their first appointment. When Gloria raised the issue of aid in dying, Sheila recalled, "The oncologist said, okay, well there's time. When we met again a month later, it came up again. There's time."

Two months later, however, when they began to pursue aid in dying seriously, time had begun to feel scarce. Gloria was now on oxygen full-time, with hospice support, and the cancer was quickly taking hold. Even while she was taking large doses of morphine, Sheila recalled, Gloria was "trying to micromanage every element" of planning for dying. Her friends begged her not to clean out her basement, promising they could deal with it after she died. "She wanted every crevice of her home gone through and distributed and organized before she died," Sheila said. "She hated leaving anything left undone. The finances, everything. She stressed about all of that right up until the end. She was the kind of person who, before she took the medication, she wanted to get up and use the bathroom first, because she didn't want to wet the bed after she took it. I mean, always mindful of everything. That's kind of her personality. But we were trying to navigate all of these things on the periphery, so as not to add an extra stress to her."

One aspect they could not navigate from the periphery was the aid-in-dying protocol. The oncologist was on board but finding a certifying physician proved more challenging. Sheila had fortuitously sold her small business weeks after Gloria's diagnosis, which gave her time to support Gloria every step of the way. Gloria and Sheila asked two other physicians on Gloria's team. Sheila was careful to point out that both were "amazing men," yet "they dragged their feet enough that it was clear they weren't quite sure." Sheila speculated that participating at that early point in the law's history "was a very bold political move in their career." Gloria and Sheila cried on the phone talking to one of these physicians, who eventually agreed to participate.

Gloria's relief after his decision was immediate. After weeks of hardly being able to move, she left the house in her pajamas and winter coat to drive with Sheila to the airport and pick up friends flying in from out of state to say their goodbyes. One was a chef, who made a decadent meal, and Gloria ate voraciously and drank wine for the first time in months. "I really think it was because she felt so good," Sheila reasoned. "You know, she felt safe. She knew that if something turned, she had her way out." That weekend proved to be her "last hurrah," and by Monday she had taken the medication. In retrospect, Sheila thought, if they had known how much bureaucracy was involved in aid in dying, and how much comfort it would bring Gloria, they would have started the process a month sooner, avoiding the "sprint" at the end.

Even under the best of circumstances, timing a death through medical aid in dying is a delicate balance, as bureaucratic time must reckon with the temporal contours of terminal illness. Patients must be close enough to death that they meet the criteria for a terminal prognosis, yet not wait so long that they will be unable to complete the labor-intensive bureaucratic protocol or become too sick to self-administer and ingest the lethal medication. Gloria's hospice nurse, Laurel Hardin, had advised Gloria, "Don't wait to the point where you're too weak to swallow four ounces of liquid." Gloria chose to ingest the lethal medication almost six months after her diagnosis. Laurel estimated that she would have otherwise died in ten to fourteen days. Laurel described the timing of Gloria's death with an approving tone: "She didn't do it early on when she was still with it and functioning and having some hours or days of quality of life or anything like that, just to get it over with. She did it right when she was really going to start to go down. I've been doing this for a long time and I kind of know when people are starting to go down." Laurel's comments illustrate how clinicians' perspectives on assisted death often reveal implicit moral assumptions about the "right time" for using it, suggesting that aid in dying is more justifiable when a person is already very close to death.

About a month before she died, Gloria had decided to create a ritual to connect the circle of women she wanted by her side when she died. She thought this would be especially important for one of her friend's teenage daughters, who she anticipated would have an especially difficult time coping with her death. Gloria's friends transformed her living-room sofa into a daybed and the coffee table into an altar, on which they placed pictures of her parents, shells, candles, and other mementos to facilitate a smooth passage. Sheila asked everyone to bring a reading to share. She also passed a ball of twine and a pair of scissors around the circle and asked each woman to tie a piece of the twine around her wrist, a symbolic gesture that would connect the women to each other, and to Gloria.

On the day Gloria took the lethal medication, the same group gathered, their twine bracelets still intact. The only addition was Laurel, who defied her agency's policy in attending Gloria's death. Hospice agencies in Vermont have unilaterally adopted a neutral stance toward Act 39, meaning that they neither advocate for nor prohibit the practice. Policies have varied, however, in the extent to which they permit staff to be present for assisted deaths. As Laurel explained to me later, "Nobody had done it. They thought people are going to be picketing out in the parking lot and everything like that. My focus is patient care. Their focus is the agency. And so, there was a real conflict there."

Before Sheila notified Laurel of Gloria's plans, Laurel had envisioned saying goodbye to Gloria and then sitting in her car across the street while Gloria took the medication. Once she arrived, however, she knew there was no way she could leave: "I walked in and they were all in a circle, and Sheila said, 'She's been waiting for you.' And there's no way I was going to leave and say, 'Call me when it's over.'" Sheila later described Laurel to me as a pioneer: "She knew that Gloria had great respect for the medical field. And knew that Gloria would have been much more comfortable with her there. So she was totally willing to be like, 'Fuck it, I'll be there. I'll break the rules and I'll deal with it later.'"[5]

If Gloria's friends had hoped for guidance from Laurel, however, they found the support she offered limited. "I followed the letter of the law,"

Laurel told me. "I read the law and I was absolutely doing nothing more or less than I should have. . . . I didn't help or hinder but I was there to support because she wanted me there." Leigh, another friend of Gloria's whom I interviewed, remembered asking Laurel a question, to which Laurel responded, "I'm not a part of this. I'm here as an observer." Laurel truly did not know any more about assisted death than anybody else. Although Gloria's death was carefully choreographed, there were no available scripts for her final moments. No one present had witnessed such a death, or had a sense of what to expect.

Despite this uncertainty, Laurel described Gloria's death as the best death she had seen, and at that point in her forty-year career as a home health nurse she had seen a lot. "If a death can be nice, it was nice," she said. "There was none of the body struggling. It was the most peaceful physiological death I've ever seen, because almost always you'll get this, what they called agonal breathing—there was none of that. It was just, she went to sleep, there was a couple little snoring noises as her airway collapsed, but no struggling with it. And I just reassured her friends that that was normal."

After Gloria's death, her friends cut the twine from their wrists, marking the dissolution of Gloria's life, and with it her circle of support. After her cremation, they stuffed the strings into the vessel with her remains. Still, they remained connected: both Sheila and Leigh noted that the experience had intensified their bonds with those present. Leigh explained to me, "There was a very, very strong connection in the time after. And it still sort of exists. . . . Whomever I already had a relationship with, maybe the closest relationship with, this was a deepening of that, and then whomever I just had a relationship with, now there's a depth to it because we shared this experience."

Gloria's death tenderly illustrates how a loving community of friends can come together to witness and stage-manage death, when given the opportunity to plan for it. For Sheila, the experience offered a striking contrast with her father's slow decline and eventual death, just months before Gloria's: "As a caregiver, experiencing two passes in the course of one season, two seasons, I have to say that Act 39 was a gift for me as well—not just for her to avoid an awful, slow, painful death. . . . Sometimes it's good to go through the ugly process of death. It has its own rite of passage. But certainly nothing easy about it, and I was grateful I didn't have to experience that again."

Such comments evoke what the public health researcher Lisa Martin and colleagues have called, in the context of abortion, "dangertalk": stories that abortion providers keep to themselves because they do not align with pro-choice messaging and therefore seem dangerous to the reproductive rights movement.[6] In this case, Sheila's comments were dangerous because suggesting that people might hasten death to avoid being a burden on caregivers threatens the autonomy-based justification for medical aid in dying: if aid in dying is not a completely independent choice, it is possible that it might not be voluntary.[7] Even though the desire to avoid being a burden on others may be a manifestation of one's autonomous wishes, acknowledging that relational concerns have shaped one's autonomy can be a politically dangerous proposition.

At the same time, Sheila's comments also demonstrate how implausible it is to consider the choice to hasten death as wholly divorced from one's social relationships. While Gloria's desire to avoid pain and suffering was paramount in her decision, she also evinced a strong desire to avoid dependency, the same desire that led her to organize her house from top to bottom and avoid leaving her friends with a mess. Proponents of aid in dying often presented a relational view of individual choice, speaking of the desire to alleviate the burden of seeing a loved one suffering through the final stages of death. For Gloria Fleming, this meant organizing a ritual that would help her community cope, or deeding her house to a friend. When these factors are silenced in advocacy movements, they obscure important realities. If pursuing aid in dying is a way of exercising one's individual choice, it is also, inescapably, a way of enacting care for others.

PEGGY BLISS

Peggy Bliss was a slight woman with an effervescent personality, a "healthy, wild, and wonderful person," in the words of her older sister, Anna. "We called her the mouse that roared," Anna explained. "She was the smartest in her class, she played the violin, she was on student council. She was probably compensating for her shortness." Peggy loved people and they loved her. She was the kind of person who could draw five hundred people to her memorial service.

Peggy married young and had two children, whom she and her husband raised in southern Vermont, on a homestead they built themselves, embracing a self-sufficient, archetypally Vermont lifestyle. They grew their own food and brewed their own beer, raising animals alongside their children, whom they taught to love nature and trees. Peggy's primary passions were nursing and art, which she pursued in some combination for much of her life, although the balance shifted over time. According to her family, she was a compassionate health care provider and a wonderful listener, who was always present for her patients.

Beneath the surface of her idyllic family life lay the seeds of an unhappy marriage, however. When her children were older and out of the home, Peggy divorced her husband. Her life unraveled, then slowly came back together. She was just finding her second act with a new partner, Henry, when she was diagnosed with a rare form of cancer. Henry asked her to move in with him, so he could take care of her. Even then, Henry later told me, he was conscious of wanting to spend whatever time he could with Peggy. "She would go off to these craft fairs and I'd go with her. She'd say, 'Really, you want to come with me?' And I said, 'Absolutely, you know, it's this time. I don't want to lose a minute of time.'"

Peggy lived nine years from her initial diagnosis, into her early sixties. After the first recurrence, she did not want further treatment, yet she acquiesced when her children protested. Anna said, "She did pretty much everything one can do. She was in the hospital for months on end, back and forth. The trajectory was more and more really horrible symptoms. It went into her lungs and she couldn't breathe. She had neuropathy from the radiation that she had in her hands. She started losing more and more of the things that she really wanted to be able to do."

Peggy began to seriously contemplate medical aid in dying about eighteen months before her death. She was not yet ready to give up, but it was also fairly obvious that she was no longer getting better. Henry recalled, "They gave her morphine, fentanyl, nothing could touch this pain. It was deep inside. . . . It was really excruciating." Initially, it was difficult for Peggy to find a physician willing to prescribe the lethal medication. Henry told me, "It seemed like people were all gung ho about it, but nobody could actually give us any concrete information about how to go about doing it." Eventually Peggy called a family doctor, who had taken care of her mother when she was dying many years earlier. Although Peggy was not his patient, he agreed to see her, and then to prescribe the medication.

Peggy did not speak much about it until one day she decided it was time. Anna reflected, "She was in the house all the time and she was hooked up to this oxygen tank. Her world was just getting smaller and smaller and smaller and she was seeing fewer and fewer and fewer people. And then I swear one day she just called me and she said, 'You better come down here because yesterday was too soon and tomorrow's too late and I'm doing it today.'" Henry said, "She would take a breath and cough. And I would hold her, and I could feel her body, her bones rattling together and her lungs just gasping for air. And one more day she would have suffocated. So she called it."

Peggy gathered her children and sisters to spend her final day with her. Peggy's daughter, Dara, described her mother's last day as beautiful. She had gotten an extra burst of energy and filled her day with a mixture of mundane tasks—calling the bank, signing over the deed to the car—and meaningful private moments with each of her loved ones. Then, at six o'clock, the time she had appointed, Peggy went upstairs to her bedroom and her family surrounded her on the bed. She was very specific about what she wanted. According to Henry, she had instructed, "I don't want there to be partying going on in the room while this is going on. No making jokes." She created a chart listing the different medications—including an anxiolytic to calm her nerves, an antinausea medication, and the active agent— so that she could cross them off as she took them, knowing that at some point her mind would start to cloud over. And she wore a diaper, so that no one would need to clean up a soiled bed if she defecated when she died.

However, while an assisted death may require less exposure to what the sociologist Julia Lawton has called "dirty dying," coaching a loved one through it can be emotionally difficult.[8] Dara recalled the courage displayed by her brother, Theo, in their mother's final moments. When Peggy started to slump over while taking the medication, Theo gently said, "Come on Mom, you can do it." Recounting this several years later, Dara's voice quivered when she got to this point in the story. "Can you imagine being so brave?" she asked me, referring to her brother's encouragement. The poignancy of this moment highlights that although aid in dying sanitizes death, it does not completely alleviate the emotional weight of assistance.

It took about seven hours for Peggy to die after she lost consciousness. Anna told me, "We started to think, 'Oh, my God, maybe he didn't prescribe the correct dosage? What if we wake up in the morning and she's like downstairs making pancakes all pissed off?' Because that's the way Peggy would be. She would like wake up and go down and make some damn pancakes." Then Anna remembered that, when their mother was dying, a hospice worker had suggested they leave the room to give their mother the space to die. Everyone left except Henry, who lay with Peggy until she died at one o'clock in the morning.

Dara and Theo were supportive of their mother's decision to use aid in dying. While they had begged her not to give up at an earlier point in her treatment, by the time she died, they appreciated the extent of her suffering and respected her personal choice. Dara told me she had been reading Cheryl Strayed's *Wild* around the time of her mother's death, and the book, a memoir that recounts the cancer death of Strayed's mother, had given her a glimpse of what Peggy's death might have otherwise been.[9] Dara was particularly moved by a part of the story in which Strayed leaned over to kiss her mother goodbye, and her mother stopped her because the pain of even receiving a kiss on the cheek was too much to bear. Peggy's choice, Dara suggested, relieved her of witnessing her mother in so much pain that she couldn't endure her children's affection.

It was also significant for Dara that Peggy had relied on medical assistance in hastening her death. After she died, a cousin posted on Facebook that Peggy had taken "a bunch of pills" and died peacefully, surrounded by family. Dara bristled at this language, which she felt distorted the circumstances of Peggy's death and did not treat it in a dignified manner. To her, it was critical that aid in dying is bestowed with medical legitimacy, differentiating it from what Dara called "straight up suicide." If her mother had committed suicide without medical assistance, it would have felt very different—in no small part because it would have most likely been a much less social experience.

Anna expressed similar sentiments about Peggy's choice, noting that it was comforting to see her sister's wishes fulfilled. "I thought, 'Oh, this will be easier for me because I know she chose it.' And that is definitely a factor. I really like the fact that I know she chose this. Nobody chose for her or forced anything on her. She was totally in her right mind, clear as a bell, and she knew this was the right thing," she explained. And yet, her grief was still overwhelming, as it was for everyone in the family. Anna continued, "That helps, but, and still—it still is kind of devastating that I lost a sibling, a younger sibling, who's so vibrant and fabulous. So in some ways it definitely helped and in other ways it's just still shocking to me that she's not around."

Peggy's death scene, like those of Tom and Gloria, suggests that medical aid in dying creates a compulsion to embrace death actively, not only for the dying person, but also for caregivers. The social phenomenology of dying relayed through these accounts offers a striking contrast to popular cultural narratives about Americans fearing dying and wanting to avoid dependency at all costs. Asking a loved one to bear witness to one's death produces a specific form of interdependency that is distinct from depending on bodily care during the slow decline of social death, and is not equally disdained. Similarly, transforming death from a messy, unpredictable process into a staged moment generates new relations of care that are structured by the procedural nature of aid in dying, including preparing the medication, offering encouragement while the person ingests it, and waiting for the medication to take effect. The social connections that cohere in these moments, in turn, generate new relations of interdependency, in which caregivers follow the dying person's lead, even as the dying person depends on caregivers to implement their choreographed vision of an aspirational death.

GOING OFF-SCRIPT

The stories recounted thus far all involve cases in which medical aid in dying proceeded relatively smoothly. Yet it was not always the case that things advanced according to plan. In some cases, people died before ingesting the lethal medication. Nora McLeod, a family medicine physician, recounted how one family had gone to considerable lengths to prepare a patient's apartment, so that she could be discharged from her nursing home to die at home with medical aid in dying. The apartment had already been cleaned out, so the family had to arrange for a hospital bed to be delivered. The patient ended up dying peacefully in the middle of the two-week waiting period. Similarly, Georgia Lewis's husband, Nick, died peacefully at home in his recliner on the morning the shipment of medication arrived at the pharmacy. Cora Tremblay, who opposed her husband's pursuit of aid in dying on the basis of religious objections, was relieved when her husband died without taking the lethal dose: "It comforts me today. So, he did have a peaceful death. We had the option in the house, but God answered my prayers and took him peacefully without that. I don't have it on my heart. It would have been heavy on my heart because I know they call it death with dignity, but he did have a death with dignity without exercising the Act 39 option." Such cases must be distinguished from the thwarted attempts, which I described in the previous chapter, of people who wanted assisted deaths but were ultimately unable to access them. Dying before ingesting lethal medication was generally considered a good outcome from the perspective of family and friends because the person obtained relief from suffering, yet did not have to undergo a stigmatized, uncertain act.

Another set of individuals strayed from choreographed scripts for dying by taking much longer than expected to die (ranging from six hours to several days), and these deaths constituted the only assisted deaths that caregivers did not praise effusively. When dying was prolonged, it was typically because the patient did not consume the medication quickly enough before losing consciousness. In Oregon, the state with the longest standing aid-in-dying statute, and one of the most comprehensive data collection programs, time between ingestion and death for 899 individuals who died between 1998 and 2019 ranged from 1 minute to 104 hours, with a median time of 30 minutes.[10] Of course, whether or not a death took "too long" depended on caregivers' expectations and subjective judgments. Peggy Bliss took seven hours to die, yet in the end her family described her death in overwhelmingly positive terms.

Two Act 39 deaths were characterized to me as unequivocally "horrible." The first was Adrienne Singleton, whose death I described at the end of chapter 2. During the nine-hour wait until Adrienne's death, conflict emerged between her family and her best friend, Susie, regarding Adrienne's wishes. The second case involved a woman in her nineties, who took several days to die. Sarabeth Grady, the primary care physician who had served as the prescribing physician, portrayed it to me as follows:

> It was hideous. [The patient's children] had taken a couple of days off from work and come in from someplace in the Midwest to be there and had expected to be there for her death, help their father through the aftermath, get their father settled in a new—he was going to be moving into an assisted living apartment because she had been doing most of the care for him. And then none of that happened and she was still alive when they had to go back home. And her husband had not been supportive of her decision to use Act 39 in the first place and then she didn't die quickly.

For Sarabeth, what made this death "hideous" was that her patient failed to die according to the projected timeline, creating uncertainty for the physician and emotional distress for the family. While time of death can rarely be anticipated with any precision, aid in dying may create false hope for taming the temporal uncertainty of death.

Lisa Withers relayed the death of her dear friend Sally, whom she had known for forty-five years. After Sally was diagnosed with ALS, she sought medical aid in dying because she was terrified that she would die from choking. No one expected it to take long for her to die: she was "on death's door," according to Lisa, and weighed barely a hundred pounds before her diagnosis. Instead, it took Sally almost nine hours to die. "Twice she turned purple. And they thought she'd gone, and she came back," Lisa told me. She stopped breathing many times, and every time this happened, "Her boys would say, 'Oh okay, she's gone. And then she would start breathing again.'" Lisa described the ordeal as terribly stressful, particularly for Sally's children. While Lisa herself had witnessed death several times, the children's closest experience was with bringing a dog to the vet to be euthanized. They expected Sally's death to be similar and were traumatized when it was not. In retrospect, Lisa said, they saw that the paperwork had warned that it could take hours, but "none of us—even the nurses did not think that it would because of her condition."

Frances Sullivan's death also strayed from the script for a swift and easy medicalized death. Her physician, Lena Rhodes, shared the events of Frances's death with me just weeks after she died. Frances had been instructed to mix the medication with applesauce and eat it quickly, and she practiced this daily in the weeks leading up to her death. In her last few days, her swallowing ability deteriorated. Eventually, it took two and a half minutes, twice as long as it had initially, for her to consume the small quantity of applesauce. Concerned about this slowdown, Lena developed a backup plan: she wrote a prescription for morphine that the nurses could deploy hourly if Frances did not consume enough of the medication to kill her. This would be enough to keep her comfortably sedated until she died.[11]

On the day of Frances's death, Lena received a phone call around five in the morning from the hospice nurse, who said that Frances had fallen asleep before swallowing all of the medication. Lena advised the nurse to start the morphine, as it might stimulate respiratory depression. The nurse was crying, yet Lena felt confident about what to do because she had discussed this scenario with Frances. "We know what she wants," Lena assured the nurse. "She wants to be very comfortable. So we'll just start her on the morphine." Frances had taken the medication around three thirty in the morning, hoping to be dead by the time her children awoke, to facilitate transportation to the crematorium first thing in the morning. She ultimately died around nine. "I do think that the majority of her death was caused by the phenobarbital," Lena surmised. "I mean, it wasn't high enough of a dose of morphine to kill her."

These three cases underscore that, while many people whose stories I heard valued the opportunity to die a carefully choreographed death, at a time of their own choosing, medical aid in dying does not guarantee a complete escape from the uncertain temporal landscape of terminal illness. Aid in dying provides an illusion of control over a process that in reality is always very uncertain, setting people up for potential disappointment when deaths do not proceed as expected. While the bureaucratic process of aid in dying might foster the impression that terminal illness can be mastered through planning and structuring death, it can also compound disappointment when there are surprises along the terminal trajectory. For families and caregivers, as well as for the dying person, death may be drawn out and painful, more of an attenuated process than a punctuated event. By focusing patients and caregivers on the pathway leading up to death, aid in dying may lead people to overlook the temporality of death itself.

THE SOCIAL PHENOMENOLOGY OF ASSISTED DEATH

In Vermont, patients who choose to die using medical aid in dying almost always die at home. This is because the law enables medical institutions to prohibit patients from taking life-ending medications while they are residents in their facilities, and nearly all hospitals and skilled nursing facilities have done so. Most of these deaths were attended by a group of family or friends (and the occasional hospice nurse, social worker, or physician)[12]— in part because Seconal, the medication most commonly used, requires someone to assist with emptying the capsules and mixing the medication with applesauce or juice. But it is also undoubtedly because many dying people want to be with others in their final moments. Choosing an assisted death creates an opportunity to say goodbye to loved ones, and to mark such goodbyes thoughtfully and meaningfully. If it is a fear of depending on others for bodily care that drives people to pursue aid in dying, then aid in dying also seems to compel their loved ones to bear witness to the moment of death in ways that revive dependency and force them all to confront death head-on.

Of the people whose assisted deaths I learned about, Jacob, Lena Rhodes's patient, whom I discussed in chapter 4, was the only one who used medical aid in dying alone. A veteran in his late sixties, he had lived a solitary life after a brief marriage ended in divorce, and he was very clear that he did not want a caregiver, or even medical treatment, for his cancer. His desire to be alone presented a logistical challenge, however, for someone would need to attend to his body and pronounce his death. This predicament highlights the ways in which bureaucratic dependencies are built into the medicolegal practice of aid in dying.

However, although the bureaucratic protocol of aid in dying shapes new possibilities for dependency and sociality, dependency and sociality in aid in dying cannot be reduced to their bureaucratic forms. As the anthropologist Lisa Stevenson convincingly illustrates, bureaucratic modes of care can be disappointingly insubstantial.[13] Instead, calling on caregivers to witness and stage-manage death requires specific forms of emotional and material labor (e.g., preparing the medication, offering support and encouragement during its ingestion, and waiting for it to take effect) that far exceed the bureaucratic demands of coordinating paperwork and prescriptions. The emotional labor required to coach a loved one through an assisted death may replace some of the physical work of providing bodily care during active dying, yet the burden remains heavy. The upbeat encouragement that Peggy Bliss's son, Theo, displayed while she struggled to ingest medication that would kill her poignantly encapsulates the emotional weight of this labor, which aims to assuage loved ones' trepidations and instill a sense of calm as they approach the moment of death.[14]

In chapter 2, I described how medical aid in dying offers terminally ill people the promise of cultivating new forms of agency by actively "making death." This chapter demonstrates how assisted dying provides caregivers with a similar opportunity, as caregivers are enrolled in stage managing and accommodating their loved one's vision for an aspirational death. In performing the emotional and material labor necessary to support a loved one's final wishes, caregivers find new relations of agency over death: rather than simply waiting for death to happen, they actively work to produce it. At times, this may create feelings of moral tension, as when Neil wondered if picking up Tom's Seconal rendered him morally complicit. Even if one does not have moral or religious objections to aid in dying, enacting it may feel wrong in other ways. Neil's discomfort was intimately tied to his having become an agent in Tom's death when he picked up the prescription—a role that defies moral and cultural norms about the nature of dying. This is not to deny the active embodied care exhibited by caregivers engaged in more conventional modes of support for the dying but rather to underscore how choosing the time of death invites powerful— and sometimes uncomfortable—forms of agency and control for oneself and one's caregivers.

Notably, the others present at the deaths were not exclusively family members. In many of the deaths I documented, including Tom's and Gloria's, a close community of friends helped organize the bureaucratic procedures and social rituals that precede and accompany death. This point reminds us that networks of care often take shape outside culturally dominant kinship structures, such as heteronormative nuclear families.[15] The stories of Gloria and Tom and others offer an important counternarrative to growing cultural concerns about eldercare in the United States, in an era during which many older adults live far away from their children and extended families. Whether their choice to pursue assisted death was influenced by living alone, and hence not having a built-in caregiver, is difficult to say.

What these deaths do convincingly show, however, is that the choice to pursue medical aid in dying is not a choice born of having no one on whom to depend. Isolated elders do exist, but this is not the population that appears to be choosing aid in dying in Vermont. Instead, many people choose aid in dying for reasons that are apparently very much embedded in their existing (and flourishing) social connections.[16] Suggesting that aid in dying may be a way of enacting care for loved ones is to engage in a form of dangertalk. It substantiates worries that aid in dying might be anything but a voluntary, independent choice. Nevertheless, grasping the complicated relationship between care, choice, and dependency is critical for absorbing the social phenomenology of assisted death. Understanding the choice for aid in dying through the autonomy-riddled advocacy rhetoric oversimplifies the nature of individual choice and obscures the extent to which choice is socially situated.

It was precisely this entanglement of care, choice, and dependency that motivated Frances Sullivan to ask two old friends from her nursing days to be present at her death. As Lena Rhodes told me, "She had taken care of ALS patients in their last moments. She knew what it was going to be like. She was very smart, and she didn't want her children and her husband seeing her suffering. . . . She wanted to spare her family that. That's why she had her friends there." Similarly, Sally Hammond wanted to make sure that her friends and family were comfortable right up to the end. On her last morning, she chose to wear silly socks to make her sons laugh. Then, on her way to her bedroom to take the lethal medication, she doubled back to the kitchen to prepare a tray of cheese and crackers for her guests to eat after her death. These examples illustrate how medical aid in dying is a deeply relational practice, one that is always embedded in existing networks of care.

Most caregivers described an intensification of intimate ties around planning for death and around the death scene itself. Yet the death they had to confront was a sanitized and domesticated kind of death that departed from the messy and disordered hospital deaths that Americans have come to fear. In most cases, the dying person simply lay back and went to sleep peacefully, often wearing a diaper to contain bodily fluids. This is death "with as little dying as possible"—that is, manageable, orderly, and subject to control.[17] This might suggest that terminally ill people are more comfortable with forms of dependency that avoid the "dirtiness" of dying.[18]

Together, these factors result in a more engaged role for loved ones in shepherding death than many contemporary Americans will face. The sociality of assisted death implicates caregivers intimately, in ways that may render them vulnerable to distress. Neil's solitude in the wake of Tom's death demonstrates that social support for the caregiver can sometimes go neglected in the social choreography of death. Hospice agencies' bereavement services, provided free of charge for up to a year after a patient's death, take an important step in addressing this gap.

Documenting the social phenomenology of these assisted deaths challenges the dominant cultural narratives and advocacy discourses that cast medical aid in dying as a rejection of dependence. People like Tom Jarvis, Gloria Fleming, and Peggy Bliss were exemplars of the fierce independence that typifies people who pursue assisted death. This profile has a particular cultural resonance in Vermont, where residents pride themselves on self-sufficiency and stoicism, values that reflect the state's rural, farming traditions. And yet, their use of aid in dying required them to embrace certain forms of dependency rather than reject it writ large. The focus of public narratives about aid in dying might be the patient at the center of the drama, but the production of aid in dying would not be possible without the caregivers' support of the dying process. This fact provides an opportunity to push back against dominant cultural narratives that view dependency at the end of life in purely negative terms.

To the extent that dependency is associated with a loss of control in the American cultural context, it may be eschewed at all costs. Yet dependencies that facilitate personal choice and control—as in the case of assisted dying—can be construed very differently.[19] From this perspective, assisted dying offers critical opportunities to reimagine the relationships between disability, dependency, and care at the end of life. The role of friends and family members in managing many aspects of bureaucratic protocol, their complicity in contributing to a stigmatized act, and their engaged presence at the scene of death all reveal how sociality might be reframed through aid in dying in unexpected ways.[20]

Choosing whom to say goodbye to, and when, also creates opportunities for secrecy and exclusion. Tom was the most private in planning his death, wanting only Neil to know the date in advance and intentionally excluding his son. In Adrienne Singleton's case, open hostility emerged at the death scene between her family and best friend, Susie, because of their conflicting understandings of Adrienne's wishes. Of course, these sorts of tensions are by no means limited to aid in dying. Yet it is important to underscore that the sociality of assisted dying, while often harmonious and unifying, is not necessarily so.

Moreover, while medical aid in dying can be seen as offering an aspirational death, there is also a danger in the aestheticization of death rendering some deaths more meaningful and valued than others.[21] Patients who seek aid in dying have been given a terminal prognosis and grasped its implications with enough time left to properly plan. Yet not everyone who dies in permissive jurisdictions will have an opportunity to plan for death, meet the other eligibility requirements, and overcome additional access barriers. And families may need support to create a meaningful death at home.[22] In this respect, the social phenomenology of aid-in-dying deaths may lay the groundwork for a politics of exclusion that highlights unequal access to preferred types of death.

Nevertheless, for those who *are* able to avail themselves of this option, hastening death under the framework of legalized medical aid in dying transforms death from a messy, unpredictable process into a staged event. People approach this process with a range of dramatic sensibilities. For Neil and Tom, moments of comic relief punctuated the somber atmosphere. Neil even wondered whether Tom had decided to die sitting up to make his friend laugh. Sally Hammond deliberately chose silly socks for this reason, while Renee Long chose to die wearing a flamboyant leopard-print outfit.[23] From a dramaturgical perspective, these choices reflect a desire to disrupt drama and heighten suspense with lighter comedic moments that push the boundaries of tragedy and deliver a genre-bending performance.[24] Peggy Bliss, in contrast, wanted no laughter or joking, yet banal acts—signing artwork, transferring the deed to her car—nevertheless broke up the dramatic tension of her final day. In different ways, these diverse approaches reveal how people script opportunities for emotional release and levity into choreographed death.

Such choreography enables the dying person to reclaim agency over the dying process and become the producer of their own death. Consequently, advocacy discourses have characterized medical aid in dying as offering terminally ill people a distinctive opportunity for an autonomous, individually controlled death and an escape from dependency. However, largely missing from the public conversation on aid in dying in the United States is the fact that choreographing one's death depends on critical support from caregivers, paradoxically revitalizing dependency, albeit in a different form.

Conclusion

If medical aid in dying offers a certain level of control to someone confronting the existential uncertainty of dying, this control is oriented not only toward relieving suffering and maintaining coherence with the life as lived but also toward achieving a "good death"—one that reflects certain aesthetic, ethical, and cultural values. In the contemporary United States, there are a variety of pathways available for scripting a good death. As the baby boomer generation ages, medical aid in dying has become both more socially acceptable and legally permissible, but American society has also witnessed a surge of interest in new ways of attaining control over death, and what happens afterward. Of course, there is a broad societal push to have "the conversation" with physicians and loved ones regarding one's end-of-life wishes, and to write advance directives if one seeks to avoid life-prolonging treatment in certain scenarios. But the potential to gain control over death stretches well beyond such advance care planning.

The 2019 HBO documentary *Alternate Endings: Six New Ways to Die in America* profiles six individuals who sought nontraditional avenues in planning for their deaths.[1] Dick Shannon pursued medical aid in dying in California, familiar territory for readers of this book. Yet the paths chosen by the other five individuals were as broad and varied as the culture of death in contemporary America currently affords. One man, an ocean lover, chose to have his cremated remains delivered to a memorial coral reef in the Gulf of Mexico, where they were mixed with cement to form new habitats for the ocean life devastated by dying coral. Another, who had been fascinated by space and time travel, elected to have his ashes launched into space by NASA. A woman with terminal cancer opted for a green burial, for which her body was wrapped in biodegradable materials and buried in a simple grave in a nature preserve, while another man hosted a living wake, at which family and friends paid tribute to him before he died. Finally, in the last and most heart-wrenching case, the parents of a five-year-old boy planned a festive celebration for their son, complete with bouncy houses and snow cones, to uphold his wishes to have a party rather than a funeral after his death from cancer.

A central contention of the film is that attaining control over death is inextricably tied to the meaning we squeeze from it. In each of these examples, death becomes more meaningful because the dying person infuses his or her plans for death, burial, or funerary rituals with personal preferences. "Death is our last great spiritual experience," writes the journalist Anne Bokma. "We want it to be meaningful, and we want as much control over it as possible."[2] As death becomes more secularized and less governed by inherited religious frameworks, there are infinitely more possibilities for personalizing it and imbuing it with specific meanings and values. It has become more common in American society for people to script their own funerals, even adding voice-overs to provide their own eulogies,[3] at the same time that the funeral industry is itself shifting dramatically, with cremation and memorial celebrations on the rise and traditional burials waning.[4] There is an aesthetic logic at play here: if a good death is a scripted death, then it is also beautiful, well edited, and often scrubbed free of the messy and complex emotions that tend to accompany grief. The cultural message is that a good death is possible—if we plan for it.

When my grandmother died in 1991 at age seventy-eight, she had a different kind of planning for death in mind. Some years before her death, she warned my mother, "Harri, when I die, make sure you check my bathrobe pockets." Several days after her sudden death from a cardiac event, my mother and uncle were stunned to find she had squirreled away seven hundred dollars in small bills, over years and years. My family found this a wildly funny manifestation of my grandmother's Depression-era mentality. She knew death would come for her eventually, and encouraging her children to check her pockets, so that her bounty would not be inadvertently thrown out, was one of the primary ways that she sought to prepare. Today, however, scripting death has shifted into the public domain, forcing more candid conversations between family members.

The current boom in alternative pathways for scripting death raises a question that I have sometimes been asked when presenting my research in academic settings: If scripting death represents a broader cultural phenomenon, what is distinctive about scripting death through medical aid in dying? While there are many other ways to script death in contemporary American society, few if any offer the same potential for control over dying. Of the six individuals profiled in *Alternate Endings,* the only case that explored the process of dying was that of Dick Shannon, who pursued medical aid in dying in California. When faced with terminal diagnoses, people may carefully script their funerals and burials and plan their final goodbyes. Under certain circumstances, they can stop dialysis, withdraw life-prolonging technologies, or stop eating and drinking to hasten the onset of active dying. Even with these choices, however, they must wait passively for the dying to begin: the primary control over the dying trajectory is achieved through medications like morphine that provide relief from symptoms, such as pain and hunger, yet do not enable anyone to pinpoint the time of death. What is unique about scripting death through medical aid in dying is both the capacity to stage the dying process with meaningful social rituals and the contracted timeline of dying itself. In the face of life's greatest uncertainty, knowing precisely when and how and where you will take your last breath is a powerful form of knowledge, one that these other pathways simply cannot afford.

STEALING TIME

As powerful an option as medical aid in dying is, the reality nevertheless remains that very few people will utilize it. For people working in the front lines of end-of-life care, the disproportionate media attention that it receives in the contemporary United States can be troubling. In July

2016, I interviewed a long-standing hospice employee who had been quite reluctant to meet with me, and did not hide her annoyance when I showed up late for our meeting after Google led me astray. At the end of our interview, I asked a boilerplate question about whether there was anything else I should know. She thought for a moment, then looked at me pointedly and said, in a somewhat rehearsed manner, "I have resented the amount of time this issue has stolen from my patients and families." She went on to describe medical aid in dying as a hot-button issue that had captivated the media's attention, even though, in her view, the benefits were small for most people. She was glad that the choice existed, but she thought putting so much time and energy into how to end their lives sent patients a harmful message. And she admitted this was why she had been experiencing some conflict coming into our meeting.

That aid in dying has "stolen time" from other pressing issues is disconcerting for some people engaged in clinical and policy work to improve end-of-life care. As Scott Connelly, a physician and medical ethicist in Vermont, put it, "It's a potent distraction from the real core issues. Vermont lags among states in terms of hospice utilization and hospice referral times. We devote full ethics conferences to aid-in-dying which is going to directly affect a half a dozen or less Vermonters a year, and we're kind of forgetting about all the other people who are dying in ways that they probably shouldn't die." Colleen McAllister, an activist who opposed medical aid in dying told me, "It creates a culture of control that I just think is unrealistic. Like I said, I keep saying this, *we're fixing the wrong problem about death.* We are really fixing the wrong problem."

"Stealing time" is in some senses a metaphor for misplaced energies and misdirected attention, particularly when used with respect to terminally ill people, whose time is in short supply. Yet there are ways in which assisted death has stolen time much more literally. According to several policy stakeholders in Vermont, the long incubation of Vermont's aid-in-dying law in the state legislature was responsible for preventing Vermont from improving its advance directive statute and clarifying issues regarding surrogate decision making. Such laws provide regulatory guidance on who should make decisions about medical care when patients lose the capacity to do so but have not filed advance directives.[5] Before 2018, if a patient lacked capacity, a health care agent, authorized medical guardian, or other individual could provide consent, but "other individual" was undefined. Beginning in 2018, section 9731 of the Vermont advance directive statute outlined a process for determining who can consent to a do-not-resuscitate order or clinicians' orders for life-sustaining treatment if a patient lacks decision-making capacity.[6] Apparently, the legislature did not want to address the issue of surrogate decision making while aid in dying was also being debated—despite the fact that surrogate decision making was poised to affect thousands more patients than aid in dying.

"Stealing time" also refers to the time lost by terminally ill patients whose attempts to use medical aid in dying were unsuccessful—like Margot Hadley's husband, Rich, whose story I told in chapter 5. This book has shown how implementing medical aid in dying in the United States encounters some of the very same challenges of America's health care system writ large: patients' choices are necessarily constrained because of inequalities underlying access to health care. Attending international conferences and presenting my research on assisted death, I have been struck by the fact that access to aid in dying is much more equitable in Canada, despite the implementation timelines being similar to those in many permissive jurisdictions in the United States. In some ways, then, the limits on aid in dying are a microcosm of the problems of the US health system more generally.

As a researcher who has devoted the past five years to studying medical aid in dying, I, too, have had to reckon with the ethics and politics of stealing time from other issues in end-of-life care. On the one hand, I firmly believe there is a pressing need to understand how the cultural imaginaries surrounding assisted death play out in real time, as terminally ill patients, their caregivers, and health care providers are faced with the daunting task of putting aid in dying into practice. On the other hand, I have also sometimes felt that focusing on aid in dying risks taking attention away from more pressing questions and challenges about death in the United States today. Part of my ambivalence about aid in dying results from the fact that our society has dedicated disproportionate time, money, and attention to an issue that will affect very few people. This is not to deny the importance of investigating and understanding the cultural significance of this growing worldwide phenomenon. But it does make me necessarily cautious about its place in the broader landscape of end-of-life care. A key premise of this book has been that aid in dying will have a greater impact than the people who ultimately use it, by shifting the cultural conversation about control over dying.[7] I see aid in dying as a canary in the coal mine: a harbinger of shifting aspirations for death in American society. It can tell us a lot about how people want (and don't want) to die, even—and perhaps especially—if they do not pursue it as an option.

When I have given lectures about this project, I have often used in my slides a photograph of Betsy Davis, a forty-one-year-old woman who died in July 2016 using California's End of Life Option Act. After living for three years with ALS, she invited friends and family to a "rebirth ceremony." The itinerary included a tamale feast and cocktail hour leading up to sunset, at which time she ingested the lethal medication. Guests were instructed not to cry in front of Betsy, and a photographer friend documented everything. I came across this story when Betsy's sister and friend published first-person accounts in the local and national media,[8] but the story was quickly picked up and reposted by other outlets.

The photograph I use in my talks shows Betsy lying on a massage table underneath a white canopy, smiling and resplendent, surrounded by elegantly dressed friends in white folding rental chairs.[9] The scene resembles nothing so much as a wedding. I use this photograph because I do not have any from my own research, and it evocatively captures the type of death scenes I have sought to describe through caregivers' retrospective accounts. To be sure, it was more theatrical and festive than the Vermont deaths I heard about, but there are key similarities: Betsy is at home, surrounded by loved ones, and she has instilled her death scene with personal values and meanings.

On one occasion when I showed this photograph to a group of bioethics experts, a physician in the audience said this image disturbed her. In her view, it promoted a sanitized, glamorized vision of death that looked far too easy, and even beautiful. I understand this perspective. Photographs can be dangerous, not only for the forms of violence and suffering they reveal and risk desensitizing us to,[10] but also for those they conceal or erase. It is easy to look at this photograph and imagine that no one *wouldn't* want this sort of a death. But the picture tells only part of the story. And one thing it does not tell is how a good death might be otherwise. This, I think, is another aspect of what the hospice employee was trying to convey when she suggested that aid in dying had stolen time from her patients and families. It had occupied the cultural imagination in such a way as to obscure certain alternatives—including the expansion of hospice and other forms of palliative care—that might offer a more realistic pathway toward a good death for a larger number of Americans.

Notwithstanding such concerns, medical aid in dying is here to stay. And if the past few years are any indication, it will continue to be adopted by a growing number of states. What, then, is the best path forward? My research points to several possible developments that might strengthen existing programs and improve access to aid in dying for people who qualify under existing state laws.[11]

First, for health care providers, better training and education in communication, clinical care, and prescribing practices are needed. In February 2020, the first National Clinicians' Conference on Medical Aid in Dying was held in Berkeley, California, with the goal of fostering clinical discussions and explorations of evidence-based knowledge regarding the clinical practice of aid in dying. The conference was spearheaded by Lonny Shavelson, a Berkeley-based former emergency medicine physician, who opened the first specialty clinic in the United States completely devoted to medical aid in dying. According to the conference website, the clinical burden of medical aid in dying in the United States has been absorbed by a small number of practitioners, who field urgent questions and concerns from across the country but have no formal training, standards of care, or organized way to share information. The conference was an important first step toward solidifying the knowledge base and organizing a professional community, and it led to the formation of the American Clinicians Academy on Medical Aid in Dying shortly after the conference.

Better education is likewise needed for patients and families regarding laws in their jurisdictions, eligibility requirements, and what to expect from the process. Some health care systems in California have offered patient navigators—hospital employees whose job is to support patients' access to assisted death. Such practices are a logical step toward equalizing access within a given institution and alleviating the burden on patients and caregivers.[12] More generally, ensuring patients have access to hospice and palliative care is a necessary prerequisite to medical aid in dying, so that terminally ill people will not choose to die because they lack better options. Ideally, hospice services and enrollment rates will grow alongside access to aid in dying, as they did in Oregon after the passage of the Death with Dignity Act.[13] Some racial and ethnic minority groups, particularly African Americans, harbor deep-seated mistrust of hospice and palliative care because of the historical legacies of unethical experimentation, mistreatment, and structural racism in medicine. For these groups, developing trust that medicine can provide high quality, end-of-life care without prematurely hastening death is an important first step in expanding access to options such as aid in dying.

Finally, we need better research on medical aid in dying in order to understand its societal effects, including utilization statistics collected by state health departments, as well as broader social and cultural studies like the one that led to this book. Data collection by state health departments has not been uniform, with some states, like Oregon, collecting a wide range of information on the utilization of aid in dying (e.g., patient ethnicity and education, time from ingestion until death, complications or adverse events, medication prescribed), and other states, like Vermont, collecting very little (e.g., diagnosis, cause of death). Such inconsistencies make it difficult to determine whether critics' concerns about patient safety and effectiveness are valid.[14] More complex questions regarding requests, care seeking, and the decision-making process may be better addressed through social research than through state health department reporting, yet NIH restrictions on research concerning morally contested medical practices have impeded the pursuit of such research.[15]

THE CULTURAL SIGNIFICANCE OF AID IN DYING

In this book, I have illustrated how the legalization of aid in dying represents an opportunity for terminally ill people to achieve aspirational deaths—deaths that reflect aesthetic and ethical values regarding what constitutes a good death. Doing so enables them to die in ways that are consonant with how they lived; the eminent psychiatrist of death and dying Elizabeth Kübler-Ross referred to this as dying in character.[16] For many contemporary Americans, the notion of end-of-life choice holds a potent cultural significance, one that renders death commensurable with other key rites of passage, in which personal values and preferences take center stage in planning. As the lobbyist Claire Ruskin put it,

> You make all these choices about your marriage. You raise your kids. You make all these choices and at your death, it seems like you don't get to make any choices. Everyone makes these choices for you and to a certain degree, you can't control your disease, but if you can decide who you want to have with you, like where you want to be when you die, what you want your day to look like, those are the kind of things that just seem to get people a lot of comfort. Whether or not they use the law, the fact that they can, they might be able to have those choices, just gives people a peace of mind at a time when there's very little else that they can hold onto as choices that they can make.

When faced with the impossibility of choosing *not* to die, choosing when and how to die is empowering. A central argument of this book has been that medical aid in dying enables ordinary people to establish control over the brute unruliness of death.

Expectations of control over death are culturally conditioned assumptions that are shaped in critical ways by personal and cultural values, habits, and practices regarding life and death. In Mumbai, India, for example, where a startling number of people die each year as a result of traffic accidents, the notion that people have a choice about death might seem patently absurd.[17] On the other hand, similar to the United States, the desire for control was a significant motivating factor in the rise of Dutch euthanasia.[18] The anthropologist and physician Scott Stonington has argued that the desire for choreography—putting death in its proper time and place—is a cultural universal.[19] Regardless of how much control is desired or expected, examining the choreography around death can tell us a lot about how people in different societies live, and the values and assumptions that guide their life projects.[20] Scripting offers an apt metaphor for the tensions between structure and agency, improvisation and control, that organize dying and lie at the heart of this book.

So what is so American about the expectation for choice and control over dying in the contemporary moment? Three elements stand out to me in this regard. First, Americans engage in planning for death as a way to tame and forestall uncertainty.[21] This tendency is particularly pronounced among the baby boomer generation, yet it can be found in younger people, from millennials on up, as well. Second, the desire to avoid end-of-life suffering at all costs is related to secular American influences that have eroded religious beliefs regarding the value of suffering.[22] Finally, the aspirational deaths carried out through medical aid in dying reveal a cultural preoccupation with individualism and self-determination with respect to the capacity to chart one's path in (and out of) the world.

Despite the American cultural fixation on individualism, one of my most basic findings is that people cannot actually accomplish assisted death on their own. Physicians' contributions to scripting death stand to change how we understand their roles in alleviating end-of-life suffering, whether or not they choose to participate in medically assisted deaths. This fact was unsettling for some physicians, as I showed in chapter 4. Yet for others, prescribing lethal medication was continuous with older forms of palliative relief and was not categorically different. How physicians and society reckon with these various possibilities depends on cultural ideas about the nature of suffering, as well as the special status accorded physicians in a highly medicalized society.

Medical aid in dying also enlists caregivers in new forms of choreographing and stage-managing death. My liberal use of theatrical metaphors in chapter 6 showcased how medically assisted deaths become staged social events that are carefully planned, timed, and controlled. The role of caregivers in coproducing these events is elided by the dominant advocacy and media rhetorics surrounding aid in dying, which champion individualism and autonomy. Aid in dying remakes sociality even as it sets about ending life, and this sticks with the caregivers, who survive assisted deaths and live on to tell their stories.

Finally, policy makers, too, are faced with new modes of regulating death through medical aid in dying. Jeff Braswell's discomfort in "handing people some bureaucracy" when they call the Department of Health and share their existential suffering, discussed in chapter 1, seems especially relevant here. Even if seeking a medically assisted death is an expression of autonomy and individual control in dying, those who pursue it cannot escape the fundamental sociality of living in the world.

When I was finishing the first draft of this book, an acquaintance of mine died in a horrific car accident, along with her six-year-old son. The news shook me. We had lost touch over the years, but our sons were born just a few weeks apart, and she was one of the first women I met in the bleary-eyed days of new motherhood. At first, I found it simply incomprehensible that this could have happened, a feeling that I am often confronted with when trying to process an unexpected death. But then it hit me, that vital fact of life that has a way of slipping out of consciousness. *We are all going to die.* Their time came way too soon, at a terrible cost to their family. But none of us will escape this fate. If writing this book taught me anything, it is that every day that I wake up, drink my coffee, kiss my husband, smell my child's hair is an astonishing privilege. Thinking, reading, and writing about death every day has made me less inclined to take these things for granted.

But death, too, can come with its own forms of privilege, and this has been an equally crucial lesson. This tragedy perversely brought home for me what a privilege it is to get to script one's death. We do not often think about a cancer diagnosis as a fortunate event, but cancer affords patients a certain mode of planning for death that many, many people will never experience—because death comes too soon or because the circumstances and context impede meaningful choice. Some will script their deaths thoroughly. Others will only show up for the curtain call. Some will succumb to senseless trauma before any script can be created. For others, there may be a certain privilege in refusing to know about death, and therefore refusing scripting and planning. I have asked myself many times while writing this book, *what would I do?* In the abstract, it is difficult to know. For now, I hold that space of wonder. Even after all this work, I remain ambivalent. I am buoyed, nonetheless, by the possibilities.

Coda

April 5, 2020

In mid-March, as millions of Americans were slowly waking up to the reality of the COVID-19 pandemic, I, like many others of my generation, was busy convincing my parents to take the situation seriously. My seventy-three-year-old mother, who lives in south Florida, told me to "relax" and "chill out," as I repeatedly pleaded with her, with increasing urgency, to cancel theater trips, card games, dinners out. Finally, as I felt the window of opportunity closing, I texted, "I have to tell you that one of my biggest concerns is that you will die and I won't be able to go to your funeral." Ten minutes later, she called me, defeated. "Okay, I did it, I canceled the dinner. I won't go."

It is quite unsettling to be finishing a book about an orderly, sanitized, and typically peaceful mode of death while a horrifying wave of fatalities is beginning to hit the world. The coronavirus pandemic brought home for me with chilling clarity one of the fundamental premises of this book: that scripting one's death through medical aid in dying is a staggering privilege, one that depends not only on socioeconomic status and medical savvy but also on dying from a predictable illness with a clearly charted terminal decline. The current situation illustrates quite painfully that most people will never have the opportunity to script their deaths by choosing when, where, and how they will die, or who will be at their side. When activists repeat such slogans as "my life, my death, my choice," they elide the many circumstances in which death sneers at human control.

The pandemic has eroded many opportunities for individual agency and control at the end of life. On the one hand, advance care planning and communication with loved ones are now more important than ever. Americans are not good at talking about death, but as a palliative care physician recently put it, "We need to be prepared for when, not if, illness will strike. The coronavirus is accelerating this need."[1] One urgent reason for these conversations is that contemplating do-not-resuscitate orders takes on heightened importance in a climate in which resuscitation is especially likely to be futile and puts health care workers at increased risk for contracting the virus. Yet while individual preferences are still relevant, when critical care resources are scarce, much decision making unfolds at the population level. Public health emergencies remind us that there is a limit to individual agency, that there is a point at which individual preferences and desires must be balanced against the needs of society as a whole.

Moreover, COVID-19 makes clear that medical aid in dying is a privilege not only for the dying person but also for the bereaved. The fears I expressed to my mother about not being able to attend her funeral have become the reality for many people. One of the biggest lessons I learned from writing this book is that dying is for most people a profoundly social experience, in addition to being an individual one. If dying in community is a fundamental component of a good death cross-culturally, one of the great tragedies of this pandemic is that hundreds of thousands of people are dying alone, quarantined in sterile hospital suites, and hundreds of thousands of families are unable to grieve according to their communities' ritual templates.

What troubles me most about these deaths is the disavowal of death's sociality. Under good circumstances, dying can be a deeply intimate and even beautiful process. But even when it is not (for death need not always be pretty), dying from illness necessarily conjures a broader collective—those who clean and care for ailing bodies, those who prepare corpses for burial or cremation, the loved ones left behind. And, as I have shown in this book, when terminally ill people craft aspirational deaths, they nearly always do so in ways that foster intimacy. If medical aid in dying accentuates the sociality of dying by marking the scene of death with ritual flourish and the strengthening of social ties, this pandemic appears to do the opposite, turning dying persons and their mourners into islands of grief. This is not to deny the critical role that health care providers, mortuary workers, and communities are playing in responding to the pandemic but rather to highlight how these support systems are operating through techniques of social distancing that strain and dehumanize conventional social practices.

These disquieting times also raise the question for me of whether it is frivolous to think about aid in dying and aspirational deaths during a global pandemic. My discomfort here returns me to the ambivalence with which I opened this book. In this moment of crisis, should we not focus our attention on more prevalent forms of illness and death? Will this book "steal time" from more pressing issues in end-of-life care? I don't know. What I do know is that today facing the reality of our deaths has taken on new urgency. If aid in dying can open up new conversations about what we want from our deaths and what matters most in the time we have left—and I firmly believe that it can—then this book can be a fitting springboard to launch these conversations. This, then, is where my ambivalence has landed me: it is a strange time to be finishing a book about death, but doing so has become even more important.

Acknowledgments

In the weeks leading up to my completing this book, I experienced an unexpected anticipatory grief about finishing the project, which has enriched my life in immeasurable ways over the past five years. Research projects, like people, have their own life cycles, and this one's has been most fortunate. When I began making the first phone calls that led to the research for this book, many people warned me that it would not be possible, that people would not want to talk with me. My first thanks go to the people in Vermont who took the risk and shared their time and stories with me, and in many cases connected me to other important interlocutors. Although I do not recognize them by name, they have my deepest gratitude. This book would not have been possible without them.

The research on which this book is based was funded with generous support from the National Science Foundation (no. 1630010), a Greenwall Faculty Scholars Award, and a University of North Carolina Junior Faculty Development Award. I drafted the manuscript with the support of a UNC Institute for Arts and Humanities Wilmer Kuck Borden Family Fellowship. My cohort of fellows— Chad Bernstein, Kia Caldwell, Maggie Chao, Elizabeth Havice, Uffe Jensen, Charlie Kurzman, and Lauren Leve, under the capable direction of Tim Marr— provided invaluable feedback about the direction of the manuscript at a critical moment. The book benefited enormously from the capable research assistance provided by Dragana Lassiter, Manisha Mishra, and Izzy Brassfield, who not only managed the banal tasks of research with ease but also offered many important

180   ACKNOWLEDGMENTS

insights as we worked on the analysis. Izzy, in particular, was an important intellectual partner and crucial assistant in the latter stages of this project.

The amazing community of the Greenwall Faculty Scholars Program challenged me intellectually and shaped my thinking on this project in countless ways. I am especially grateful for the leadership and mentorship of Bernard Lo, former president of the Greenwall Foundation, during this time. Dan Sulmasy, Keith Wailoo, Jeremy Greene, and Scott Kim were helpful consultants at various points, and James Tulsky deserves special credit for planting the seed that led to this project.

Two wonderful writing groups sustained, encouraged, and challenged me during my most intensive period of writing. I thank my Greenwall colleagues— Jenny Blumenthal-Barby, Lori Freedman, and Efthimios Parasidis—and my medical anthropology colleagues—Dörte Bemme, Jocelyn Chua, Nadia El-Shaarawi, and Harris Solomon—for their friendship, collegiality, and enthusiasm for this project. For offering astute comments on portions of the manuscript and the ideas presented within, I am grateful to Jill Fisher, Gili Hammer, Anita Hannig, Gail Henderson, Sharon Kaufman, Carol Kidron, Barbara Koenig, stef shuster, and Kathryn Tucker. Naomi Richards and Janelle Taylor generously reviewed the complete manuscript for the University of California Press and provided important feedback and support for the project. I presented some of the material to audiences at Columbia University; Duke University; Harvard University; the University of Glasgow, Dumfries campus; McGill University; the University of Montreal; the University of Ghent; the University of Colorado—Denver; and the van Leer Institute, Jerusalem. I give particular thanks to the individuals who hosted me at these institutions, including James Colgrove, Rebecca Brendel, Naomi Richards, Thomas Schlich, Jennifer Fishman, Samuel Blouin, Karen Lutfey Spencer, Inna Leykin, Anat Rosenthal, and Guy Shalev.

I am very fortunate to be housed in a medical school department that values the publication of academic books. My colleagues in the Department of Social Medicine at the University of North Carolina at Chapel Hill have been very supportive of this work. I am especially grateful to my department chair, Jon Oberlander, for granting me protected time to write while I was finishing the manuscript. I presented portions of the manuscript to the Bioethics at UNC Working Group; I thank my colleagues for their excellent insights and feedback. Kathy Crosier is an expert copy editor, who graciously offered to read my manuscript in full, even though it does not really fit into her job description. I also involved my medical students, Laila Knio, Eni Ojo, and Conny Morrison, in data analysis and manuscript preparation in the later phases of this project, which is all the better for their contributions. My editors at UC Press, Kate Marshall and Enrique Ochoa-Kaup, and the editor of the California Series in Public Anthropology, Ieva Jusionyte, seamlessly shepherded the book through production. I am grateful to them for their support and encouragement.

Studying death made me acutely aware of how precious life is and instilled in me gratitude for how rich my own life has been. My family—particularly Jesse Summers, Simon Summers, Harriet and Marty Yogel, Steve Buchbinder, Emily Hutton, Joanna and Fred Bogin, and Debby Cohen—has provided a steady stream of support for this project. Harriet and Debby deserve special mention for reviewing the complete manuscript and providing helpful comments and encouragement. This book is for my parents, Harriet and Steve, who gave me the gift of life and have continued to enrich it over the years in countless quiet ways. I am happy to be sharing it these days with Jesse and Simon, who fill my days with laughter and share with me an abiding sense of the pleasure found in books.

Appendix: About the Research

"You're going to have hard times getting people to talk to you," said the woman on the other end of the line. "Have you considered going to Oregon? They've been doing this a lot longer than we have." And so went several humbling conversations when I embarked on this project. I had not considered this possibility; it was the novelty of medical aid in dying in Vermont that drew me there as a field site.

The origins of this project stretch back several years, to when I studied clinicians' adaptations to a new abortion law in my home state of North Carolina. I was fascinated by the intersections of medicine and law, and, after that study, I was eager to look at other contexts in which law and medicine collide. A fortuitous meeting with a palliative care physician at a neighboring academic institution set me on the path to studying medical aid in dying.

I began my research with a series of phone calls in the winter of 2015, using existing contacts from my undergraduate years in New Hampshire as a starting point and snowballing out from there. (Snowball sampling is a recruitment method in social research in which study participants are asked to provide names and contact information for additional prospective participants in hard-to-reach categories, especially experts, and are sometimes asked to facilitate introductions.) In an early phone call, the physician I call Amanda Townshend warned me that I would need to position myself carefully because many journalists had been interested in Vermont's aid-in-dying law and how it was working. Moreover, she said, lots of people wanted patient stories and had been calling around looking for people to interview. She advised me that people would be sensitive about sharing their perspectives on this controversial issue, and I would have better success if others could vouch for me. This advice turned out to be prescient.

With a small grant from my university, I made my first fieldwork trip in summer 2015, towing along my husband, mother-in-law, and toddler son, who embraced the opportunity to head north for the summer. After gathering preliminary data, I gained additional funding from the Greenwall Foundation for Bioethics and the National Science Foundation. The bulk of my fieldwork took place during the summers of 2015, 2016, and 2017. I also conducted five-day research trips each month between November 2016 and May 2017. It was important for me to visit Vermont in the winter, when the weather forces many people indoors and changes the tempo of social life. More than once, I got stuck driving in snowstorms with low visibility, feeling out of my element, despite my New England upbringing.

The bulk of my research materials consists of 144 interviews. I relied on a variety of methods to recruit interview participants. I generated lists of physicians from hospitals across the state, choosing those in specialties having the highest numbers of patients who seek aid in dying (i.e., palliative care, oncology, and neurology), and wrote them emails and letters. I circulated a recruitment advertisement in the Vermont Medical Society listserv, and to various hospice agencies and support groups. I hung flyers in libraries, cafes, hospitals, and senior centers. I placed one advertisement through Front Porch Forum, a Vermont weekly e-newsletter targeting people in specific neighborhoods. My most successful methods by far, however, were snowball sampling and approaching people in person at professional conferences or advocacy events.

My final interview sample included physicians (n = 29); nurses, chaplains, and social workers (n = 22); terminally ill people (n = 9); caregivers (n = 34); and activists, legislators, and other policy stakeholders (n = 37). During my first summer of fieldwork, as I was developing my research objectives, I also conducted formative interviews with thirteen Vermont residents who did not have a stake in medical aid in dying to discuss their general perspectives on it.

Initially, I hoped to interview more terminally ill people contemplating the option of using medical aid in dying. For several reasons, this proved far more difficult than I anticipated. First, although I was an experienced medical anthropologist, my studies had to this point been tied to specific clinical settings. Because aid in dying is so rare, I could not base my project within a particular clinic, or even hospital, and expect to obtain a large enough sample. Consequently, I could not follow my usual strategy of partnering with a physician to facilitate access to patients. Second, many providers and lay people were appropriately cautious about introducing me to terminally ill individuals with limited time left, and were protective of their privacy. Finally, in many cases, the timing simply did not work out. It was a huge boon for me when the physician I call Lena

Rhodes introduced me to her patient "Frances Sullivan" late in 2017, but I was ultimately unable to interview anyone else who was actively pursuing assisted death. On the plus side, however, my reliance on retrospective accounts of aid in dying afforded the opportunity to obtain narratives about a particular death from multiple perspectives—for example, a physician and family member, or a hospice nurse and best friend. In some cases, I obtained the story of a particular death from three or four different standpoints.

I adapted the semistructured interview guide from guides I had created for earlier research projects, including my study of the North Carolina abortion law.[1] I tailored the interview guide to the specific participant category, but all of them generally included the following domains: (1) professional background, (2) ideas about a "good death," (3) views on the provider's role in end-of-life care, (4) attitudes toward aid in dying, (5) experiences with aid in dying, and (6) views on the consequences of the aid-in-dying law. Interview questions were broad and open-ended to capture a breadth of responses, and to ensure I remained open to the possibility of negative or positive effects of legalization.

I conducted nearly all of the interviews in person, in a location of the participant's choosing, such as the person's home or place of employment or a local cafe. One interview was conducted by telephone when a suitable in-person meeting time could not be arranged. At the outset of the interviews, participants provided written informed consent. Interviews were recorded using digital audio recorders, but participants could opt out of recording and still participate; five declined to be recorded. I supplemented recordings with written field notes that included contextual details and interpretations of key points. Interviews lasted between 39 and 106 minutes, and I did not compensate participants for their time.

The largest concentration of interviews took place around the metropolitan areas of Burlington (the largest city and the location of the only teaching hospital in Vermont, the University of Vermont Medical Center), Montpelier (the capital city), and Brattleboro (a large city in southern Vermont), but I interviewed people across the state. During the summers, my home base was in Burlington, but I often drove several hours for interviews. It was important to me to obtain a geographically diverse sample because access to medical aid in dying varies significantly from county to county in Vermont.

After interview recordings were transcribed verbatim and deidentified, I coded the transcripts with the assistance of three research assistants, using an inductive, iterative approach guided by the tenets of grounded theory.[2] We first read transcripts to identify emergent themes. We defined themes broadly to capture depth and variation across participants' experiences and then organized the themes into a structured coding dictionary that included a definition for each of the forty-four codes (e.g., control, good death, social support, temporality). We assigned codes to excerpts or "chunks" of interview text that matched the code definition using NVivo 11 Software (QSR International, Melbourne, Australia).

Two coders blinded to the other's work coded each transcript (and field notes of unrecorded interviews). We discussed and resolved discrepancies, so that understanding of concepts and codes remained in agreement. After coding was complete, I generated coding reports for each coding category and further examined these to identify patterns across the larger data.

In addition to interviews, I also conducted ethnographic observations in several settings in which medical aid in dying was discussed. Ethnography, the hallmark method of cultural anthropology, is premised on the notion that immersing oneself in a particular setting enables a deeper understanding of social phenomena. I wanted to understand how aid in dying comes up in naturally occurring conversations, as opposed to the formal context of elicited interviews. Here again, I knew the familiar methods of clinically based ethnography I had used in past studies were unlikely to be successful because I could not be sure which patient encounters would yield discussions of assisted death. Consequently, it did not make sense to observe clinical interactions. Instead, I attended professional medical conferences in Vermont and nationwide on topics in ethics and palliative care. Occasionally, these conferences directly addressed the topic of medical aid in dying, but even when they did not, the topic was often raised. As I continued to work on this research, I also began to be invited to present my research at conferences, which provided more fodder for analysis.

In addition to medical conferences, I also attended advocacy and educational events to understand how lay people received and responded to information about medical aid in dying. During my research, Compassion & Choices held several screenings of the documentary film *How to Die in Oregon* in churches and community centers in Vermont. I attended several of these screenings and the question and answer sessions that followed them. I volunteered for two summers with the Wake Up to Dying Project, a multimedia exhibit aimed at fostering public conversations about the fact that we all die. This exhibit, which featured a sound tent that amplified stories about death and dying, was installed on the lawn of the Burlington Public Library in the summers of 2014, 2015, and 2016. It also included public workshops by local experts on various topics related to death. I attended as many of these as I could.

Early in my research, I attended Death Cafes—informal gatherings where people drink tea, eat cake, and discuss death in a respectful, confidential space—in cities across Vermont. I hoped these gatherings would give me a lens onto the culture of death and dying in Vermont. I found that each of these groups had a distinctive flavor and culture. I kept returning to one based in a small town, over the course of my fieldwork, because I enjoyed the company of the core group of members; I appreciated their sense of humor and their not treating the topic of death too seriously. The topic of aid in dying occasionally came up in this group, and over time some of these members connected me with interview participants and listened to me speak about my emergent findings.

Finally, in July 2016, several conservative physicians' groups filed a lawsuit against the Vermont Board of Medical Practice and Office of Professional Regulation. The plaintiffs alleged that Act 39 required physicians to inform terminally ill patients that aid in dying was a legal option in Vermont, and that this violated their constitutionally protected right to free speech. I traced how the lawsuit unfolded during my fieldwork, analyzing the legal briefs contributed by each side and attending a public hearing in November 2016. I also interviewed key figures on both sides of the case. Eventually, the lawsuit was dismissed—because the state argued that Act 39 held no such affirmative duty to inform, and the federal judge overseeing the case determined that the two sides had come to a mutually agreeable position.

Ethics approval for this research was obtained by the Internal Review Board at the University of North Carolina at Chapel Hill. In keeping with anthropological ethics conventions, all names that I use in this book are pseudonyms. In some cases, I have changed specific details about people's lives and backgrounds in an effort to maintain confidentiality.

Notes

INTRODUCTION

1. Mancini 2014.

2. They are Oregon, Washington, Montana, Vermont, California, Colorado, Hawaii, the District of Columbia, Maine, and New Jersey.

3. Emanuel et al. 2016.

4. Biehl 2007; Epstein 1996, 2009; Timmermans and Buchbinder 2012.

5. See the appendix for further information about the data and methods of this project, the Vermont Study on Aid in Dying.

6. Vermont Department of Health 2018. Beginning in 2018, the state health department has been legally required to submit a statistical report on aid-in-dying utilization to the state legislature every two years, and to make the report publicly available. The first reporting period coincided with my data collection, which was completed in Vermont in July 2017. The second report, released in 2020, confirmed an additional thirty-four prescriptions were written between July 1, 2017, and June 30, 2019; all thirty-four individuals had a death certificate on file, and twenty-eighty had used the patient choice prescription (Vermont Department of Health 2020).

7. Hedberg and New 2017.

8. Centers for Disease Control and Prevention 2020.

9. Back et al. 2002; Dobscha et al. 2004; Norwood 2009.

10. Voluntarily stopping eating and drinking (VSED) is a method of hastening death (Quill et al. 2018). Patients are kept comfortable with pain medication and by swishing water in their mouths to prevent the sensation of thirst. Some terminally ill people and health care providers view this as a preferable alternative to medical aid in dying, in some cases, because it seems more "natural." Some clinicians in my study touted VSED as a quicker alternative to aid in dying because people who stop eating will typically die within ten to fourteen days, whereas Vermont's legal process takes a minimum of seventeen days. Several nurses explicitly told me they were more comfortable discussing VSED after Vermont's medical aid-in-dying law was enacted.

11. Canada has authorized both practices since 2016 and has adopted the language of physician-administered death and patient-administered death to avoid the stigma of euthanasia.

12. All names of research participants in this book are pseudonyms.

13. On scripting birth in American society, see Han (2013) and Lyerly (2014).

14. Final Exit Network, Mission Statement (https://finalexitnetwork.org /about/mission-and-vision/). Assisting with this type of death is a criminal act in many US states. Final Exit Network volunteers circumvent these legal restrictions by maintaining that they "guide" rather than "assist," but the group was convicted in Minnesota in 2015 for assisting a suicide. State of Minnesota, Respondent, v. Final Exit Network, Inc., Appellant, A15-1826 (2016). See https://caselaw.findlaw.com/mn-court-of-appeals/1761968.html.

15. A sizable social scientific literature has investigated this very question. On the "good death" in an American context, see Cain and McCleskey (2019), Good et al. (2004), Neumann (2016), and Steinhauser et al. (2000). For cross-cultural perspectives, see Counts and Counts (2004), Krikorian, Maldonado, and Pastrana (2020), and Pool (2004).

16. Desjarlais 2016; van der Geest 2004; Koksvik 2020.

17. Long 2004; Richards and Krawczyck, forthcoming; Seale 1998.

18. Walter 1993.

19. This conceptual framework builds on my previous work on the use of scripts and scripting in abortion medicine. See Buchbinder (2016) and Buchbinder and Lassiter (2019). The anthropologist Scott Stonington (2020) similarly suggests that the concept of choreographing death invokes a dance that is partly planned and partly improvised.

20. Lock 2001; Kaufman 2015.

21. Miller and Truog 2009.

22. Kaufman 2020, n.p.

23. Miller and Truog 2009.

24. Biehl 2005; Buch 2015b; Kaufman 2000; Timmermans 1998.

25. Borgstrom 2017.

26. Norwood 2009.

27. Bird-David and Israeli 2010; Kaufman 2000. An important exception to this trend is the significant body of anthropological literature on dementia (e.g., Taylor 2008; Leibing and Cohen 2006; McLean 2007).

28. See Seymour (1999) and Floersch and Longhofer (1997) for critiques of the medicalization-of-dying argument, which holds technology responsible for impeding "natural death." These authors caution against adopting a romanticized notion of dying in premodern times and blaming technology for society's ills.

29. Fox, Kamakahi, and Capek 1999; Hillyard and Dombrink 2001; McInerney 2000.

30. Lavi 2005.

31. Richards and Krawcyzk, forthcoming, 1. Notably, Richards and Krawcyzk here distinguish between death—the cessation of life—and dying, the period of social and bodily decline leading up to it.

32. Lawton 1998.

33. I thank Jocelyn Chua for encouraging me to develop this point.

34. Some anthropologists have critiqued bioethics' emphasis on autonomy for privileging the individual patient as the primary unit of analysis and neglecting the relational and structural context in which much decision making unfolds (e.g., Das 1996; Drought and Koenig 2002; Ikels 2013; Kleinman 1995; Sargent and Smith-Morris 2006; Scheper-Hughes 2005). The relational turn in bioethics has addressed some of these critiques. See, in particular, Jennings (2016, 15), whose call on bioethicists to "defamiliarize autonomy" will resonate with many anthropologists.

35. Here, I follow Ortner (2006, 135) in suggesting that intentions play an important role in agency because without intentions, enactments of agency may become habituated routine practices.

36. Ortner 2006, 145.

37. Ahearn 1999, 13.

38. When California passed its End of Life Options Act via the state legislature three years later, it challenged the notion that this type of achievement would not be possible in a larger state.

39. US Census Bureau 2018.

40. Newport 2017.

41. Pew Research Center 2014.

42. US Census Bureau 2018.

43. Vanderbeck 2006, 650.

44. Evancie and Sananes 2017.

45. The reasons for this disparity are not entirely clear. A report commissioned by the Visiting Nurse Association of Chittenden and Grand Isle Counties, a

Vermont hospice agency, suggests a combination of factors, including: inadequate knowledge about hospice and palliative care among both professionals and lay people; the misperception that hospice is equivalent to morphine and death; reluctance among physicians to refer patients to hospice; fiscal barriers to in-home care, including challenges to obtaining hospice for nursing-home residents; and the availability of other in-home care services (Bolda and Eager 2015).

46. McCullum 2018.

47. Vanderbeck 2006, 646. These characteristics, Vanderbeck argues, are implicitly racially marked.

48. Cain et al. 2019; Nguyen et al. 2018; Harman and Magnus 2017; Petrillo et al. 2017.

49. Egelko 2017; McCormick-Cavanagh 2019.

50. Gillespie 2017.

51. Vanderbeck 2006.

52. There is a rich tradition in medical anthropology and related fields of examining how people mobilize stories of personal experience to make sense of illness and suffering. See, for example, Frank (1995), Good (1994b), Kleinman (1998), Mattingly (1998), and Mattingly and Garro (2000).

53. Egan 2014.

54. Knight 2015.

55. Desjarlais 2016, 30.

56. I thank Jocelyn Chua and Harris Solomon for pushing me to develop this point.

57. On the relationship between narrative and experience, see Good (1994a), Mattingly (1998), and Throop (2003).

58. Here, the writing of one of my mentors, Sharon Kaufman, has been particularly influential on my thinking. In her brilliant ethnography of hospital death, Sharon writes that adopting the perspective of an activist researcher "would have meant paying closest attention to an agenda for political and social change and compromising my goal of 'seeing,' as comprehensively as one person working alone could, the multiple strands of cultural formation, institutional constraint, and production of power that make hospital death happen. To the extent I could, I needed to stand outside the logic of the hospital world, including its desire for change" (Kaufman 2005, 19).

59. American Academy of Hospice and Palliative Medicine 2016b; Compassion and Choices 2019.

60. American Academy of Family Physicians 2018.

61. Field note excerpt, July 14, 2015.

62. Burt 2004.

63. On ambivalence as anthropological method and analytic strategy, see Kierans and Bell (2017).

CHAPTER 1

1. Greenhouse 2006.

2. For more comprehensive reviews of the aid-in-dying advocacy movement, see Ball (2012) and Fox, Kamakahi, and Capek (1999).

3. Neumann 2016.

4. Hillyard and Dombrink 2001, 69–98.

5. In Canada, by way of contrast, the Supreme Court's 2015 decision in *Carter v. Canada* authorized both physician-administered medication and patient-administered medication out of concerns for equality of opportunity (that is, patients with certain disabilities would not be capable of self-administering the medication) (Karsoho et al. 2016).

6. Oregon's law has served as a model for all subsequent states that have legalized aid in dying, but states vary in their requirements regarding waiting periods, state residency, and reporting practices (Abbott, Glover, and Wynia 2017). Hawaii's law, passed in 2018, broke with the Oregon model in establishing the most restrictive set of safeguards, including increasing the minimum waiting period from fifteen to twenty-two days and requiring that every patient undergo a mental health consultation before obtaining the lethal prescription. See Buchbinder and Pope (2018).

7. The Department of Veterans Affairs offers health care to military veterans in the United States. Federally qualified health centers are safety net providers in underserved areas that receive federal funding.

8. Ball 2012.

9. For a more extended analysis of these decisions, see Ball (2012, 67–104) and Hillyard and Dombrink (2001, 119–62). Ball shows, interestingly, that the justices' reasoning rested largely on a technicality: in both *Washington* and *Vacco*, all of the terminally ill plaintiffs died before their cases arrived at the Supreme Court. Consequently, the cases became "facial challenges," which entail a stricter standard. If the plaintiffs had survived, the cases would have been "as applied" challenges. See Ball (2012, 97).

10. Neumann 2016.

11. See Tucker (2019) for a review of the *Baxter* case and the legal context of aid in dying in Montana.

12. Death with Dignity National Center, n.d.

13. In this chapter, I use politicians' real names. All other names are pseudonyms.

14. Death with Dignity National Center, n.d.

15. This remains the case ten years after the *Baxter* decision.

16. I describe these barriers in chapter 5.

17. State of Vermont 2013.

18. Oregon's text reads, "'Capable' means that **in the opinion of a court or in the opinion of the patient's attending physician or consulting physician, psychiatrist or psychologist,** a patient has the ability to make and communicate health care decisions to **health care providers,** including communication through persons familiar with the patient's manner of communicating if those persons are available" (State of Oregon 1997, bolded text denotes a difference from Vermont's text).

19. State of Oregon 1997.

20. Hedberg and New 2017.

21. Vermont Department of Health 2018.

22. Associated Press 2013.

23. Buchbinder 2016; Sharma 2013.

24. Lipsky 1980. See also Giordano (2015) and Gupta (2012).

25. Thyden 2017.

26. Walter 1993.

27. Sociologists have examined the social and political forces that shape "right to die" movements and countermovements in several national settings (Fox, Kamakahi, and Capek 1999; Hillyard and Dombrink 2001; McInerney 2000). By documenting activists' political struggles to legalize aid in dying, these studies have depicted legalization as a key moment of cultural and historical rupture. Consequently, the literature on "right to die" movements implicitly treats the passage of aid-in-dying legislation as a de facto endpoint of social scientific inquiry, with less attention paid to the implementation process.

CHAPTER 2

1. Sandomir 2017.

2. See Kaufman, Russ, and Shim (2006) and Russ, Shim, and Kaufman (2007) for a discussion of life on dialysis in the United States. For a perspective from Egypt, see Hamdy (2008).

3. While my focus in this chapter is on the cultural significance of this distinction, it is also worth noting that this has been a philosophically meaningful (if contested) distinction as well. See, for example, Asscher (2008), Kuhse (1998), and Rachels (1975).

4. Biehl 2007; V-K Nguyen 2010.

5. Franklin 2000; Rabinow and Rose 2006.

6. Dumit 2012; Rose 2006; Sunder Rajan 2006.

7. Foucault 1990; Lemke 2011.

8. Stevenson 2016, 713.

9. Kline 2018.

10. Murray 2006, 197.

11. For other relevant critiques of biopolitics, see Marsland and Prince (2012) and Lamb (2019).

12. Stevenson 2016, 714.

13. Murray 2018, 718.

14. Murray 2006.

15. Andriolo 2006.

16. Hannig 2019.

17. Hannig 2019, 58.

18. Drought and Koenig 2002; Kaufman 2015; Kaufman, Russ, and Shim 2006.

19. On the ethical nature of timing death, see Kaufman (2010, 2015) and Kaufman and Fjord (2011). On the aesthetics of death, see Richards (2017).

20. Das 2007.

21. Yip-Williams 2019, 297.

22. The gold standard and most frequently prescribed medication for assisted death in the United States is Seconal. Because a hundred capsules are needed to form a lethal dose, most patients are advised to empty the capsules and mix the powder with juice, applesauce, or another beverage to cut the bitter taste.

23. Carhartt is a clothing company that makes utilitarian clothes for outdoor work.

24. Doughty 2014; M. Harris 2007; Mitford 1998.

25. I discuss this further in chapter 5.

26. Kaufman 2005.

27. Kaufman 2015.

28. Kaufman 2005.

29. I describe assisted deaths in more detail in chapter 6.

30. Romain 2010.

31. Memmi (2003) suggests that individuals in contemporary France have more control over life and death decisions, and that the state is loosening its grip over these processes. A number of anthropologists have observed similar tensions between state sovereignty with regard to biopolitical regulations, on the one hand, and neoliberalizing trends in health care, which increasingly defer responsibility for life and death decision making to individuals, on the other (Bernstein 2016).

CHAPTER 3

1. Portions of this chapter first appeared in Buchbinder (2019).

2. Picard 2014.

3. Christakis 1999, 179.

4. Singer et al. 1998.

5. Connors et al. 1995. The primary outcome measures were the timing of written do-not-resuscitate (DNR) orders; agreement between patients and physicians on DNR status; the number of days patients spent in an intensive care unit, comatose, or receiving mechanical ventilation; pain; and hospital resource use. There was no effect on any of these outcomes except for a small effect on patient-physician agreement on DNR status and a slight *increase* in pain for the intervention group.

6. Connors et al. 1995, 1596.

7. Institute of Medicine 2014.

8. Dresser 2016.

9. Halpern et al. 2013.

10. This point has been challenged by cross-cultural research demonstrating preferences for nondisclosure of prognosis and family-based decision making among certain ethnic groups (see, for example, Zivkovic 2018).

11. Dresser 2016, 6.

12. Perkins 2007.

13. Lavi 2005.

14. Quill 1991. No legal charges were brought against Quill after the essay was published. He did become the lead plaintiff in a lawsuit against the State of New York regarding the state's prohibition against physician-assisted suicide. As I described in chapter 1, this case eventually reached the Supreme Court, which determined in *Vacco v. Quill* that states have a right to ban physician-assisted death, and there is no constitutionally protected "right to die."

15. The Hemlock Society was a US-based right-to-die advocacy organization founded by Derek Humphrey in 1980.

16. Quill 1991, 693.

17. As with all medical aid-in-dying statutes in the United States, Vermont's law requires that the prescribing physician refer the patient to a second physician, who will confirm the diagnosis, prognosis, and patient's mental competence. This physician must also verify that the patient is acting voluntarily and has made an informed decision, and attest to these facts with written documentation submitted to the Vermont Department of Health.

18. American Academy of Hospice and Palliative Medicine 2016b; Quill, Back, and Block 2016; Tulsky, Ciampa, and Rosen 2000.

19. Interestingly, while opponents of medical aid in dying have been particularly worried that financial concerns make the socioeconomically marginalized vulnerable, participants suggested that such concerns crop up more often among more affluent populations.

20. Ganzini et al. 2001; Lee and Tolle 1996. An alternative explanation is that palliative care was already expanding throughout the United States at this time and thus the increase in hospice enrollment was not caused by the legalization of aid in dying.

21. American Academy of Hospice and Palliative Medicine 2016a; Quill, Back, and Block 2016; Tulsky et al. 2000.

22. See Duranti (1997, 214–44) and Buchbinder (2016, 2019).

23. Norwood (2009) suggests Dutch physicians may introduce the topic of euthanasia in the Netherlands, but it is relatively infrequent.

24. Digoxin is a medication used to treat heart failure.

25. Irvine 1989; Woolard and Schieffelin 1994. Language ideologies reflect much more than understandings of language per se. Their enactments also provide a rich source of information about social norms, hierarchy, identity, and social reproduction and change within a cultural system.

26. Cohen-Almogar 2004, 97.

27. State of Vermont 2009.

28. Vermont Department of Health 2015. This document was updated after the lawsuit was settled and is no longer available online, but it is available from the author upon request.

29. Buchbinder 2016. In this article, I also complicate the concept of the state, noting that it is not a monolithic actor but a cultural construction that takes shape through social practices and imaginings of legislative intent.

30. Vermont Alliance for Ethical Healthcare, Inc. et al. v. Hoser et al. 2016a, 19.

31. Vermont Alliance for Ethical Healthcare, Inc. et al. v. Hoser et al. 2016c, 8.

32. Vermont Alliance for Ethical Healthcare, Inc. et al. v. Hoser et al. 2016b, 2.

33. Vermont Alliance for Ethical Healthcare, Inc. et al. v. Hoser et al. 2017, 10.

34. The legal precedent for conscientious objection from authorized health care services can be traced to the emergence of "conscience clause" legislation after the Supreme Court's decision to legalize abortion in *Roe v. Wade*. See Stahl and Emanuel (2017) for a historical review of conscientious objection in health care. I discuss these issues in further detail in the next chapter.

35. National Academies of Sciences, Engineering, and Medicine 2018, 7–3. Sharon Kaufman, Ann Russ, and Janet Shim (2006) documented an inverse relationship in their study of living kidney donation, in which many end-stage kidney patients felt that a donor kidney may be offered but may never be requested from a relative.

36. National Academies of Sciences, Engineering, and Medicine 2018, 3–14.

37. Interestingly, such views are not quite so tenacious in Canada. The Canadian Association of Medical Aid-in-Dying Assessors and Providers (CAMAP) recommends that physicians and nurse practitioners involved in care planning and informed consent processes bring up medical aid in dying as a care option for patients when it is medically relevant and they are likely eligible (Daws et al. n.d.).

38. Calam, Far, and Andrew 2000; Casarett and Quill 2007; Mrig and Spencer 2018.

39. Hancock et al. 2007; Hagerty et al. 2005; Christakis 1999.

40. Byock 1998; Gawande 2014; Kalanithi 2016; Zitter 2017.

41. The anthropologist Frances Norwood (2009) makes a similar observation about euthanasia in the Netherlands, in which she argues that euthanasia discourse only rarely culminates in euthanasia death, and that the cultural value of euthanasia functions more as a social discourse about control, independence, and the prevention of social death.

CHAPTER 4

1. Hillyard and Dombrink 2001.

2. American Medical Association 2019; L.S. Sulmasy and Mueller 2017.

3. L.S. Sulmasy and Mueller 2017.

4. American Medical Association 2019.

5. Hafferty and Levinson (2008) characterize medical professionalism as a modern social movement dating to the 1980s, initially arising as a backlash against the rise of managed care and corporate interests in medicine. They observe that the emphasis on professionalism in medical school curricula emerging in the early aughts has stressed individual motives and behaviors, to the exclusion of the organizational forces shaping professionalism at a macrolevel.

6. *ASCO Post* 2018.

7. Gerson et al. 2020.

8. Text of the Hippocratic oath can be found at the National Library of Medicine, National Institutes of Health, https://www.nlm.nih.gov/hmd/greek/greek_oath.html.

9. Quill and Cassel 1995.

10. Quill and Cassel 1995, 371.

11. Pellegrino 1995.

12. Pellegrino 1995, 377.

13. Rapp 1987.

14. This case description first appeared in Buchbinder, Brassfield, and Mishra (2019).

15. Boston Women's Health Book Collective 1973.

16. See, for example, Pollitt (2015).

17. Quill, Arnold, and Youngner 2017; Quill, Lo, and Brock 1997. A smaller number have questioned whether this need be the case (Battin 2005).

18. D. Sulmasy 1999. Critics have challenged the idea that there is a morally relevant distinction between intended and foreseen effects (e.g., Lindblad, Lynöe, and Juth 2014).

19. Fohr 1998; Portenoy et al. 2006.

20. Most hospices in Oregon have adopted a similar position, which likely reflects hospice's ideological commitment to avoid hastening death, in addition to concerns about possible legal retributions for assistance (Campbell and Cox 2012).

21. See Berlinger (2016).

22. I discuss such cases further in the next chapter. The risk results from ambiguity in Act 39 concerning the residency requirement for aid in dying. The law ultimately leaves it to the physician's discretion to determine who counts as a resident, a power that makes some physicians uncomfortable.

23. Gilligan 1987.

24. Held 2006; Noddings 2002; Tronto 1993.

25. The sociological concept of dirty work can be traced to Hughes's (1971) discussion of the extermination of Jews in Nazi Germany. More recently, sociologists of professional work have applied this concept to medical care. See, for example, Bosk (1992), Chiappetta-Swanson (2005), and Martin et al. (2017).

26. A longer version of this case was first published in Brassfield, Manishra, and Buchbinder (2019).

27. Typically, barbiturates or benzodiazepines are used for palliative sedation, also known as terminal sedation (Quill, Lo, and Brock 1997). The patient dies of starvation, dehydration, or underlying disease process after days or weeks. The legalization of aid in dying has revitalized bioethical debates about palliative sedation, which some see as a preferable alternative because the primary intent is to relieve the patient of suffering, not to hasten death. For a countervailing view, see Battin (2008).

28. This distinction is closely related to lively debates within the bioethics literature about the distinction between killing and letting die. See Asscher (2008), Kuhse (1998), Rachels (1975), and Merkel (2016).

29. Arnold did not end up taking the medication and ultimately died of his cancer. I discuss this case in Buchbinder (2019).

30. For example, most abortions are provided in freestanding abortion clinics, rather than hospital-based women's health clinics (Freedman 2010). This pattern contrasts with other liberal democracies, most notably, Britain and Canada, which both have a long history of public funding for abortion, including hospital-based procedures (Halfmann 2011).

31. Childress 1979.

32. See, for example, Brock (2008), Cantor and Baum (2004), Card (2011), and Wicclair (2011). For critiques of how such debates elide considerations of conscience-based reasons for *offering* care, see Dickens and Cook (2011), L. Harris (2012), and Buchbinder et al. (2016).

33. See also Czarnecki et al. (2019) for a related discussion of how health care professionals' decisions to participate in abortion provision are not binary

decisions. Participants in their study differentiated between various aspects of abortion work, including intake, medication, and aftercare.

34. In his ethnography of Dutch euthanasia, Pool (2000) found that patients' requests for assistance were met favorably by physicians when made by specific patients and families in specific circumstances. In some cases, personality differences were consequential to physicians' decisions.

35. See Buchbinder et al. (2016), which draws on the philosopher Carolyn McLeod's (2009) relational account of conscience.

36. Brock 2008. It is also important to note that some find the conventional compromise unsatisfying because they believe even the act of referral renders one complicit in morally controversial medical care. Brock responds to this objection by arguing physicians have a professional obligation to fulfill this threshold level of care, even though it may render them partially complicit.

37. Vermont Department of Health 2018.

CHAPTER 5

1. Portions of this chapter first appeared in Buchbinder (2018a).

2. Margot's email has been edited slightly to preserve her confidentiality.

3. Exposure to Agent Orange, an herbicide and defoliant used by the US military in the Vietnam War, has been linked to a large swath of health problems.

4. In accordance with federal restrictions, the VA prohibits employees from participating in medical aid in dying, even in states where it is legally authorized.

5. Switzerland has been a destination for assisted death, or "suicide tourism," because the Swiss penal code permits aid in dying even for non-Swiss citizens. Most assisted deaths in Switzerland are arranged by privately run nonprofit companies. See Richards (2017) for a discussion of the motivations of British right-to-die proponents who planned to "go to Switzerland."

6. Offord 2017; Sanburn 2013.

7. Dembosky 2016; Offord 2017.

8. Petrillo et al. 2017.

9. In addition to being referenced by multiple physicians and one pharmacist I interviewed, this medication protocol is available online. See Eighmey (2016) and Shavelson (2018).

10. Buchbinder 2018a.

11. As I discussed in chapter 1, the self-administration requirement does not expressly prohibit patients from ingesting medication via a gastrointestinal tube (Thyden 2017).

12. I suggest the term *thanatological tourism* as an alternative to the more pejorative *suicide tourism*, which is more commonly used in the popular media.

13. Long 2004; Seale 1998.

14. Borovoy 2005; E. A. Davis 2012; Jenkins 1991; Kitanaka 2012; Scheper-Hughes and Lock 1986.

15. Shim 2010; Dubbin, Chang, and Shim 2014.

16. Shim 2010, 8.

17. When justice has been considered with respect to aid in dying, it is typically out of concerns about the vulnerability of disadvantaged groups to coercion or abuse (Coleman 2002; Sneddon 2006)—that is, that they will be involuntarily subjected to aid in dying—or in the context of distributive justice arguments. Regarding the latter, in a climate of scarce resources, terminally ill patients desiring to hasten death should be permitted to do so, if they act voluntarily, to free up limited health care goods for other patients in need (Battin 1994; Savulescu 2015).

18. Luna and Luker 2013; Ross and Solinger 2017.

19. Bridges 2011; Galvez 2011; Roberts 1997.

20. This point parallels similar scholarly critiques regarding the role of individual choice in end-of-life decision making. Drought and Koenig (2002) argue that the bioethical discourse on choice presupposes a patient who is actively engaged in their care and who has recognized and accepted death well in advance of its arrival. However, as they point out, this model may be unrealistic or even undesirable for patients from certain socioeconomic and racial/ethnic backgrounds.

21. Buchbinder, Rivkin-Fish, and Walker 2016.

22. Battin et al. 2007.

23. In the first twenty-one years of Oregon's Death with Dignity law, 2,518 prescriptions for lethal medication were written and 1,657 people (66%) took the medication to hasten death (Oregon Health Authority 2020).

24. Carter 2011.

25. In fact, the architects of the reproductive justice framework made a similar point in arguing that the right to have a child and the right to parent are just as important as the right to abortion, which often eclipses other issues in reproductive politics (Luna and Luker 2013).

26. Hosseini 2017; Simpson 2017.

27. See, for example, Bay Area End of Life Options (https://bayareaendof lifeoptions.com/) and Integrated MD Care (https://integratedmdcare.com/) in San Diego. These clinics charge a set fee of about three thousand dollars to help patients through all components of the process and associated end-of-life care.

CHAPTER 6

1. Portions of this chapter first appeared in Buchbinder (2018b).

2. This is one prevalent concern among many. Other major concerns include the difficulty of ensuring that medical aid in dying remains voluntary, the

possibility that individuals with disabilities may be coerced into aid in dying involuntarily, and the fear that legalizing aid in dying may be a "slippery slope" toward euthanizing people with disabilities to reduce health care costs. It is worth noting, however, that not all disability rights advocates oppose aid in dying.

3. On middle-class American conceptions of personhood, see Lamb (2014) and Ramirez et al. (2014). On how certain forms of slow dying erode personhood, see Bird-David and Israeli (2010) and Kaufman (2000).

4. Arlie Hochschild (1983) introduced the concept of emotional labor to describe the process of managing one's emotional expression to fulfill one's job requirements, typically with respect to paid employment—her original case concerned flight attendants. The concept resonates here because of the deliberate work that caregivers performed to manage their own emotional response to a loved one's impending death and thus avoid overburdening the dying person with expressions of grief and suffering.

5. Of the fourteen aid-in-dying deaths direct witnesses described to me, health care providers were present for eight. For some patients, having a health care provider present provided a sense of security about dealing with potential complications, such as vomiting. Nurses have served in this role more frequently than doctors, primarily because nurses' frequent visits afford deeper connections with patients. After Gloria's death, Laurel's agency changed its policy and permitted nurses to be present for medical aid in dying.

6. Martin et al. 2017.

7. Hannig 2017.

8. Lawton (1998) used this term to describe the messy disintegration and decay that often accompany the dying body.

9. Strayed 2012.

10. The total number of patients who utilized the law during this period was 1,657, but this information was unavailable for 758 of them. The time between ingestion and death has increased slightly over time as certain more quick-acting medications (pentobarbital and secobarbital) have become unavailable (Oregon Health Authority 2020).

11. Physicians in my study told me about several other failed attempts at assisted death that proceeded along similar lines. Effectively, this approach amounts to a shift from aid in dying to palliative sedation.

12. One way in which these Vermont deaths differed from the euthanasia deaths described by Norwood (2009) is that physicians were infrequently present, typically to honor the dying person's wishes. Only six providers (two nurses and four physicians), or 16 percent of my sample, reported having attended a patient's death. Norwood describes a much more intimate relationship between Dutch euthanasia patients and *huisarten* (family doctors). Of course, in the Dutch cases, the physician's presence is also necessary because

most Dutch people pursuing assisted death choose physician-administrated medication, as opposed to patient-administrated medication. (Both are legally authorized in the Netherlands.)

13. Stevenson 2009.

14. Hochschild (1983) argued that emotional labor is as much about producing certain feelings in one's interactional partners as it is about modulating one's own emotional expressions.

15. See, for example, Borneman (2001), Buch (2015a), and Wool (2017).

16. This situation contrasts with recent anthropological work on the growing phenomenon of "lonely death" among older adults in Japan (e.g., Allison 2016, 2017; Danely 2019). Allison (2017) shows how the increasing dispersion of Japanese kin networks has facilitated the development of new social ties: Japanese elders can now contract with private companies promising to save them from social abandonment in death.

17. Chapple 2010, 17.

18. Lawton 1998.

19. Kulick and Rydstrom (2015) similarly show that Danish policies around disability and sexuality, which help to facilitate sex for individuals with cognitive and physical disabilities, reveal an ethics of engagement and social responsibility that reframes dependency as something to manage and work around, rather than something to avoid.

20. Anthony Stavrianakis (2020) makes a similar point in his ethnography of assisted death in Switzerland, in which he shows that the decision to end one's life is always mediated and cannot be undertaken alone.

21. Lovell 2016. See also Richards (2017).

22. Coe 2019.

23. See Buchbinder (2018b) for a description of Renee's death.

24. In her beautiful ethnography of a cancer ward in Botswana, Julie Livingston (2012, 2016) argues that laughter can alleviate the isolation of pain, a paradigmatic incommensurate experience, by transforming it into a shared experience. Livingston (2016, 199) writes, "Sociality is potentially tenuous for these patients, and laughter all the more powerful for its potential not only to facilitate autopalliation, but also to strengthen and animate benign social connectivity, which is healing and care for Batswana." Humor plays a similar role in medical aid in dying, by collectivizing the solitary work of dying.

CONCLUSION

1. Peltz and O'Neill 2019.

2. Bokma 2019.

3. In the documentary film *How to Die in Oregon,* the journalist and radio personality Ray Carnay is depicted recording a eulogy for his funeral (Richardson 2011).

4. Heller 2019.

5. DeMartino et al. 2017.

6. Vermont General Assembly, the Vermont Statutes Online, Title 18, chapter 231, Advance Directives for Health Care, Disposition of Remains, and Surrogate Decision Making, https://legislature.vermont.gov/statutes/fullchapter/18/231.

7. Norwood's (2009) argument about the social function of euthanasia talk in the Netherlands has influenced my thinking here.

8. K. Davis 2016; Pantera 2016.

9. Bever 2016.

10. Sontag 1977.

11. Experts and advocates have also discussed expanding current laws to include larger populations of eligible patients, including those who cannot self-administer or self-ingest medication and those who cannot meet the six-month prognostic criteria, but I leave these issues aside for now.

12. Nguyen et al. 2018.

13. Campbell and Cox 2012.

14. Abbott, Glover, and Wynia 2017.

15. I was able to obtain funding for my own research from the National Science Foundation, but doing so required some creative thinking. Even with that grant, I would not have been able to pursue this work without additional generous support from the Greenwall Foundation.

16. Kübler-Ross [1969] 2011.

17. Solomon 2017.

18. Pool 2000.

19. Stonington 2020.

20. Ortner 2006.

21. See also Richards and Rotter (2013).

22. Lavi 2005.

CODA

1. Puri 2020.

APPENDIX

1. Mercier et al. 2015.
2. Corbin and Strauss 2007.

References

Abbott, Jean, Jacqueline Glover, and Matthew Wynia. 2017. "Accepting Professional Accountability: A Call for Uniform Data Collection on Medical Aid-in-Dying." *Health Affairs* (blog). November 20, 2017. https://www .healthaffairs.org/do/10.1377/hblog20171109.33370/full/.

Ahearn, Laura. 1999. "Agency." *Journal of Linguistic Anthropology* 9 (1–2): 12–15.

Allison, Anne. 2016. "Lonely Death: Possibilities for a Not-Yet Sociality." In *Living and Dying in the Contemporary World: A Compendium*, edited by V. Das and C. Han, 662–74. Oakland: University of California Press.

———. 2017. "Greeting the Dead: Managing Solitary Existence in Japan." *Social Text* 35 (1): 17–35.

American Academy of Family Physicians. 2018. "COD Addresses Medical Aid in Dying, Institutional Racism." https://www.aafp.org/news/2018-congress-fmx/20181010cod-hops.html.

American Academy of Hospice and Palliative Medicine. 2016a. "Advisory Brief: Guidance on Responding to Requests for Physician-Assisted Dying." http:// aahpm.org/positions/padbrief.

———. 2016b. "Statement on Physician-Assisted Dying." http://aahpm.org /positions/pad.

American Medical Association. 2019. "Opinions on Caring for Patients at the End of Life." https://www.ama-assn.org/system/files/2019–06/code-of-medical-ethics-chapter-5.pdf.

Andriolo, Karin. 2006. "The Twice-Killed: Imagining Protest Suicide." *American Anthropologist* 108 (1): 100–113.

ASCO Post. 2018. "AMA Rejects Recommendation to Reaffirm Opposition to Medical Aid in Dying." June 18, 2018. https://www.ascopost.com/News/58962.

Asscher, Joachim. 2008. "The Moral Distinction between Killing and Letting Die in Medical Cases." *Bioethics* 22 (5): 278–85.

Associated Press. 2013. "First Lethal Prescription Requested." *Boston Globe*, December 15, 2013. https://www.bostonglobe.com/metro/2013/12/15/vermont-man-received-lethal-prescription/tothzhfH0y2lWoOT4xP0LI/story.html.

Back, Anthony, Helene Starks, Clarissa Hsu, Judith Gordon, Ashok Bharucha, and Robert Pearlman. 2002. "Clinician-Patient Interactions about Requests for Physician-Assisted Suicide." *Archives of Internal Medicine* 162 (11): 1257–65.

Ball, Howard. 2012. *At Liberty to Die: The Battle for Death with Dignity in America*. New York: New York University Press.

Battin, Margaret. 1994. *The Least Worst Death: Essays in Bioethics on the End of Life*. Oxford: Oxford University Press.

———. 2005. "Safe, Legal, Rare? Physician-Assisted Suicide and Cultural Change in the Future." In *Ending Life: Ethics and the Way We Die*, 321–31. Oxford: Oxford University Press.

———. 2008. "Terminal Sedation: Pulling the Sheet over Our Eyes." *Hastings Center Report* 38 (5): 27–30.

Battin, Margaret, Agnes van der Heide, Linda Ganzini, Gerrit van der Wal, and Bregje D. Onwuteaka-Philipsen. 2007. "Legal Physician-Assisted Dying in Oregon and the Netherlands: Evidence concerning the Impact on Patients in 'Vulnerable' Groups." *Journal of Medical Ethics* 33 (10): 591–97.

Berlinger, Nancy. 2016. *Are Workarounds Ethical? Managing Moral Problems in Health Care Systems*. Oxford: Oxford University Press.

Bernstein, Anya. 2016. "Love and Resurrection: Remaking Life and Death in Contemporary Russia." *American Anthropologist* 118 (1): 12–23.

Bever, Lindsey. 2016. "A Terminally Ill Woman Had One Rule at Her End-of-Life Party: No Crying." *Washington Post*, August 16, 2016. https://www.washingtonpost.com/news/inspired-life/wp/2016/08/16/a-terminally-ill-woman-had-one-rule-at-her-end-of-life-party-no-crying/.

Biehl, João. 2005. *Vita: Life in a Zone of Social Abandonment*. Berkeley: University of California Press.

———. 2007. *Will to Live: AIDS Therapies and the Politics of Survival*. Princeton, NJ: Princeton University Press.

Bird-David, Nurit, and Tal Israeli. 2010. "A Moment Dead, a Moment Alive: How a Situational Personhood Emerges in the Vegetative State in an Israeli Hospital Unit." *American Anthropologist* 112 (1): 54–65.

Bokma, Anne. 2019. "How Boomers Are Planning to Die." *Vice*, October 16, 2019. https://www.vice.com/en_ca/article/ne89px/how-boomers-are-planning-to-die.

Bolda, Elise, and Eliza Eager. 2015. *Vermont Hospice Study Report*. https://www.uvmhomehealth.org/wp-content/uploads/2015/11/FINAL-VHS-REPORT-pdf-version.pdf.

Borgstrom, Erica. 2017. "Social Death." *QJM: An International Journal of Medicine* 110 (1): 5–7.

Borneman, John. 2001. "Caring and Being Cared For: Displacing Marriage, Kinship, Gender and Sexuality." In *The Ethics of Kinship*, edited by J. D. Faubion, 29–46. Lanham, MD: Rowman and Littlefield.

Borovoy, Amy. 2005. *The Too-Good Wife: Alcohol, Dependency, and the Politics of Nurturance in Postwar Japan*. Berkeley: University of California Press.

Bosk, Charles. 1992. *All God's Mistakes: Genetic Counseling in a Pediatric Hospital*. Chicago: University of Chicago Press.

Boston Women's Health Book Collective. 1973. *Our Bodies, Ourselves*. New York: Simon and Schuster.

Brassfield, Elizabeth, Manisha Mishra, and Mara Buchbinder. 2019. "Responding to Requests for Aid-in-Dying: Rethinking the Role of Conscience." *Narrative Inquiry in Bioethics* 9 (1): 67–72.

Bridges, Khiara. 2011. *Reproducing Race: An Ethnography of Pregnancy as a Site of Racialization*. Berkeley: University of California Press.

Brock, Dan. 2008. "Conscientious Refusals by Physicians and Pharmacists: Who Is Obligated to Do What, and Why?" *Theoretical Medicine and Bioethics* 29 (3): 187–200.

Buch, Elana. 2015a. "Anthropology of Aging and Care." *Annual Review of Anthropology* 44:277–93.

———. 2015b. "Postponing Passages: Doorways, Distinctions, and the Thresholds of Personhood among Older Chicagoans." *Ethos* 43 (1): 40–58.

Buchbinder, Mara. 2016. "Scripting Dissent: US Abortion Laws, State Power, and the Politics of Scripted Speech." *American Anthropologist* 118 (4): 772–83.

———. 2018a. "Access to Aid-in-Dying in the United States: Shifting the Debate from Rights to Justice." *American Journal of Public Health* 108 (6): 754–59.

———. 2018b. "Choreographing Death: A Social Phenomenology of Medical Aid-in-Dying in the United States." *Medical Anthropology Quarterly* 32 (4): 491–97.

———. 2019. "The Power of Suggestion: Disclosure Ideologies in Assisted Death." *Medical Anthropology Theory* 6 (1): 5–29.

Buchbinder, Mara, Elizabeth Brassfield, and Manisha Mishra. 2019. "Health Care Providers' Experiences with Implementing Medical Aid-in Dying in Vermont: A Qualitative Study." *Journal of General Internal Medicine* 34 (4): 636–41.

Buchbinder, Mara, and Dragana Lassiter. 2019. "Script." In *The Social Medicine Reader*, edited by Jonathan Oberlander, Mara Buchbinder, Larry Churchill, Sue Estroff, Nancy King, Barry Saunders, Ronald Strauss, and Rebecca Walker, 145–48. Vol. 1. 3rd ed. Durham, NC: Duke University Press.

Buchbinder, Mara, Dragana Lassiter, Rebecca Mercier, Amy Bryant, and Annie Lyerly. 2016. "Reframing Conscientious Care: Providing Abortion Care When Law and Conscience Collide." *Hastings Center Report* 46 (2): 22–30.

Buchbinder, Mara, and Thaddeus Pope. 2018. "Medical Aid in Dying in Hawaii: Appropriate Safeguards or Unmanageable Obstacles?" *Health Affairs* (blog). August 13, 2018. https://www.healthaffairs.org/do/10.1377/hblog 20180808.14380/full/.

Buchbinder, Mara, Michele Rivkin-Fish, and Rebecca Walker, eds. 2016. *Understanding Health Inequalities and Justice: New Conversations across the Disciplines.* Chapel Hill: University of North Carolina Press.

Burt, Robert. 2004. *Death Is That Man Taking Names: Intersections of American Medicine, Law, and Culture.* Berkeley: University of California Press.

Byock, Ira. 1998. *Dying Well: Peace and Possibilities at the End of Life.* New York: Riverhead Books.

Cain, Cindy, Barbara Koenig, Helene Starks, Judy Thomas, Lindsay Forbes, Sara McCleskey, and Neil Wenger. 2019. "Hospital Responses to the End of Life Option Act: Implementation of Aid in Dying in California." *JAMA Internal Medicine* 179 (7): 985–87.

Cain, Cindy, and Sara McCleskey. 2019. "Expanded Definitions of the 'Good Death'? Race, Ethnicity and Medical Aid in Dying." *Sociology of Health and Illness* 41 (6): 1175–91.

Calam, Betty, Susan Far, and Rodney Andrew. 2000. "Discussions of 'Code Status' on a Family Practice Teaching Ward: What Barriers to Family Physicians Face." *CMAJ: Canadian Medical Association Journal* 163 (10): 1255–59.

Campbell, Courtney, and Jessica Cox. 2012. "Hospice-Assisted Death? A Study of Oregon Hospices on Death with Dignity." *American Journal of Hospice and Palliative Medicine* 29 (3): 227–35.

Cantor, Julie, and Ken Baum. 2004. "The Limits of Conscientious Refusal— May Pharmacists Refuse to Fill Prescriptions for Emergency Contraception?" *New England Journal of Medicine* 351 (19): 2008–12.

Card, Robert. 2011. "Conscientious Objection, Emergency Contraception, and Public Policy." *Journal of Medicine and Philosophy* 36 (1): 53–68.

Carter, Zoe Fitzgerald. 2011. "What Assisted Suicide Really Looks Like." Salon, May 25, 2011. https://www.salon.com/2011/05/25/how_to_die_ in_oregon/.

Casarett, David, and Timothy Quill. 2007. "'I'm Not Ready for Hospice': Strategies for Timely and Effective Hospice Discussions." *Annals of Internal Medicine* 146 (6): 443–49.

Centers for Disease Control and Prevention. National Center for Health Statistics. 2020. "Underlying Cause of Death 1999–2018." CDC WONDER Online Database. Data from the Multiple Cause of Death Files, 1999–2018. Compiled from Data Provided by the 57 Vital Statistics Jurisdictions through the Vital Statistics Cooperative Program. http://wonder.cdc.gov /ucd-icd10.html.

Chapple, Helen. 2010. *No Place for Dying: Hospitals and the Ideology of Rescue.* Walnut Creek, CA: Left Coast Press.

Chiappetta-Swanson, Catherine. 2005. "Dignity and Dirty Work: Nurses' Experiences in Managing Genetic Termination for Fetal Anomaly." *Qualitative Sociology* 28 (1): 93–116.

Childress, James. 1979. "Appeals to Conscience." *Ethics* 89 (4): 315–35.

Christakis, Nicholas. 1999. *Death Foretold: Prophecy and Prognosis in Medical Care.* Chicago: University of Chicago Press.

Coe, Cati. 2019. "Meaningful Deaths: Home Health Workers' Mediations of Deaths at Home." *Medical Anthropology* 39 (1): 1–13.

Cohen-Almogar, Raphael. 2004. *Euthanasia in the Netherlands: The Policy and Practice of Mercy Killing.* Dordrecht, The Netherlands: Kluwer Academic Press.

Coleman, Carl. 2002. "The 'Disparate Impact' Argument Reconsidered: Making Room for Justice in Assisted Suicide Debate." *Journal of Law, Medicine and Ethics* 30 (1): 17–23.

Compassion & Choices. 2019. "Physician Support for Medical Aid in Dying Is Strong." https://compassionandchoices.org/resource/medical-associations-medical-aid-dying/.

Connors, Alfred, Neal Dawson, Norman Desbiens, William Fulkerson Jr., Lee Goldman, et al. 1995. "A Controlled Trial to Improve Care for Seriously Ill Hospitalized Patients: The Study to Understand Prognoses and Preferences for Outcomes and Risks of Treatments (SUPPORT)." *Journal of the American Medical Association* 274 (20): 1591–98.

Corbin, Jill, and Anselm Strauss. 2007. *Basics of Qualitative Research: Techniques and Procedures for Developing Grounded Theory.* Thousand Oaks, CA: Sage.

Counts, Dorothy Ayers, and David Counts. 2004. "The Good, the Bad, and the Unresolved Death in Kaliai." *Social Science and Medicine* 58 (5): 887–97.

Czarnecki, Danielle, Renee Anspach, Raymond DeVries, Mercedez Dunn, Katrina Hauschildt, and Lisa Harris. 2019. "Conscience Reconsidered: The Moral Work of Navigating Participation in Abortion Care on Labor and Delivery." *Social Science and Medicine* 232:181–89.

Danely, Jason. 2019. "The Limits of Dwelling and the Unwitnessed Death." *Cultural Anthropology* 34 (2): 213–39.

Das, Veena. 1996. "Public Good, Ethics, and Everyday Life: Beyond the Boundaries of Bioethics." *Daedalus* 128 (4): 99–134.

———. 2007. *Life and Words: Violence and the Descent into the Ordinary.* Berkeley: University of California Press.

Davis, Elizabeth Anne. 2012. *Bad Souls: Madness and Responsibility in Modern Greece.* Durham, NC: Duke University Press.

Davis, Kelly. 2016. "What I Learned Helping My Sister Use California's New Law to End Her Life." *Voice of San Diego.* August 9, 2016. http://www.voiceofsandiego.org/all-narratives/state-government/what-i-learned-helping-my-sister-use-californias-new-law-to-end-her-life/.

Daws, T., J. T. Landry, P. Viens, et al., for the Canadian Association of MAID Assessors and Providers. n.d. "Bringing Up Medical Assistance in Dying (MAID) as a Clinical Care Option." https://cpsm.mb.ca/cjj39alckF30a/wp-content/uploads/MAID/CAMAP%20Guidance%20document%20Bringing%20up%20Medical%20Assistance%20In%20Dying.pdf.

Death with Dignity National Center. 2019. *Take Action in Your State: Death with Dignity around the US.* https://www.deathwithdignity.org/take-action/.

———. n.d. "Death with Dignity in Vermont: A History." https://www.deathwithdignity.org/death-with-dignity-vermont-history/.

DeMartino, Erin, David Dudzinski, Cavan Koyle, Beau Sperry, Sarah Gregory, Mark Siegler, Daniel Sulmasy, Paul Mueller, and Daniel Kramer. 2017. "Who Decides When a Patient Can't? Statutes on Alternate Decision Makers." *New England Journal of Medicine* 376 (15): 1478–82.

Dembosky, April. 2016. "Drug Company Jacks Up Cost of Aid-in-Dying Medication." *Shots: Health News* from KQED. National Public Radio. March 23, 2016. https://www.npr.org/sections/health-shots/2016/03/23/471595323/drug-company-jacks-up-cost-of-aid-in-dying-medication.

Desjarlais, Robert. 2016. *Subject to Death: Life and Loss in a Buddhist World.* Chicago: University of Chicago Press.

Dickens, Bernard, and Rebecca Cook. 2011. "Conscientious Commitment to Women's Health." *International Journal of Gynaecology and Obstetrics* 113 (2): 163–66.

Dobscha, Steven, Ronald Heintz, Nancy Press, and Linda Ganzini. 2004. "Oregon Physicians' Responses to Requests for Assisted Suicide: A Qualitative Study." *Journal of Palliative Medicine* 7 (3): 451–61.

Doughty, Caitlin. 2014. *Smoke Gets in Your Eyes: And Other Lessons from the Crematory.* New York: W. W. Norton.

Dresser, Rebecca. 2016. "Medicare and Advance Planning: The Importance of Context." *Hastings Center Report* 46 (3): 5–6.

Drought, Theresa, and Barbara Koenig. 2002. "'Choice' in End-of-Life Decision Making: Researching Fact or Fiction." *Gerontologist* 42 (30): 114–28.

Dubbin, Leslie, Jamie Chang, and Janet Shim. 2014. "Cultural Health Capital and the Interactional Dynamics of Patient-Centered Care." *Social Science and Medicine* 93:113–20.

Dumit, Joseph. 2012. *Drugs for Life: How Pharmaceutical Companies Define our Health*. Durham, NC: Duke University Press.

Duranti, Alessandro. 1997. *Linguistic Anthropology*. Cambridge: Cambridge University Press.

Egan, Nicole. 2014. "Cancer Patient Brittany Maynard: Ending My Life—My Way." *People*, October 27, 2014.

Egelko, Bob. 2017. "California's Assisted Dying Loophole: Some Doctors Won't Help Patients Die." *San Francisco Chronicle*. August 12, 2017. https://www .sfchronicle.com/news/article/California-s-assisted-dying-loophole-Some-11761312.php.

Eighmey, George. 2016. "New Formula as Alternative to Seconal and Nembutal." Death with Dignity National Center. https://www.nvve.nl/files/5614/6530 /8019/George-Eighmey-G104–14–05–2016.pdf.

Emanuel, Ezekiel, Bregie Onwuteaka-Philipsen, John Urwin, and Joachim Cohen. 2016. "Attitudes and Practices of Euthanasia and Physician-Assisted Suicide in the United States, Canada, and Europe." *Journal of the American Medical Association* 316 (1): 79–90.

Epstein, Steven. 1996. *Impure Science: AIDS Activism and the Politics of Knowledge*. Chicago: University of Chicago Press.

———. 2009. *Inclusion: The Politics of Difference in Medical Research*. Chicago: University of Chicago Press.

Evancie, Angela, and Rebecca Sananes. 2017. "Why Is Vermont So Overwhelmingly White?" *Brave Little State*. Vermont Public Radio. https://www.vpr.org /post/why-vermont-so-overwhelmingly-white#stream/0.

Floersch, Jerry, and Jeffrey Longhofer. 1997. "The Imagined Death: Looking to the Past for Relief from the Present." *Omega* 35 (3): 243–60.

Fohr, Susan Anderson. 1998. "The Double Effect of Pain Medication: Separating Myth from Reality." *Journal of Palliative Medicine* 1 (4): 315–28.

Foucault, Michel. 1990. *The History of Sexuality*. Vol I. Translated by R. Hurley. New York: Vintage Books.

Fox, Elaine, Jeffrey Kamakahi, and Stella Capek. 1999. *Come Lovely and Soothing Death: The Right to Die Movement in the United States*. New York: Twayne.

Frank, Arthur. 1995. *The Wounded Storyteller: Body, Illness, and Ethics*. Chicago: University of Chicago Press.

Franklin, Sarah. 2000. "Life Itself: Global Nature and the Genetic Imaginary." In *Global Nature, Global Culture*, edited by S. Franklin, C. Lury, and J. Stacey, 188–227. London: Sage.

Freedman, Lori. 2010. *Willing and Unable: Doctors' Constraints in Abortion Care*. Nashville: Vanderbilt University Press.

Galvez, Alyshia. 2011. *Patient Mothers, Patient Citizens: Mexican Women, Public Prenatal Care, and the Birth-Weight Paradox*. New Brunswick, NJ: Rutgers University Press.

Ganzini, Linda, Heidi Nelson, Melinda Lee, Dale Kramer, Terri Schmidt, and Molly Delorit. 2001. "Oregon Physicians' Attitudes about and Experiences with End-of-Life Care since Passage of the Oregon Death with Dignity Act." *Journal of the American Medical Association* 285 (18): 2363–69.

Gawande, Atul. 2014. *Being Mortal: Medicine and What Matters in the End*. New York: Metropolitan Books.

Gerson, Sheri Mila, Gitte Koksvik, Naomi Richards, Lars Johan Materstvedt, and David Clark. 2020. "The Relationship of Palliative Care with Assisted Dying Where Assisted Dying Is Lawful." *Journal of Pain and Symptom Management* 59 (6): 1287–1303.

Gillespie, Kelly. 2017. "Before the Commission: Ethnography as Public Testimony." In *If Truth Be Told: The Politics of Public Ethnography*, edited by Didier Fassin, 69–95. Durham, NC: Duke University Press.

Gilligan, Carol. 1987. "Moral Orientation and Moral Development." In *Women and Moral Theory*, edited by Eva Feder Kittay and Diana Meyers, 19–33. Savage, MD: Rowman and Littlefield.

Giordano, Cristiana. 2015. "Lying the Truth: Practices of Confession and Recognition." *Current Anthropology* 56 (S12): S211–21.

Good, Byron. 1994a. *Medicine, Rationality, and Experience: An Anthropological Perspective*. Cambridge: Cambridge University Press.

———. 1994b. "The Narrative Representation of Illness." In *Medicine, Rationality, and Experience: An Anthropological Perspective*, 135–65. Cambridge: Cambridge University Press.

Good, Mary-Jo DelVecchio, Nina Gadmer, Patricia Ruopp, Matthew Lakoma, Amy Sullivan, Ellen Redinbaugh, Robert Arnold, and Susan Block. 2004. "Narrative Nuances on Good and Bad Deaths: Internists' Tales from High-Technology Work Places." *Social Science and Medicine* 58 (5): 939–53.

Greenhouse, Carol. 2006. "Fieldwork on Law." *Annual Review of Law and Social Science* 2:187–210.

Gupta, Akhil. 2012. *Red Tape: Bureaucracy, Structural Violence, and Poverty in India*. Durham, NC: Duke University Press.

Hafferty, Frederic, and Dana Levinson. 2008. "Moving beyond Nostalgia and Motives: Toward a Complexity Science View of Professionalism." *Perspectives in Biology and Medicine* 51 (4): 599–615.

Hagerty, R. G., P. N. Butow, P. M. Ellis, S. Dimitry, and M. H. N. Tattersall. 2005. "Communicating Prognosis in Cancer Care: A Systematic Review of the Literature." *Annals of Oncology: Official Journal of the European Society for Medical Oncology* 16 (7): 1005–53.

Halfmann, Drew. 2011. *Doctors and Demonstrators: How Political Institutions Shape Abortion Law in the United States, Britain, and Canada.* Chicago: University of Chicago Press.

Halpern, Scott, George Loewenstein, Kevin Volpp, Elizabeth Cooney, Kelly Vranas, Caroline M. Quill, Mary S. McKenzie, Michael O. Harhay, Nicole B. Gabler, Tatiana Silva, Robert Arnold, Derek C. Angus, and Cindy Bryce. 2013. "Default Options in Advance Directives Influence How Patients Set Goals for End-of-Life Care." *Health Affairs* 32 (2): 408–17.

Hamdy, Sherine. 2008. "When the State and Your Kidneys Fail: Political Etiologies in an Egyptian Dialysis Ward." *American Ethnologist* 35 (4): 553–69.

Han, Sallie. 2013. *Pregnancy in Practice: Expectation and Experience in the Contemporary US.* New York: Berghahn Books.

Hancock, Karen, Josephine M. Clayton, Sharon M. Parker, Sharon Wal der, Phyllis N. Butow, Sue Carrick, David Currow, Davina Ghersi, Paul Glare, Rebecca Hagerty, and Martin H. N. Tattersall. 2007. "Truth-Telling in Discussing Prognosis in Advanced Life-Limiting Illnesses: A Systematic Review." *Palliative Medicine* 21 (6): 507–17.

Hannig, Anita. 2017. "'Becoming a Burden': Examining Relational Suffering in Medically-Assisted Dying." Paper presented at the Annual Meeting of the American Anthropology Association, Washington, DC, December.

———. 2019. "Author(iz)ing Death: Medical Aid-in-Dying and the Morality of Suicide." *Cultural Anthropology* 34 (1): 53–77.

Harman, Stephanie, and David Magnus. 2017. "Early Experience with the California End of Life Option Act: Balancing Institutional Participation and Physician Conscientious Objection." *JAMA Internal Medicine* 177 (7): 907–98.

Harris, Lisa. 2012. "Recognizing Conscience in Abortion Provision." *New England Journal of Medicine* 367 (11): 981–83.

Harris, Mark. 2007. *Grave Matters: A Journey through the Modern Funeral Industry to a Natural Way of Burial.* New York: Scribner.

Hedberg, Katrina, and Craig New. 2017. "Oregon's Death with Dignity Act: 20 Years of Experience to Inform the Debate." *Annals of Internal Medicine* 167 (8): 579–83.

Held, Virginia. 2006. *The Ethics of Care: Personal, Political, Global.* Oxford: Oxford University Press.

Heller, Karen. 2019. "The Funeral as We Know It Is Becoming a Relic—Just in Time for a Death Boom." *Washington Post,* April 15, 2019. https://www.washingtonpost.com/lifestyle/style/the-funeral-as-we-know-it-is-becoming-a-relic—just-in-time-for-a-death-boom/2019/04/14/a49003c4-50c2-11e9-8d28-f5149e5a2fda_story.html.

Hillyard, Daniel, and John Dombrink. 2001. *Dying Right: The Death with Dignity Movement*. London: Routledge.

Hippocrates. 2002. The Hippocratic Oath. Translated by M. North. https://www.nlm.nih.gov/hmd/greek/greek_oath.html.

Hochschild, Arlie. 1983. *The Managed Heart: Commercialization of Human Feeling*. Berkeley: University of California Press.

Hosseini, Raheem. 2017. "The Uncounted Dead: California Doesn't Want to Know Who's Falling through the Cracks of Its Assisted Death Law." *Sacramento News and Review*, July 6, 2017. https://www.newsreview.com/sacramento/uncounted-dead-california-doesnt/co.

Hughes, C. Everett. 1971. *The Sociological Eye: Selected Papers*. Chicago: Aldine.

Ikels, Charlotte. 2013. "The Anthropology of Organ Transplantation." *Annual Review of Anthropology* 42:89–102.

Institute of Medicine. 2014. *Dying in America: Improving Quality and Honoring Individual Preferences Near the End of Life*. Washington, DC: National Academies Press.

Irvine, Judith. 1989. "When Talk Isn't Cheap: Language and Political Economy." *American Ethnologist* 16 (2): 248–67.

Jenkins, Janis. 1991. "The State Construction of Affect: Political Ethos and Mental Health among Salvadoran Refugees." *Culture, Medicine, and Psychiatry* 15 (2): 139–65.

Jennings, Bruce. 2016. "Reconceptualizing Autonomy: A Relational Turn in Bioethics." *Hastings Center Report* 46 (3): 11–16.

Kalanithi, Paul. 2016. *When Breath Becomes Air*. New York: Random House.

Karsoho, Hadi, Jennifer Fishman, David Wright, and Mary Ellen McDonald. 2016. "Suffering and Medicalization at the End of Life: The Case of Physician-Assisted Dying." *Social Science and Medicine* 170:188–196.

Kaufman, Sharon. 2000. "In the Shadow of 'Death with Dignity': Medicine and Cultural Quandaries and the Vegetative State." *American Anthropologist* 102 (1): 69–83.

———. 2005. *. . . And a Time to Die: How American Hospitals Shape the End of Life*. Chicago: University of Chicago Press.

———. 2010. "Time, Clinic Technologies, and the Making of Reflexive Longevity: The Cultural Work of Time Left in an Ageing Society." *Sociology of Health and Illness* 32 (2): 225–37.

———. 2015. *Ordinary Medicine: Extraordinary Treatments, Longer Lives, and Where to Draw the Line*. Durham, NC: Duke University Press.

———. 2020. "Neither Person nor Cadaver." *Aeon*. February 6, 2020. https://aeon.co/essays/why-medics-and-the-law-clash-with-family-in-brain-death-cases.

Kaufman, Sharon, with Lakshmi Fjord. 2011. "Medicare, Ethics, and Reflexive Longevity: Governing Time and Treatment in an Aging Society." *Medical Anthropology Quarterly* 25 (2): 209–31.

Kaufman, Sharon, Ann Russ, and Janet Shim. 2006. "Aged Bodies and Kinship Matters: The Ethical Field of Kidney Transplant." *American Ethnologist* 33 (1): 81–99.

Kierans, Ciara, and Kirsten Bell. 2017. "Cultivating Ambivalence: Some Methodological Considerations for Anthropology." *HAU: Journal of Ethnographic Theory* 7 (2): 23–44.

Kitanaka, Junko. 2012. *Depression in Japan: Psychiatric Cures for a Society in Distress*. Princeton, NJ: Princeton University Press.

Kleinman, Arthur. 1988. *The Illness Narratives*. New York: Basic Books.

———. 1995. "Anthropology of Bioethics." In *Writing at the Margins: Discourse between Anthropology and Medicine*, 41–67. Berkeley: University of California Press.

Kline, Nolan. 2018. "Life, Death, and Dialysis: Medical Repatriation and Liminality among Undocumented Kidney Failure Patients in the United States." *Political and Legal Anthropology Review* 41 (2): 216–30.

Knight, Kelly Ray. 2015. *addicted. pregnant. poor.* Durham, NC: Duke University Press.

Koksvik, Gitte. 2020. "Medically Timed Death as an Enactment of the Good Death: An Ethnographic Study of Three European Intensive Care Units." *OMEGA—Journal of Death and Dying* 81 (1): 66–79.

Krikorian, Alicia, Camilo Maldonado, and Tania Pastrana. 2020. "Patient's Perspectives on the Notion of a Good Death: A Systematic Review of the Literature." *Journal of Pain and Symptom Management* 59 (1): 152–64.

Kübler-Ross, Elizabeth. (1969) 2011. *On Death and Dying: What the Dying Have to Teach Doctors, Nurses, Clergy, and Their Own Families*. New York: Scribner.

Kuhse, Helga. 1998. "Critical Notice: Why Killing Is Not Always Worse—and Is Sometimes Better—Than Letting Die." *Cambridge Quarterly of Healthcare Ethics* 7 (4): 371–74.

Kulick, Don, and Jens Rydstrom. 2015. *Loneliness and Its Opposite: Sex, Disability, and the Ethics of Engagement*. Durham, NC: Duke University Press.

Lamb, Sarah. 2014. "Permanent Personhood or Meaningful Decline? Toward a Critical Anthropology of Successful Aging." *Journal of Aging Studies* 29:41–52.

———. 2019. "On Being (Not) Old: Agency, Self-Care, and Life Course Aspirations in the United States." *Medical Anthropology Quarterly* 33 (2): 263–81.

Lavi, Shai. 2005. *The Modern Art of Dying: A History of Euthanasia in the United States*. Princeton, NJ: Princeton University Press.

Lawton, Julia. 1998. "Contemporary Hospice Care: The Sequestrations of the Unbounded Body and 'Dirty Dying.'" *Sociology of Health and Illness* 20 (2): 121–43.

Lee, Melinda, and Susan Tolle. 1996. "Oregon's Assisted Suicide Vote: The Silver Lining." *Annals of Internal Medicine* 124 (2): 267–69.

Leibing, Annette, and Lawrence Cohen. 2006. *Thinking about Dementia: Culture, Loss, and the Anthropology of Senility.* New Brunswick, NJ: Rutgers University Press.

Lemke, Thomas. 2011. *Biopolitics: An Advanced Introduction.* Translated by E. Trump. New York: New York University Press.

Lindblad, Anna, Niels Lynöe, and Niklas Juth. 2014. "End-of-Life Decisions and the Reinvented Rule of Double Effect: A Critical Analysis." *Bioethics* 28 (7): 368–77.

Lipsky, Michael. 1980. *Street-Level Bureaucracy: Dilemmas of the Individual in Public Service.* New York: Russell Sage.

Livingston, Julie. 2012. *Improvising Medicine: An African Oncology Ward in an Emerging Cancer Epidemic.* Durham, NC: Duke University Press.

———. 2016. "The Social Phenomenology of the Next Epidemic: Pain and the Politics of Relief in Botswana's Cancer Ward." In *Living and Dying in the Contemporary World: A Compendium,* edited by Veena Das and Clara Han, 185–204. Oakland: University of California Press.

Lock, Margaret. 2001. *Twice Dead: Organ Donation and the Reinvention of Death.* Berkeley: University of California Press.

Long, Susan. 2004. "Cultural Scripts for a Good Death in Japan and the United States: Similarities and Differences." *Social Science and Medicine* 58 (5): 913–28.

Lovell, Anne M. 2016. "'God Isn't Finished with This City Yet': Disputing Katrina-Related Deaths in Post-disaster New Orleans." In *Living and Dying in the Contemporary World: A Compendium,* edited by Veena Das and Clara Han, 559–75. Oakland: University of California Press.

Luna, Zakiya, and Kristin Luker. 2013. "Reproductive Justice." *Annual Review of Law and Social Sciences* 9:327–52.

Lyerly, Anne Drapkin. 2014. *A Good Birth: Finding the Positive and the Profound in Your Childbirth Experience.* New York: Avery.

Mancini, Barbara. 2014. Interview by Anderson Cooper. *60 Minutes.* CBS. Aired October 17, 2014. https://www.cbsnews.com/video/60-minutes-preview-nurse-prosecuted-for-helping-father-take-own-life/.

Marsland, Rebecca, and Ruth Prince. 2012. "What Is Life Worth? Exploring Biomedical Interventions, Survival, and the Politics of Life." *Medical Anthropology Quarterly* 26 (4): 453–69.

Martin, Lisa, Jane Hasinger, Michelle Debbink, and Lisa Harris. 2017. "Dangertalk: Voices of Abortion Providers." *Social Science and Medicine* 184:75–83.

Mattingly, Cheryl. 1998. *Healing Dramas and Clinical Plots: The Narrative Structure of Experience.* Cambridge: University of Cambridge Press.

Mattingly, Cheryl, and Linda Garro. 2000. *Narrative and the Cultural Construction of Illness and Healing.* Berkeley: University of California Press.

Mbembe, Achilles. 2003. *Necropolitics. Public Culture* 15 (1): 11–40.

McCormick-Cavanagh, Conor. 2019. "Even with an Aid-in-Dying Law on the Books, Death Is No Certainty in Colorado." *Westword,* May 7, 2009. https://www.westword.com/content/printView/11332857.

McCullum, April. 2018. "Vermont Will Pay Remote Workers $10,000 to Work Here." *Burlington Free Press,* May 31, 2018. https://www.burlingtonfreepress.com/story/news/local/vermont/2018/05/31/vermont-pay-remote-workers-move-incentive/659553002/.

McInerney, Fran. 2000. "'Requested Death': A New Social Movement." *Social Science and Medicine* 50 (1): 137–54.

McLean, Athena. 2007. *The Person in Dementia: A Study of Nursing Home Care in the US.* Toronto: University of Toronto Press.

McLeod, Carolyn. 2009. "Referral in the Wake of Conscientious Objection to Abortion." *Hypatia* 23 (4): 30–47.

Memmi, Dominique. 2003. "Governing through Speech: The New State Administration of Bodies." *Social Research* 70 (2): 645–58.

Mercier, Rebecca, Mara Buchbinder, Amy Bryant, and Laura Britton. 2015. "The Experiences and Adaptations of Abortion Providers Practicing under a New TRAP Law: A Qualitative Study." *Contraception* 91 (6): 507–12.

Merkel, Reinhard. 2016. "Killing or Letting Die? Proposal of a (Somewhat) New Answer to a Perennial Question." *Journal of Medical Ethics* 42 (6): 353–60.

Miller, Franklin, and Robert Truog. 2009. "The Incoherence of Determining Death by Neurological Criteria: A Commentary on *Controversies in the Determination of Death.*" White Paper, President's Council on Bioethics. *Kennedy Institute of Ethics Journal* 19 (2): 185–93.

Mitford, Jessica. 1998. *The American Way of Death Revisited.* New York: Knopf.

Mrig, Emily Hammad, and Karen Lutfey Spencer. 2018. "Political Economy of Hope as a Cultural Facet of Biomedicalization: Qualitative Examination of Constraints to Hospice Utilization among U.S. End-Stage Cancer Patients." *Social Science and Medicine* 200:107–13.

Murray, Stuart. 2006. "Thanatopolitics: On the Use of Death for Mobilizing Life." *Polygraph* 18:191–215.

———. 2018. "Thanatopolitics." In *Bloomsbury Handbook to Literary and Cultural Theory,* edited by J. R. DiLeo, 718–19. London: Bloomsbury.

National Academies of Sciences, Engineering, and Medicine. 2018. *Physician-Assisted Death: Scanning the Landscape: Proceedings of a Workshop.* Washington, DC: National Academies Press. https://doi.org/10.17226/25131.

Neumann, Anne. 2016. *The Good Death: An Exploration of Dying in America.* Boston: Beacon Press.

Newport, Frank. 2017. "Mississippi Retains Standing as Most Religious State." *Gallup News,* February 8, 2017. https://news.gallup.com/poll/203747/mississippi-retains-standing-religious-state.aspx.

Nguyen, Huong, Eduard Gelman, Tracey Bush, Janet Lee, and Michael Kanter. 2018. "Characterizing Kaiser Permanente Southern California's Experience with the California End of Life Options Act in the First Year of Implementation." *JAMA Internal Medicine* 178 (3): 417–21.

Nguyen, Vinh-Kim. 2010. *The Republic of Therapy: Triage and Sovereignty in West Africa's Time of AIDS*. Durham, NC: Duke University Press.

Noddings, Nel. 2002. *Starting at Home: Caring and Social Policy*. Berkeley: University of California Press.

Norwood, Frances. 2009. *The Maintenance of Life: Preventing Social Death through Euthanasia Talk and End-of-Life Care—Lessons from the Netherlands*. Durham, NC: Carolina Academic Press.

Offord, Catherine. 2017. "Accessing Drugs for Medical Aid-in-Dying." *Scientist*, August 16, 2017. https://www.the-scientist.com/bio-business/accessing-drugs-for-medical-aid-in-dying-31067.

Oregon Health Authority. 2020. *Oregon Death with Dignity Act 2019 Data Summary*. Salem: Oregon Health Authority. https://www.oregon.gov/oha/PH/PROVIDERPARTNERRESOURCES/EVALUATIONRESEARCH/DEATHWITHDIGNITYACT/Documents/year21.pdf.

Ortner, Sherry. 2006. "Power and Projects: Reflections on Agency." In *Anthropology and Social Theory: Culture, Power, and the Acting Subject*. Durham, NC: Duke University Press.

Pantera, Kestrin. 2016. "I Arrived at My Friend's Party: A Few Hours Later She Died, Exactly as Planned." Vox, August 28, 2016. https://www.vox.com/2016/8/22/12552940/assisted-suicide-california.

Pellegrino, Edmund. 1995. "Nonabandonment: An Old Obligation Revisited." *Annals of Internal Medicine* 122 (5): 377–78.

Peltz, Perri, and Matthew O'Neill, dirs. 2019. *Alternate Endings: Six New Ways to Die in America. AXIOS*. HBO, 68 minutes.

Perkins, Henry. 2007. "Controlling Death: The False Promise of Advance Directives." *Annals of Internal Medicine* 147 (1): 51–57.

Petrillo, Laura, Elizabeth Dzeng, Krista Harrison, Lindsay Forbes, Benjamin Scribner, and Barbara Koenig. 2017. "How California Prepared for Implementation of Physician-Assisted Death: A Primer." *American Journal of Public Health* 107 (6): 883–88.

Pew Research Center. 2014. "Religious Composition of Adults in Vermont: From the Religious Landscape Study." https://www.pewforum.org/religious-landscape-study/state/vermont/.

Picard, Ken. 2014. "The 'Wake Up to Dying Project' Brings Death Out of the Closet. *Seven Days*, July 21, 2014. https://www.sevendaysvt.com/LiveCulture/archives/2014/07/21/the-wake-up-to-dying-project-brings-death-out-of-the-closet.

Pollitt, Katha. 2015. *Pro: Reclaiming Abortion Rights*. New York: Picador.

Pool, Robert. 2000. *Negotiating a Good Death: Euthanasia in the Netherlands.* London: Routledge.

———. 2004. "'You're Not Going to Dehydrate Mom, Are You?' Euthanasia, *Versterving,* and Good Death in the Netherlands." *Social Science and Medicine* 58 (5): 955–66.

Portenoy, Russell, Una Sibirceva, Randall Smouth, Susan Horn, Stephen Connor, Ronald Blum, Carol Spence, and Perry Fine. 2006. "Opioid Use and Survival at the End of Life: A Survey of a Hospice Population." *Journal of Pain and Symptom Management* 32 (6): 532–40.

Puri, Sunita. 2020. "It's Time to Talk about Death." *New York Times,* March 27, 2020. https://www.nytimes.com/2020/03/27/opinion/covid-end-of-life.html ?referringSource=articleShare.

Quill, Timothy. 1991. "Death and Dignity: A Case of Individualized Decision Making." *New England Journal of Medicine* 324 (10): 691–93.

Quill, Timothy, Robert Arnold, and Stuart Youngner. 2017. "Physician-Assisted Suicide: Finding a Path Forward in a Changing Legal Environment." *Annals of Internal Medicine* 167 (8): 598–99.

Quill, Timothy, Anthony Back, and Susan Block. 2016. "Responding to Patients Requesting Physician-Assisted Death: Physician Involvement at the Very End of Life." *Journal of the American Medical Association* 315 (3): 245–46.

Quill, Timothy, and Christine Cassel. 1995. "Nonabandonment: A Central Obligation for Physicians." *Annals of Internal Medicine* 122:368–74.

Quill, Timothy, Linda Ganzini, Robert Truog, and Thaddeus Mason Pope. 2018. "Voluntarily Stopping Eating and Drinking among Patients with Serious Advanced Illness—Clinical, Ethical, and Legal Aspects." *JAMA Internal Medicine* 178 (1): 123–27.

Quill, Timothy, Bernard Lo, and Daniel Brock. 1997. "Palliative Options of Last Resort: A Comparison of Voluntarily Stopping Eating and Drinking, Terminal Sedation, Physician-Assisted Suicide, and Voluntary Active Euthanasia." *Journal of the American Medical Association* 278:2009–2104.

Rabinow, Paul, and Nikolas Rose. 2006. "Biopower Today." *BioSocieties* 1 (2): 195–217.

Rachels, James. 1975. "Active and Passive Euthanasia." *New England Journal of Medicine* 292 (2): 78–80.

Ramirez, Michelle, Andrea Altschuler, Carmit McMullen, Marcia Grant, Mark Hornbrook, and Robert Krouse. 2014. "'I Didn't Feel Like I Was a Person Anymore': Realigning Full Adult Personhood after Ostomy Surgery." *Medical Anthropology Quarterly* 28 (2): 242–59.

Rapp, Rayna. 1987. "Moral Pioneers: Women, Men, and Fetuses on a Frontier of Reproductive Technology." *Women and Health* 13 (1–2): 101–16.

Richards, Naomi. 2015. "Dying to Go to Court: Demanding a Legal Remedy to End-of-Life Uncertainty." In *The Clinic and the Court: Law, Medicine, and*

Anthropology, edited by Ian Harper, Tobias Kelly, and Akshay Khanna, 214–38. Cambridge: Cambridge University Press.

———. 2017. "Assisted Suicide as a Remedy for Suffering? The End-of-Life Preferences of British 'Suicide Tourists.'" *Medical Anthropology* 36 (4): 348–62.

Richards, Naomi, and Marian Krawczyk. Forthcoming. "What Is the Cultural Value of Dying in an Era of Assisted Dying?" *Medical Humanities*.

Richards, Naomi, and Rebecca Rotter. 2013. "Desperately Seeking Certainty? The Case of Asylum Applicants and People Planning an Assisted Suicide in Switzerland." *Sociological Research Online* 18 (4): 250–65.

Richardson, Peter, dir. 2011. *How to Die in Oregon*. Distributed by Clearcut Productions. Documentary, 108 minutes.

Roberts, Dorothy. 1997. *Killing the Black Body: Race, Reproduction, and the Meaning of Liberty*. New York: Pantheon.

Romain, Tiffany. 2010. "Extreme Life Extension: Investing in Cryonics for the Long, Long Term." *Medical Anthropology* 29 (2): 194–215.

Rose, Nikolas. 2006. *The Politics of Life Itself: Biomedicine, Power, and Subjectivity in the 21st Century*. Princeton, NJ: Princeton University Press.

Ross, Loretta, and Rickie Solinger. 2017. *Reproductive Justice: An Introduction*. University of California Press.

Russ, Ann, Janet Shim, and Sharon Kaufman. 2007. "The Value of 'Life at Any Cost': Talk about Stopping Kidney Dialysis." *Social Science and Medicine* 64:2236–47.

Sanburn, Josh. 2013. "The Hidden Hand Squeezing Texas' Supply of Execution Drugs." *Time*, August 7, 2013. http://nation.time.com/2013/08/07/the-hidden-hand-squeezing-texas-supply-of-execution-drugs/.

Sandomir, Richard. 2017. "Howard Frank Mosher, Whose Novels Evoked Hardscrabble Vermont, Dies at 74." *New York Times*, February 7, 2017. www.nytimes.com/2017/02/07/books/howard-frank-mosher-whose-novels-evoked-hardscrabble-vermont-dies-at-74.html.

Sargent, Carolyn, and Carolyn Smith-Morris. 2006. "Questioning Our Principles: Anthropological Contributions to Ethical Dilemmas in Clinical Practice." *Cambridge Quarterly of Healthcare Ethics* 15 (2): 123–34.

Savulescu, Julian. 2015. "Autonomy Interests, Justice, and Active Medical Euthanasia." In *New Directions in the Ethics of Assisted Suicide and Euthanasia*, edited by M. Cholbi and J. Varelius, 41–58. New York: Springer.

Scheper-Hughes, Nancy. 2005. "The Last Commodity: Post-human Ethics and the Global Traffic in 'Fresh' Organs." In *Global Assemblages: Technology, Politics, and Ethics as Anthropological Problems*, edited by A. Ong and S. Collier, 145–68. Malden, MA: Blackwell.

Scheper-Hughes, Nancy, and Margaret Lock. 1986. "Speaking Truth to Illness: Metaphors, Reification, and a Pedagogy for Patients." *Medical Anthropology Quarterly* 17 (5): 137–40.

Seale, Clive. 1998. *Constructing Death: The Sociology of Dying and Bereavement*. Cambridge: Cambridge University Press.

Seymour, Jane Elizabeth. 1999. "Revisiting Medicalisation and 'Natural' Death." *Social Science and Medicine* 49 (5): 691–704.

Sharma, Aradhana. 2013. "State Transparency after the Neoliberal Turn: The Politics, Limits, and Paradoxes of India's Right to Information Law." *Political and Legal Anthropology Review* 36 (2): 308–25.

Shavelson, Lonny. 2018. "Best Practices for Aid-in-Dying: Recommendations from the Bedside." *San Francisco Marin Medicine* 91 (4): 17–19.

Shim, Janet. 2010. "Cultural Health Capital: A Theoretical Approach to Understanding Health Care Interactions and the Dynamics of Unequal Treatment." *Journal of Health and Social Behavior* 51 (1): 1–15.

Simpson, Kevin. 2017. "Getting to Goodbye: an Aurora Couple's Struggle to Employ Colorado's New Aid-in-Dying Law." *Denver Post*, April 2, 2017. https://www.denverpost.com/2017/04/02/getting-to-goodbye-an-aurora-couples-struggle-to-employ-colorados-new-aid-in-dying-law/.

Singer, Peter, Douglas Martin, James Lavery, Elaine Thiel, Merrijoy Kelner, and David Mendelssohn. 1998. "Reconceptualizing Advance Care Planning from the Patient's Perspective." *Archives of Internal Medicine* 158 (8): 870–84.

Sneddon, Andrew. 2006. "Equality, Justice, and Paternalism: Recentreing Debate about Physician-Assisted Suicide." *Journal of Applied Philosophy* 23 (4): 387–404.

Solomon, Harris. 2017. "Shifting Gears: Triage and Traffic in Urban India." *Medical Anthropology Quarterly* 31 (3): 349–64.

Sontag, Susan. 1977. *On Photography*. New York: Farrar, Straus, and Giroux.

Stahl, Ronit, and Ezekiel Emanuel. 2017. "Physicians, Not Conscripts—Conscientious Objection in Health Care." *New England Journal of Medicine* 376 (14): 1380–85.

State of Oregon. 1997. Death with Dignity Act. Pub. L. No. 127.800–127.995. https://www.oregon.gov/oha/PH/PROVIDERPARTNERRESOURCES/EVALUATIONRESEARCH/DEATHWITHDIGNITYACT/Documents/statute.pdf.

State of Vermont. 2009. Patient's Bill of Rights for Palliative Care and Pain Management. 18V.S.A. § 1871.

———. 2013. Vermont Act 39: An Act Relating to Patient Choice and Control at End of Life. http://www.leg.state.vt.us/docs/2014/Acts/ACT039.pdf.

Stavrianakis, Anthony. 2020. *Leaving: A Narrative of Assisted Suicide*. Oakland: University of California Press.

Steinhauser, Karen, Elizabeth Clipp, Maya McNeilly, Nicholas Christakis, Lauren McIntyre, and James Tulsky. 2000. "In Search of a Good Death: Observations of Patients, Families, and Providers." *Annals of Internal Medicine* 132 (10): 825–32.

Stevenson, Lisa. 2009. *Life beside Itself: Imagining Care in the Canadian Arctic.* Berkeley: University of California Press.

———. 2016. "Life beside Itself." In *Living and Dying in the Contemporary World: A Compendium,* edited by V. Das and C. Han, 712–28. Oakland: University of California Press.

Stonington, Scott. 2020. *The Spirit Ambulance: Choreographing the End of Life in Thailand.* Oakland: University of California Press.

Strayed, Cheryl. 2012. *Wild: From Lost to Found on the Pacific Crest Trail.* New York: Alfred Knopf.

Sulmasy, Daniel. 1999. "The Rule of Double Effect: Clearing Up the Double Talk." *Archives of Internal Medicine* 159:545–50.

Sulmasy, Lois Snyder, and Paul Mueller, for the Ethics, Professionalism and Human Rights Committee of the American College of Physicians. 2017. "Ethics and the Legalization of Physician-Assisted Suicide: An American College of Physicians Position Paper." *Annals of Internal Medicine* 167 (8): 576–78.

Sunder Rajan, Kaushik. 2006. *Biocapital: The Constitution of Postgenomic Life.* Durham, NC: Duke University Press.

Taylor, Janelle. 2008. "On Recognition, Caring, and Dementia." *Medical Anthropology Quarterly* 22 (4): 313–35.

Throop, C. Jason. 2003. "Articulating Experience." *Anthropological Theory* 3 (2): 219–41.

Thyden, Amanda. 2017. "Death with Dignity and Assistance: A Critique of the Self-Administration Requirement in California's End of Life Option Act." *Chapman Law Review* 20 (2): 421–44.

Timmermans, Stefan. 1998. "Social Death as Self-Fulfilling Prophecy: David Sudnow's *Passing On* Revisited." *Sociological Quarterly* 39 (3): 453–72.

Timmermans, Stefan, and Mara Buchbinder. 2012. *Saving Babies? The Consequences of Newborn Genetic Screening.* Chicago: Chicago University Press.

Tronto, Joan. 1993. *Moral Boundaries: A Political Argument for an Ethic of Care.* New York: Routledge.

Tucker, Kathryn. 2019. "Aid in Dying in North Carolina." Addendum 1. *North Carolina Law Review* 97: 1–20.

Tulsky, James, Ralph Ciampa, and Elliott Rosen, for the University of Pennsylvania Center for Bioethics Assisted Suicide Consensus Panel. 2000. "Responding to Legal Requests for Physician-Assisted Suicide." *Annals of Internal Medicine* 132 (6): 494–99.

US Census Bureau. 2018. Quick Facts: Vermont. https://www.census.gov/quickfacts/VT.

Vanderbeck, Robert. 2006. "Vermont and the Imaginative Geographies of American Whiteness." *Annals of the Association of American Geographers* 96 (3): 641–59.

Van der Geest, Sjaak. 2004. "Dying Peacefully: Considering Good Death and Bad Death in Kawhu-Tafo, Ghana." *Social Science and Medicine* 58 (5): 899–911.

Van Gennep, Arnold. 1960. *The Rites of Passage.* Translated by M. Vizedom and G. Caffee. Chicago: University of Chicago Press.

Vermont Alliance for Ethical Healthcare, Inc. et al. v. Hoser et al. 2016a. Complaint. 5:16-cv-00205-gwc (D. Vt., July 19, 2016). https://compassionandchoices.org/wp-content/uploads/2016-07-19.-0001-COMPLAINT-wm.pdf.

———. 2016b. Defendants' Memorandum of Law in Support of a Motion to Dismiss. 20175:16-cv-00205-gwc (D. Vt., September 25, 2016). https://compassionandchoices.org/wp-content/uploads/2018/06/2016-09-25.-0031-MOTION-to-Dismiss-for-Failure-to-State-a-Claim-filed-by-Colin-R.-Benjamin-Richard-Bernstein-Gary-B-5-2016-cv-00205-vtd.pdf.

———. 2016c. Plaintiffs' Memorandum of Law in Support of Motion for a Preliminary Injunction. 5:16-cv-00205-gwc (D. Vt., September 26, 2016). http://www.adfmedia.org/files/VermontAllianceMotionBriefPI.pdf.

———. 2017. Opinion and Order re: Defendants' Motion to Dismiss and Plaintiffs' Motion for Preliminary Injunction. 5:16-cv-00205-gwc (D. Vt., April 5, 2017). http://www.adfmedia.org/files/VermontAllianceDismissalOrder.pdf.

Vermont Department of Health. 2015. The Patient Choice and Control at End of Life Act; Frequently Asked Questions. http://healthvermont.gov/family/end_of_life_care/documents/Act39_faq.pdf.

———. 2018. *Report Concerning Patient Choice at the End of Life.* January 15. https://legislature.vermont.gov/assets/Legislative-Reports/2018-Patient-Choice-Legislative-Report-12–14–17.

———. 2020. *Report Concerning Patient Choice at the End of Life 2.0.* January 15. https://legislature.vermont.gov/assets/Legislative-Reports/2020-Patient-Choice-Legislative-Report-2.0.pdf.

Walter, Tony. 1993. "Death in the New Age." *Religion* 23 (2): 127–45.

Wicclair, Mark. 2011. *Conscientious Objection in Medical Care: An Ethical Analysis.* Cambridge: Cambridge University Press.

Wool, Zoe. 2017. "In-Durable Sociality: Precarious Life in Common and the Temporal Boundaries of the Social." *Social Text* 35 (1): 79–99.

Woolard, Kathryn, and Bambi Schieffelin. 1994. "Language Ideology." *Annual Review of Anthropology* 23:55–82.

Yip-Williams, Julie. 2019. *The Unwinding of the Miracle: A Memoir of Life, Death, and Everything that Comes After.* New York: Random House.

Zitter, Jessica Nutnik. 2017. *Extreme Measures: Finding a Better Path to the End of Life.* New York: Avery.

Zivkovic, Tanya. 2018. "Forecasting and Foreclosing Futures: The Temporal Dissonance of Advance Care Directives." *Social Science and Medicine* 215:16–22.

Index

Founded in 1893,
UNIVERSITY OF CALIFORNIA PRESS
publishes bold, progressive books and journals
on topics in the arts, humanities, social sciences,
and natural sciences—with a focus on social
justice issues—that inspire thought and action
among readers worldwide.

The UC PRESS FOUNDATION
raises funds to uphold the press's vital role
as an independent, nonprofit publisher, and
receives philanthropic support from a wide
range of individuals and institutions—and from
committed readers like you. To learn more, visit
ucpress.edu/supportus.